# THRIVE IN OVERDRIVE

## How to Navigate Your Overloaded Lifestyle

Patrick K. Porter, PhD

Other Books, CDs & MP3s by Patrick K. Porter, PhD

*Awaken the Genius—Mind*
*Technology for the 21st Century*

*Discover the Language of the Mind*
*The Hypnotist's Guide to Psycho-Linguistics*

**For Online CVR Certification Go To:**
http://www.QuantumUniversity.com

For information about Dr. Porter's creative visualization audio programs
please visit: **www.PorterVision.com**

Cover Art: Robert Johnson at www.johnsondesign.org
Editor: Lauran Strait at lauran-strait@cox.net

*First Edition: Jan 2009*

ISBN: 978-1-4507-3815-6
Library of Congress Control Number: 2008911632

# TABLE OF CONTENTS

*"I still need more healthy rest in order to work at my best. My health is the main capital I have and I want to administer it intelligently."*

**Ernest Hemingway (1899 - 1961)**

To my talented wife, Cynthia.
Without her motivation, skill and love this
work would never have been completed.

*"You must be the change
you want to see in the world."*

**- Mahatma Gandhi (1869 - 1948)**

# ACKNOWLEDGEMENT

In my previous book, Awaken the Genius, I described genius as a higher order of thinking. Beyond survival and success there is a synergy that we all draw upon. This work is a continuation of that message and didn't start with me and most certainly won't end with me.

I am grateful to have been born into such a phenomenal time known as the "information explosion," and to share with you, the reader, the techniques that helped me to awaken my learning potential. I am grateful for the inspiration and wisdom of the many great minds and teachers who have shaped my life.

I would like to personally acknowledge all my teachers, some of whom I have met, and some of whom I have not met (yet). The most important include Swami Sri Sathya Sai Baba, Paramahansa Yoganada, Hamid Bey, James Allen, Paul Adams, Gil Gilly, J. J. Hurtak, Milton Erickson, Richard Bandler, John Grinder, Walter Cannon, Dr. Herbert Benson, and Jerry DeShazo. I am grateful for the many students, friends, and clients who have continually proven the effectiveness of these techniques.

I am grateful to have been born into a family with eight brothers and sisters. Michael, Michelle, David, Walter, Sarah, Bill, John and Fran -- all truly awakened geniuses. I was blessed to have witnessed the courage of my father who used these principles to overcome alcoholism and was thus motivated to enter the field of mental wellness. Through his example, he taught his nine children to live proactive lifestyles. I am grateful to my mother, who spent the greater part of her short life taking care of such a tribe. She was a fearless leader.

I am grateful to my wife, Cynthia, who spent endless hours helping to put together the *Thrive In Overdrive* book. Without her special creativity we would all miss out.

I humbly thank Dr. George Grant, a great author and scientist, for his thoughtful foreword to this book. Gratitude to Dr. Scott Newman for the use of his research in the chapter on stress as well as Dr. Dan Smith for his wisdom and expertise in the area of neurotransmitters. A big thank you goes out to Greg, Stephanie, Marina and Morgan Mulac for helping get this message out to the world.

Special thanks to Jerry DeShazo, Mitzi Lynton, Jennifer Severo, John Shoecraft, Rev. Michele Whittington, Steve Francisco, Gail Larson, Inna Komarovsky, Beverly Nadler, Bill Bartmann and the others who chose to remain nameless for their time, talent, and for sharing their stories that prove the value of the concepts in this book and how they can be used in the real world.

With deep gratitude I wish to acknowledge my amazing editor, Lauran Strait, whose fresh perspective and insight brought this text to life. Special thanks also go to Heidi Porter for her hard work in transcribing and formatting large sections of the first draft.

I am grateful to you, the reader, for giving me the motivation to finish this book. I confidently await your contribution to this remarkable planet as you learn to thrive in overdrive.

-- Patrick Porter

*"He felt that his whole life was some kind of dream and he sometimes wondered whose it was and whether they were enjoying it."*

**- Douglas Adams (1952 - 2001)**
*"The Hitchhiker's Guide to the Galaxy"*

# FOREWORD

What a great honor to write the foreword for Dr. Patrick Porter's new book, *Thrive in Overdrive, How to Navigate Your Overloaded Lifestyle.* As I read through the manuscript for this book, I realized that Dr. Porter had identified a need that no one else was addressing: the need we all have to meet the demands of today's high-tech, fast-paced world and still enjoy a healthy, stress-free lifestyle.

We are a society that wants to have it all, and this book is a how-to for doing just that. Inside these pages you will discover the blueprint for leading a healthy, balanced life physically, mentally, and spiritually and at the same time enjoy success and financial rewards.

After completing both my masters and doctoral work in stress management, I came to realize that stress is, in fact, deadly. Stress is responsible for over eighty-five percent of all illness in our modern society.

In these pages you will discover an accurate and practical guide to managing stress, improving your life, or even overcoming unwanted habits, all while maintaining your hectic daily schedule. The book is loaded with tips to help readers lead a balanced life. When I reviewed the book, I found it inspiring, particularly the chapter on the connection between stress and the immune system and hormone balance.

This book is a must-read for every parent, scientist, student, and teacher to help us move from imperfection to perfection, from imbalance to balance, from being a victim to a victor and to transform illness to wellness.

Every chapter provides deep insight into the quest for achieving balance in one's life. Of particular interest is the section entitled *Can Stress Harm or Destroy Relationships?* This section is like a GPS guide for any couple to reach harmony and equanimity within their relationship.

Another key section for every working adult is *Why is There So Much Stress in the Workplace?* As Dr. Porter points out, Twenty-first Century living offers little time for rest or relaxation. Every day we feel pressure to keep up with the frenetic pace of modern life. Today this is true in nearly every culture. For this reason, I believe these principles should be taught in every school, corporation, and place of worship worldwide.

Today's technology-based world is one of the greatest paradoxes of human history. The very gadgets we've invented to simplify our lives have also complicated our lives to the extent that our human bodies are suffering the ravages of chronic stress like never before. Yet Dr. Porter has found a way to use technology to combat high-tech stress and it's called *visual/auditory entrainment*. In Chapter Four, Dr. Porter describes this light and sound relaxation device in detail and outlines the benefits to the user. I have been using with great success these very devices at my clinics in Toronto, Canada as well as during the Lunch & Learn lectures I offer for Fortune 500 companies worldwide.

I strongly recommend this eye opening, inspiring, and easy-to-read guide to everyone who is serious about reaching maximum potential. *Thrive in Overdrive* is truly a handbook for life and is, in my opinion, the best antidote for thriving in our modern stress-filled world.

Dr. George Grant, B.Sc., M.Sc., M.Ed., Ph.D., D.N.M., C.Chem., R.M.

Printed in the United States of America
10 9 8 7 6 5 4 3 2

## INTRODUCTION

### Why did I write this book?

*I have the ability to change the world.* To some I know this makes me sound like an egomaniac, but the truth is, I have indeed happened upon what I consider to be a magic elixir that has the potential to transform our world into a place of peace, harmony, and plentitude, even as we continue to live our lives in overdrive. It's an elixir so abundant that it's within the reach of every human being. It doesn't cost a penny and you don't have to earn it.     Best of all, it's so easy to use, even a child can do it.

If I told you it was possible for you to be free from your overloaded life of stress, anger, and frustration, and at the same time you could have abundant energy, feel optimistic each day, sleep like a child every night, and be able to follow your passions and live your dreams, would you believe me? Most people would tell me I have a few loose screws. And why wouldn't they? Everywhere they turn they see stress. In their personal lives they have mortgages, credit card debt, housework, taxes, crying babies or wayward teens, marital troubles, and more. On the job they have difficult co-workers, lengthy meetings, disagreements with management, technology meltdowns, cell phones that now keep them chained to work no matter where they go, and more activities to do than is humanly possible. They look into the world and see overloaded people taking desperate, unthinkable actions. They see terrorism, violence in their neighborhoods, shootings in schools, corrupt and immoral politicians, behemoth corporations taken down by a handful of crooked leaders, soaring gas prices, global warming, and deadly diseases that didn't even exist just a few decades ago. Where can anyone find freedom from stress in all that?

Yet I contend that this kind of freedom exists, and I believe everyone has the right to have it, along with the right to follow his or her own passions, and enjoy a healthy, happy, abundant life. You hold in your hands the guide that will take you to this magic elixir. Within these pages you will discover exactly where to go to get it, how to use it, why it works, and how others have used it to change their lives and the world.

Looking back over my life, I now realize that my journey to self-discovery started when I was twelve years old. Like most pubescent boys, I'd been getting into mischief. My dad tried to tame me by grounding me and by taking away prized possessions, yet I remained undaunted. When all else failed, Dad got an idea—an idea that changed my life.

After overcoming alcoholism through relaxation, visualization, and positive affirmation techniques, my dad started teaching others the methods he was using. By learning how to manage his own overloaded life, he was able to help other people do the same. He helped them stop smoking, lose weight, control stress before, during, and after surgery, give birth with less pain, and sleep better at night.

Instead of punishing me, which wasn't working anyway, he purchased a cassette player and taught me how to record my own positive affirmations. I was then required to listen to these recordings twice a day. At first I felt embarrassed hearing my own voice on the tape. Since I didn't really know what to say, the tapes were nothing more than a jumble of words I'd overheard my dad using. The entire process still felt like a punishment. Then one day I read in a magazine that one of my favorite sports figures had used visualization to prepare for competition. *Now that got my attention.* I had already set the goal of being captain of the football team, and I could use my dad's affirmation techniques to get me there.

If you've read my first book, *Awaken the Genius, Mind Technology for the 21st Century*, you already know that I not only attained my goal of being football captain, but also made captain of my school's wrestling and track teams.

By the time I was twenty, I had achieved far more than I could have dreamed possible when Dad had bought that tape recorder for me eight years earlier. I was so excited about the techniques I'd been using, even though I was barely into college, I wanted to share what I had discovered with others. "I'd like to help in your practice," I said to my dad one day.

"You're too young," he immediately said. "You're still in college. Who's going to listen to a kid?"

"If I share my story, I think they'll listen." I said.

While Dad was dubious about my ability to inspire anyone, he gave me the title of relaxologist, which was a designation I'm sure my dad made up, and which meant my job was simply to help people relax. Dad set me up with appointments with a few of his more challenging clients and told me to see what I could do. Not a single one of those clients, or any others I later helped, complained about my youth. I suppose they were too busy improving their lives.

Those years I spent as a relaxologist gave me a rare glimpse at the inner workings of humanity. I learned what makes people tick. I got a glimpse into how value systems and beliefs influence people's thoughts and actions. I learned to recognize the physical, mental and emotional effects of stress, which were devastating for some of my clients. Most importantly, it made me proficient at helping people uncover their sources of stress, tune into their bodies and, by using the proper sequence of words and suggestions, to reach deep, meaningful levels of relaxation so they could improve their lives.

Later, I founded and painstakingly built an international self-improvement chain that focused on helping people lose weight, stop smoking, and reduce stress. I learned from the inside out exactly what goes on inside the human mind. I listened to the hopes, dreams, and fears of my clients. I encouraged them, lent a strong shoulder, and dried their tears. I gave them motivation to stick to their commitment, tough love when they made excuses, and high-fives when they melted off pounds and inches or kicked their smoking addictions once and for all. And, through it all, I learned the magic elixir that I'll teach you in this book—the magic elixir that you will use to transform your overloaded lifestyle into one of inner calm and self-satisfaction—a new lifestyle that will help to create a new reality for the world. Living in overdrive isn't bad; it's how we get things done in this fast-paced world. The trick is to learn how to thrive while in overdrive, rather than letting stress overload you.

## How can you get the most out of the book?

One of the greatest benefits I gained by using creative visualization to excel in sports was the athletic scholarship I earned for college. Since the coaches knew their athletes were losing precious study time due to the rigors of training, and because we were required to keep our grades at a certain level in order to participate in athletics, they wisely enrolled each of us in a special accelerated learning program. The tools I learned there were so effective, I was able to get my studying done in half the time it took most students. I was so amazed by the results, and fascinated by the mind's ability to learn, I've continued to study accelerated learning techniques throughout my career. To this day, I can't figure out why this powerful method of learning is reserved for athletes, and why colleges, or high schools for that matter, don't teach these techniques to all students.

This book is written with the premise of accelerated learning in mind. It's written for every type of learner. In other words, there is more than one way you can read the book. In my prior book, *Awaken the Genius*, I describe at length a highly effective method for speed-reading. What follows is a short-cut version of that technique.

The first thing you'll notice about this book is that almost all of the headings are written as questions instead of statements of fact. Your mind works best with questions because, as human beings, we seem to have an insatiable desire for answers. If I present questions such as, "Why is stress called the silent killer?" I pique your curiosity. If I simply write, "Stress is the silent killer," I have not engaged your inquisitive nature.

Therefore, I recommend that you start by reading the chapter heading and, if it's not already stated in question form, change it to a question. For example, the heading for Chapter 3 is titled, "The Stress Solution – Creative Visualization and Relaxation." Your goal is to change that to a question such as, "Why is creative visualization and relaxation the stress solution?" Now your mind is engaged—it's curious to find the answer.

As you go through this process, your mind sets up a kind of hopper system at the *other-than-conscious* level that stores, categorizes, and organizes the information. You'll actually know what you'll be reading before you read it, which makes the entire process faster and dramatically increases your comprehension.

Gaining and retaining useful new information is the primary goal in reading any self-help book. The way you store what you read and learn at the other-than-conscious level of your mind will determine your level of retention and comprehension. Everything you've learned from the moment you first heard your parents' voices is still available to you today. However, you can't keep all that information available at the conscious level of your thinking; it would be so much information you couldn't function. This is where your other-than-conscious mind comes in.

Every day you are bombarded with over 50,000 different messages, some of which are positive, and many of which are negative. Therefore, your brain has created a strategy for forgetting rather quickly what's unimportant so you can focus on what's needed at the present moment. To get the most out of this book, read every heading, search out terms that are bold or italicized, look at pictures or captions, and take note of anything that jumps off the page and into your awareness. Next close the book, take one to three deep, cleansing breaths, and then reopen the book at the start of the chapter. As you start reading, you'll be amazed to discover how much you already know before you've even read the first paragraph. Best of all, you can use this strategy to read just about any non-fiction book or textbook.

Be sure to repeat this process with each chapter. It may seem as if it will take you longer to get through the book, but in reality you will read much faster because the material is no longer completely foreign to you. Additionally, your retention of information will astound you.

## What Are Thought Experiments and Why Should You Do Them?

Throughout this book and at the end of most chapters you will find thought experiments, which are exercises designed to help you fully grasp each of the concepts and make them relevant in your own life. I didn't come up with the term thought experiment on my own; I borrowed it from the man I consider to be the greatest mind of our time—Albert Einstein.

At sixteen years of age, Einstein applied for admittance to the Zurich Polytechnic. Although the school's director was skeptical that one so young could gain admission, he allowed Einstein to take the entrance exam. Not surprisingly, Einstein easily passed the math and science sections of the exam. The general sections, unfortunately, were beyond the grasp of the child prodigy, and, therefore, he was denied admission.

His failure to gain admittance, however, proved to be an important turning point in his life for it was then that he decided to attend a school founded by a Swiss educational reformer of the early nineteenth century, Johann Heinrich Pestalozzi. While a student at this unique school in the village of Aurau, Einstein's teachers regularly encouraged him to visualize images. It was there that Einstein came up with his first thought experiment—he visualized himself riding alongside a light beam—which eventually led him to postulate the Theory of Relativity.

In the book, *Einstein, His Life and Universe*, Walter Isaacson writes: "This type of visualized thought experiments—*Gedankenexperiment*—became a hallmark of Einstein's career. Over the years, he would picture in his mind such things as lightning strikes and moving trains, accelerating elevators and falling painters, two-dimensional blind beetles crawling on curved branches, as well as a variety of contraptions designed to pinpoint, at least in theory, the location and velocity of speeding electrons." [1]

The thought experiments you find in this book not only will help you hone your skills as a *creative visualizer*, but also will fully engage your mind in creating what you want for your life.

Each thought experiment is designed to engage all your senses—sight, hearing, smell, taste, and touch—so the changes you want for your life come easily, and so the experience is rich, enjoyable, and complete. Reading this book without doing the thought experiments would be like reading the description of a mouth-watering dessert and then never having the sensual pleasure of tasting it, or like seeing musical notes on a page, but never hearing the beautiful melody those notes represent. The thought experiments are the icing on the cake, so please be okay with giving yourself the time to learn, play, experiment, and discover the true you waiting to come to life.

**What outcome do I have for you, the reader?**

My goal for you, my dear reader, is for you to change your life so that together we can change the world. I know this is possible because, just like me, *you have the ability to change the world.* The reality, however, is that we can't change the world until we learn how to change our own lives. As you read through these pages, I see you experiencing an awakening; I see you discovering how, by using the power of your mind, along with certain universal principles, you can change your life far more easily than you ever dreamed possible. I see you living a life of awe and wonder as you realize that your mind need only see an image of what you truly want for you to have it. I also see you experiencing the true joy that comes when you fall in love with your life and the world in which you live, when you discover the limitlessness of the boundless universe.

Don't worry; it's easier than you think. Solutions to your every problem are available to you right now. In fact, those solutions have always been there, waiting for you to wake up and break free from the limitations you learned during childhood, to let go of the narrow mental attitude that you absorbed from the people around you, and release the stress and confusion that kept you mired in longing, despair, and the illusion of lack. I want you to realize how, when you see what you want and truly believe you can have it, the unseen forces of your mind will go about proving you right, creating a way for you to solve any problem, overcome any obstacle, and get *anything* and *everything* you want out of life.

*"Reality is the leading cause of stress amongst those in touch with it."*

**- Lily Tomlin**

# C H A P T E R

# O N E

## Stress – The Silent Killer

*"Visual understanding is the essential and only true means of teaching how to judge things correctly."*

Johann Heinrich Pestalozzi

## Stress - The Silent Killer

Stress may be the most pervasive malady of our time. The constant pressure associated with living in a fast-paced world has created an environment where almost everyone suffers from stress. Stress comes at you from every aspect of your life. Your home life is a complicated balance between fragile family relationships, never ending household duties, career, and finances. In your work life you must deal with unreasonable customers, equipment breakdowns, uncooperative co-workers, stalled traffic, an impossible to please boss, or unattainable deadlines. At the same time, the media offers up daily doses of violence, terrorism, natural disasters, political and corporate scandals, and a host of horrors beyond imagining. With all that stress, is it any wonder that anxiety disorders are the most common mental illness in the United States affecting approximately forty million American adults (age eighteen or older), or about 18.1 percent of the adult population. [2]

Sure we can say to ourselves, *pull yourself together*, or *get a grip*, but if it were that simple we wouldn't be feeling anxious or stressed out in the first place. Once stress gets its hooks in you, it can be pretty hard to shake. You may feel its effects in the form of headaches, insomnia, anxiety, depression, indigestion, irritable bowel syndrome, chronic fatigue syndrome, fibromyalgia, allergies, or any myriad of other physical ailments.

## So what exactly is stress anyway?

For starters, I can tell you what it's not. It's not tangible; it's not something you can point to and say, "There, over there, that's stress." You can't go to the corner drug store and ask the pharmacist for a quart of stress. So stress isn't *real*. It's a symptom of cause and effect. It's created out of our reactions to situations or events.

It may surprise you to know that the circumstances of our lives don't determine our level of stress. Our *thoughts* and *actions* are what control the amount of stress in our lives. Therefore, stress is not something that happens to us; rather, it happens through us. In other words, stress is something we create in our own lives.

The medical community defines stress as a physical or psychological stimulus that produces a physiological reaction. These reactions may lead to poor physical, mental, or emotional health. When the human body is healthy, it's in a state of *homeostasis*, which means it is in a continuous stable condition. Stress disrupts homeostasis and is usually triggered by distressing or fear related experiences, either real or imagined.

How many times have you uttered these words: "I'm really stressed out today"? These are not words to be ignored. The effects of stress on our health, productivity, and quality of life are more devastating than most people want to admit. In fact, according to the National Institutes of Health, eighty to ninety percent of all illnesses are caused by direct or indirect stress.

How often do you complain about that aching shoulder, pain in your neck, nagging headache, or upset in your stomach? Before you shrug it off as "just stress," think again. Stress typically shows up at your weakest point, though it actually affects your entire body. Long-term stress can make you old before your time or, worse yet, can make you ill. Not a single part of your body is safe from stress's devastating effects—the heart, brain, muscles, immune system, joints—every single cell of your body is affected by stress, making you vulnerable to illness, disease, pain, or all three. A variety of variables will determine where stress shows up in your body including genetics, lifestyle, and the kinds of stress you experience each day.

The stress of work, family life, and personal challenges suppress the immune system. Therefore, it is of vital importance that we all incorporate a program of stress reduction and relaxation into our everyday life experience. By minimizing anxiety and stress, and facilitating relaxation, we can optimize our immune systems and operate from a place of unlimited resources.

Some people are born with the ability to remain calm in a stress-filled world. This book is for the rest of us—those of us who need help to relax, revitalize, and rejuvenate. It's also for those of us who want to stay positive in a world filled with negativity, and it is for those of us who yearn to make the world a better place in which to live. In the upcoming pages, we'll discuss in more detail how stress can harm your body and well-being, and then we'll go over exactly what you can do to protect your body and mind from the ravages of stress.

It should be noted, however, that some stress is good. There is a type of stress called eustress. It's the kind of stress we feel when we are faced with opportunities or challenges. Healthy levels of eustress provide motivation and drive and allow us to grow and develop as human beings. Without a little kick of eustress, we would never achieve self-fulfillment. Examples of eustress include situations such as graduating from college, getting married, buying a new home, or winning a competition. However, when eustress turns into distress, the stress becomes undesirable.

## Why is Stress the Silent Killer?

Our bodies have a built-in response to stress that is a natural part of our physiology. This physical reaction, known as the *fight-or-flight response*, is triggered whenever we encounter a stressful or fearful event.

Harvard physiologist Walter Cannon coined the term fight-or-flight response. He says that our brains are hard-wired to fight or flee as a part of the genetic wisdom that protects us from physical harm. External circumstances trigger the fight-or-flight response, but it can also be set off by extreme worry or fear.

This response actually corresponds to an area of our brain called the hypothalamus, which, when activated by a stressful event, starts a sequence of nerve cell firings and chemical releases that prepare our body to either run or fight.

The release of chemicals into the bloodstream, like adrenaline, noradrenalin and cortisol creates a dramatic physical change. The respiratory rate increases. Blood is directed away from the digestive tract and into muscles and limbs where added energy is needed to run or fight. The pupils dilate and sight sharpens. Awareness intensifies and impulses quicken. The perception of pain diminishes. In other words, the body prepares itself—physically and mentally—for fight-or-flight.

Throughout early human development the fight-or-flight response was critical to survival. When a caveman encountered a man-eating tiger, he needed the energy and intensified awareness to fight off the animal or run away.

In our modern world filled with high-pressure jobs, traffic, family challenges, and financial concerns, but very few wild tigers, the fight-or-flight response is rarely triggered by actual physical danger. Instead, worry and anxiety prompt most instances of fight-or-flight today.

By its very nature, the fight-or-flight response bypasses the logical left-brain. This is because our early ancestors didn't have time for a logical debate when a man-eating tiger was a few feet away licking its chops. In today's world, however, bypassing the logical mind can cause distorted thinking and exaggerated feelings of anxiety or fear. One may overreact to the slightest comment, or fall into the habit of *catastrophizing* even the smallest concerns.

Catastrophizing is the habit of building a fear up in your mind until you come to *expect* disaster. For instance, you hear on the radio that a severe storm is approaching. While taking precautions is a good idea, the *catastrophizing* person starts creating *what if* scenarios until the fear becomes irrational or turns into panic. *What if* a tornado hits? *What if* your spouse gets in an accident on the way home? *What if* your home is blown to bits with you in it?

It's next to impossible to foster a positive attitude while catastrophizing or when trapped in survival mode. When access to the logical part of your mind is denied, it's not realistic to expect you to make clear choices or understand the consequences of those choices.

Researchers are now finding that when there is a collective buildup of stress hormones that are not properly metabolized over time, toxicity and disorders of the autonomic nervous system can occur, often resulting in chronic illnesses such as migraine headaches, irritable bowel syndrome, or high blood pressure. One is also at higher risk for disorders of the hormonal and immune systems, resulting in chronic fatigue, depression, and diseases such as rheumatoid arthritis, lupus, allergies and, yes, even cancer.

You may be thinking, "I really never feel that stressed out." This is because excess stress doesn't always show up as the *feeling* of being stressed. Stress often goes directly to the body and may only be recognized by the symptoms it creates such as headaches, depression, anxiety, or disease.

Are you starting to understand why stress is a silent killer?

## How Does Stress Affect Your Body?

As I mentioned earlier, stress is not something that happens to us, it is something we create in our own lives. Let's take a look at some of the physical responses your body can have to stress, how getting overloaded affects your health, and why reducing stress is so essential to your well-being.

### Overload Trouble Spot #1: The Heart

Whenever the fight-or-flight response is triggered, whether through real or imagined stress, an increase in heart rate, blood pressure, and breathing delivers more oxygen faster throughout the body. At the same time, a rapid release of glucose and fatty acids into the bloodstream occurs. This is how your body can respond with strength and stamina during an emergency.

Chronic stress, however, can lead to high blood pressure and undue strain on the heart. The added glucose, if unused by the body, can cause elevated or erratic blood sugar levels. These blood sugar swings can make you feel fatigued and can lead to diabetes. Stress also prompts the body to release cortisol, which can cause a build up of cholesterol in the arteries. The bottom line: Stress can contribute to cardiovascular disease.

### Overload Trouble Spot #2: The Brain

Are you one of those people who work best on deadlines? Do you use stress as a motivator? If so, you may be doing long-term harm to your brain that could cause early memory loss or may even lead to Alzheimer's Disease.

You may thrive on stress because of the short-term brain boost of glucose your brain gets when you're under the gun. When this happens, your senses are heightened and your memory improves. Problems start when stress lasts more than two hours. That's when the body assumes you need more physical strength than brainpower and starts sending the glucose back to the muscles, leaving your brain short of glucose. At the same time, stress hormones impair neuron functioning. Another part of the brain, the hippocampus, associated with learning and memory, can get smaller over time due to the loss of glucose and damage to neurons. Researchers don't know the full effect of a shrinking hippocampus, but they do know that it can make you forgetful and muddle your thinking.

## Overload Trouble Spot #3: The Immune System

Whenever the fight-or-flight response is triggered, stress hormones course through your body and signal the non-essential functions to stop or slow down so that all systems essential to dealing with an emergency receive an extra boost of energy. Your immune system is not required for urgent activity. Therefore, it temporarily stops or slows down during peak stress periods. This system works out fine when the stress is short term, but when the stress hormones keep pouring in, your immune system suffers, making you vulnerable to infection.

Dr. Marc Schoen, an assistant clinical professor at UCLA's David Geffen School of Medicine, began studying the affects of stress on the immune system in 2001 after falling ill on a trip to Hawaii—a trip that he took after a long period of stress. In his research, Schoen identified a stress disorder he calls the *let-down effect*, an illness that strikes after a stressful period when one finally has time to rest. *3*

Inna Komarovsky, a graduate student at Clemson University, says the let-down effect strikes like clockwork every time exams roll around. Between her already overloaded schedule of classes, job, fiancé, and internship, she must find time to study. "There's just not enough time in the day," she says, "so I end up pulling all-nighters." When she finally finishes her last exam, and the stress is gone, she's ready for a weekend of relaxation but invariably gets sick.

According to Schoen, Komarovsky's experience is more common than most people realize. When the immune system is suppressed, it doesn't just go back to baseline, it goes below baseline, leaving the body vulnerable to just about any infection it may have been exposed to while under stress. "While it is well known in medicine that stress is hazardous to our health," says Schoen, "what is less well-known is that many of us do not begin suffering from stress related illness until *after* the stress is over. Many of us get sick *after* we finish a demanding project at work, *during* or *after* we go on vacation, or after we retire from a lifetime of fast paced living."

## Overload Trouble Spot #4: Body Fat

I once wrote an article called, "Why Stress is More Fattening than Chocolate." During my years of running weight loss clinics, I heard client after client ask me, "Why is it that my friends can gobble up everything in sight and not gain a pound, while I nibble on salads and the scale won't budge?"

With a little research, I found the answer in a powerful hormone called cortisol. Cortisol's job is to signal the body to relax and refuel after periods of stress; it's the body's way of slowing us down so that we don't burn out. After reviewing my client files, I realized that almost everyone who complained that he or she couldn't lose weight, even while dieting, lived with at least one high-stress factor that was likely causing high cortisol levels. Cortisol's message to slow down tends to make us feel tired, lethargic, and hungry. Therefore, while under the powerful influence of cortisol, our tendency is to want to lie around, watch television, and snack, thus the term, stress-eater, and the reason stress can be more fattening than chocolate.

Cortisol also triggers fat storage in the adipose tissue of the abdomen. When the majority of weight is in the abdomen it gives one an apple appearance. More importantly, it can lead to *Cushing's Syndrome*, which involves storage of fat on the inside of the abdominal cavity. *Cushing's Syndrome* can be dangerous and may lead to diabetes and heart disease.

### *What is the Relationship Between Hormones and Stress?*

Anti-aging specialists now know that hormone levels are affected by two factors: aging and stress. While we can't do much about the ticking clock, we certainly can control our stress factors. When hormone levels drop, the diseases regularly associated with aging appear. These diseases, including obesity, heart attack, stroke, osteoporosis, cancer, and dementia are all accepted as the natural ravages of aging. Studies on aging, however, now show that we can greatly reduce our risk of these diseases by reducing the level of stress in our lives.

Have you ever noticed how some people seem to get old before their time, or been shocked to hear about a thirty-eight year old having a fatal heart attack? In all likelihood, their bodies were the victims of chronic stress that depleted their hormones and forced their bodies into early aging.

Most people are familiar with the sex hormones, estrogen, progesterone, and testosterone, but few are aware of the hormones that drive the metabolism and fight off the affects of stress.

## Thyroid Hormones

Blood circulation, body temperature, metabolism, and brain function are all driven by thyroid hormones. Energy levels and sex drive are influenced by thyroid hormones as well. When the thyroid is working optimally, it protects against heart disease and strokes, lowers cholesterol, improves brain metabolism, and helps prevent memory problems. When the body is too frequently in fight-or-flight mode, the thyroid function can decrease, or in some instances may stop producing hormones.

## Insulin

Almost everyone knows someone who developed Type II diabetes later in life. Type II diabetes is called the lifestyle disease because it is caused by lifestyle choices, such as poor diet, lack of exercise, obesity, and *chronic stress*. Appropriate lifestyle changes can prevent or even reverse Type II diabetes. When the hormone insulin is depleted, the result is Insulin Resistance Syndrome (IRS). Gone unchecked, IRS can quickly turn into diabetes, or it may lead to other serious health conditions such as high blood pressure, abnormal cholesterol and/or triglycerides, stroke, and gout.

## Cortisol

Cortisol has recently been touted as the new wonder weight loss remedy. Because low cortisol levels can lead to fat storage, the assumption is that if you stimulate the body to produce more cortisol, you'll lose weight. This is a dangerous assumption. Most people don't realize that cortisol is a hormone produced naturally by the body, or that stress is what caused its depletion in the first place. Cortisol is the body's stress management system, but it has its limits.

Cortisol is secreted by the adrenals, tiny glands located just above each kidney. Don't let the adrenal glands' diminutive size fool you. The hormones produced here are absolutely essential to human life. For instance, when my sister-in-law's lung cancer spread to her adrenal glands, she struggled even to lift her fingers. Powerful steroids extended her life by a few months, but the reality is, too many of her body's systems required the important hormones secreted by the adrenal glands. Our bodies simply can't function without these hormones, especially cortisol.

Chronic or acute states of fight-or-flight increase the body's cortisol secretion. When cortisol levels are high, it can actually lead to weight gain because cortisol is your body's signal to slow down. Other symptoms may include anxiety, mental fogginess, insomnia, and high blood pressure. If this goes on for too long, the body's stores of cortisol become depleted and *adrenal fatigue* sets in—a weak immune system, depression, and chronic fatigue result.

# DHEA

*DHEA* is another stress-reactive hormone  secreted by the adrenal glands. When secreted at proper levels, it aids in lowering cholesterol, thus reducing the risk of heart attacks and stroke. DHEA also helps to reduce body fat, stimulates the metabolism and immune systems, maintains sexual vitality, and boosts the mood. Considered an anti-stress hormone, DHEA can help prevent anxiety and depression.

## Melatonin

*Melatonin*, the hormone associated with sleep patterns, influences the body's ability to rejuvenate and repair. It is secreted by the pineal gland, located at the base of the brain. Melatonin is produced from serotonin, the hormone associated with mood. You'll learn more about serotonin in the next section. When high stress levels disturb sleep, the production of melatonin is inhibited, the immune system is compromised, and the rejuvenation and repair of cells is impaired. During the deeper sleep stages, the body produces natural killer cells—the cells that devour cancers and other free radicals in the body. Insufficient or depleted melatonin can put you at higher risk of developing cancer or other immune deficiency diseases. Additionally, melatonin deficits can result in irritability and premature aging.

As you can see, chronic stress can cause early depletion of nearly every hormone your body produces. And depletion of hormones equates to early aging and disease. In the next section, we'll discuss how stress affects the neurotransmitters in your brain, impacting your emotions and cognitive (thought process) abilities.

## How Can Stress Harm or Destroy Relationships?

Every year, when my children were young, my wife and I would take them on long summer vacations. For four to six weeks we camped, hiked, and saw sights throughout the country. Once the kids got older, we decided to travel from one end of Canada to the other. One day, while driving through a winding road in the Canadian Rockies, we came upon a line of cars stopped along the shoulder of the highway.

People hung out of their cars snapping photographs. Our eyes followed the direction of the photographers' cameras, but we couldn't spot anything. Then, there along the side of the road, we saw two bear cubs tumbling around in the tall grass. Just like the other tourists, I pulled out my camera and started snapping photos. Mama Bear was nowhere in sight, but we knew she wasn't far from her cubs.

Everyone watched from the safe confines of their cars, until one intrepid tourist decided he just had to get a little closer. He ventured across the road to where the baby cubs romped. Within moments Mama Bear appeared from behind a shrub. Surprisingly, her presence didn't dissuade the determined tourist. The closer the man walked, the more the mama bear showed signs of agitation. Though people yelled to the man to turn back, he persisted. Finally, Mama Bear reared up on her hind legs and let out a roar that shocked even those of us sitting in our vehicles. The photographer was so startled that he threw down his camera and raced toward his car.

I realized then what takes place when we're under stress. Just like the bear, people think and act differently when involved in a stressful event. Mama Bear was perfectly content to let her cubs frolic and play in front of all those people as long as the onlookers stayed at a safe distance. As soon as the bear felt threatened, or that her babies were vulnerable, she immediately reacted.

While the bear was feeling safe, she was in what we term a *resourceful state*; she was calm and more than happy to let her cubs play. Once she sensed danger, she moved into an *unresourceful state*; in other words, *all* she could do is react. This is related to the fight-or-flight response discussed earlier.

When you're in a resourceful state, it means that you have access to all the resources available to you. In other words, you have time to think things through. While in a resourceful state, you can easily be loving, caring, and patient with people.

Let's take the story of Judy Jones for an example. She is both vice president of a successful software firm and a single mother. One warm spring day while Judy was driving home from work her favorite song came on the radio. But Judy, unfortunately, didn't hear it, nor did she notice any of the beauty around her. She had a meeting in forty-five minutes and was unforgivably late. The way traffic moved it would take her thirty minutes just to get home. She had to change clothes, gather a dozen files together, then race across town for the meeting. Even though there was no possible way for her to make it on time, she was determined to try anyway. She started catching red lights and every driver around her seemed determined to get in her way. When she finally made it home, she ran through the door and slammed it behind her. Her son, Jimmy, was so startled he dropped a plate and it shattered. What do you think happened to little Jimmy?

Because she was under so much stress, Judy didn't react the way she would in normal circumstances. She got furious with Jimmy. She yelled and said things she deeply regretted and later felt ashamed and guilty.

On another day a few weeks later, Judy got a second chance. It was a Friday evening and she was driving home. Her favorite music played on the radio and she hummed along. Earlier that day she'd had a meeting with her boss and was given a raise and a promotion. She looked forward to spending the weekend with Jimmy. She had no other place she needed to be. As she drove, it seemed as if all the lights turned green just for her. She felt relaxed and comfortable. When she walked in the door, little Jimmy dropped a cup and it broke into a dozen pieces. How did Judy react this time? She patted his head and told him it was okay. She moved him out of harm's way and picked up the pieces. This time, it was no big deal. Why? Because this time Judy was in a resourceful state. She didn't overreact because she wasn't overloaded.

The relationship between Judy and Jimmy is harmed in the first scenario and enhanced in the second. If Judy had been able to maintain a resourceful state even when she felt rushed, she could have prevented Jimmy's hurt feelings and her own resultant guilt and shame.

Was it possible for Judy to remain calm and logical in the first scenario? Some people would say, "No way." However, I know that it's not only possible but also likely, when one has the right tools. In fact, I believe it so strongly that I'd venture so far as to say we could positively change the entire world—could create a new reality—if everyone on the planet learned and practiced what I show you in this book.

**Why Is It So Important to Discharge Stress?**

Let's look at the effect of stress on relationships in another way. Try thinking of your body like electric circuitry. In an electric circuit, a component called a capacitor is designed to hold its charge to a preset point. Once it reaches that point, it has to release the energy and fills the circuit with it.

Our bodies work in a similar way in that they build up energy throughout the day. Normally, that energy is processed and released while we sleep. If you have a high stress job, however, this energy builds faster than normal. You periodically need to release that charge. You can't discharge it at work because you'll lose your job. By the time you get home, you're ready to blow. Without you knowing it, your body seeks a way to vent. Road rage occurs when people discharge energy while driving. Most people hold the energy in until they get home and then, at the first opportunity, they unload it on people with whom they feel the safest, on the people who will forgive them and take them back. In most cases, these people are their family members and closest friends.

Well, this may be all right once, and we may even get away with it twice, but what happens when we continually discharge on family members?

Let's take a look at the currently stressful relationship between David and Maureen. The couple met in college at a local watering hole. Much of their early relationship involved partying with friends. After graduation they decided to tie the knot. Several of their college friends married at about the same time, and the party went on. After a few years, Maureen was ready to have children. She decided she needed to take better care of her health and gave up drinking. David, on the other hand, had unwittingly become dependent on alcohol as a way to discharge his stress. And so for David the partying and drinking continued. David's drinking caused countless arguments between the couple. One day, out of fear of losing his wife, David committed to drinking less. He wasn't ready to give it up entirely, but he agreed to do his best.

For several weeks David was able to say no to his Friday night drinking buddies. He went home and spent the evenings watching television with Maureen. Then, on one particular Friday, David found out he had earned a promotion and a significant pay raise. His friends convinced him that he simply had to go out with them for a celebratory drink. In the midst of all the fun and excitement at the bar, he lost track of time. It didn't matter, though, since he had some pretty exciting news to share with his wife.

Grinning, he walked in the door at midnight. Maureen smelled the alcohol on his breath. He put his arms around her. "I've got great news," he said.

Maureen didn't hear him. She could only think about all the other times David had tried to hug her when he'd had alcohol on his breath. She realized that David hadn't touched her in weeks; he seemed to need to be intoxicated to show intimacy. Maureen pushed him away and stormed out of the room. David hadn't yet recognized how the stress of his job had inhibited his intimacy or that he sought release in alcohol.

In this scenario, David and Maureen are headed for big trouble. Unless David learns another way to release his stress, he will remain incapable of loving himself and others.

David's story is just one example of how people release stress in negative ways. Some people use prescription drugs, others get addicted to television, or food, or sex. As you read through this book, you will find simple techniques for releasing the stress that builds up in your life—from your job, relationships, work, traffic, the environment—so you can avoid causing permanent harm to your relationships. As human beings living in the Twenty-first Century we must be vigilant about releasing our stress in positive ways, or it can leak into our lives, and, like two radio stations that overlap, keep us from hearing the beautiful music that is our world.

## Why is There So Much Stress in the Workplace?

Maggie Wood is employed by one of the largest companies in Silicon Valley. Maggie happened to sit down next to me at a conference and we started to chat. When she told me that she had four grandchildren, I nearly fell off my chair. "Wow," I said, "You look thirty-five."

"Oh, no, I'm in my mid-fifties," she said. "I work in Silicon Valley. I have to look young. If I don't, I'm out of a job."

"Wow, that's intense," I said. "How do you do it?"

"I do what everyone else in the high tech industry does. When I take my vacation, I quietly go off and have plastic surgery. I've had two facelifts," she said with a shrug. "I haven't had a real vacation in six years. I also get up at five every morning and run three miles. Gotta stay fit, too."

"Well, you look great," I said. "But how long do you think you can keep up that pace?"

"Oh, that's not the half of it." She frowned. "I just landed this dream job last year. At least I thought it was a dream job. Now I'm not so sure. Everyone's expected to work twelve-hour days. You work nine hours at the office and then go home and log in again for two or three hours. You don't dare skip the working-at-home part, either. They know exactly when you're logged in and when you're not. It's never said aloud, but if you don't put in the hours, you usually don't keep your job."

"Silicon Valley sounds pretty stressful to me," I said.

Maggie went on to tell me that she'd always dreamed of being a novelist. Just before taking her "dream job" she had joined a writing club and started working on her craft. "I miss writing," she said. "But there's just no time."

"Why don't you look for a less stressful job?" I asked.

"Are you kidding? I live in California. It's what everyone has to do to get by."

Maggie agreed that I could write about her story, provided I didn't use her real name. She was convinced she'd be fired if anyone at her company saw it.

In my opinion, Maggie is a victim of the high-pressure society we've collectively created for ourselves. Twenty-first Century living, especially in the United States, offers little time for rest or relaxation. Every day we feel pressure to keep up with the frenetic pace of life. Stress and burnout not only have increased, but also have become epidemic. We live in fear of being left behind. As a result, physical, emotional, and psychological illnesses are also on the rise. According to a survey by the American Psychological Association, Fifty-four percent of Americans are concerned about the level of stress in their everyday lives." [4] Furthermore, "sixty-two percent of Americans say work has a significant impact on stress levels." [4]

Statistics show that one million employees are absent on an average workday due to stress-related problems. This epidemic costs companies \$200–300 billion annually, as assessed by absenteeism, diminished productivity, employee turnover, accidents, and direct medical, legal, and insurance costs. According to the National Institute for Occupational Safety and Health, "Job stress can be defined as the harmful physical and emotional responses that occur when the requirements of the job do not match the capabilities, resources, or needs of the worker." [4]

Let's take a look at some frightening statistics that show just how far over the top our stress levels have become.

## Stress in America

- The American worker has the least vacation time of any modern, developed society.
- In 2005, 33% of workers said they felt a great deal of stress.
- One-half of workers reported they felt a great deal of stress on the job.
- 44% of working moms admitted to being preoccupied about work while at home and one-fourth said they brought home projects at least one day a week.
- 19% of working moms reported they often or always worked weekends.
- 37% of all working dads said they would consider the option of taking a new job with less pay if it offered a better work/life balance.
- 36% of working dads reported they brought work home at least one day a week and 30% said they often or always worked weekends. [5]

These grim statistics demonstrate how little time people are taking for themselves. Jobs like Maggie's, where people work twelve-hour, overloaded, stress-packed days with little or no time for unwinding and rejuvenating are more commonplace than ever. And, like Maggie, people think they have to work and live in overdrive just to stay ahead of the curve. No one stops to think about how out of balance our lives have become.

### Why Does Stress Sabotage You When You Want to Make a Change?

Stress is our worst saboteur because we operate just like that mama bear who grew more anxious as the threat moved closer. Our bodies react; it's either fight-or-flight. If, on the other hand, you're in an open and resourceful state, time, energy, or resources do not confine you. The change you want to make gains your full focus and attention.

Let's use David's drinking problem as a further example. One day David decided he no longer wanted to be an alcoholic. He wanted to salvage his suffering marriage. David committed himself to a rehabilitation center for thirty days. In his usual overachiever style, he gave his all to the program. He was the star of every group therapy session. He walked out of rehab alcohol free and feeling better than he had in years. The counselors encouraged him to continue his therapy through Alcoholics Anonymous. But David didn't think he needed that. He was cured.

Then David returned to his old life. Maureen was not as optimistic about his so-called cure, and insisted he go to AA meetings. Her nagging made him furious. He wasn't about to spend time with a bunch of old lushes. When he returned to his job, backlogged work stood in piles all over his desk. It would take him weeks to sort it all out. His drinking buddies started subtly enticing him with stories of the good old days. Every trigger that had driven him to drink in the past seemed ten times more powerful. Soon the stress, anger, and confusion pushed him over the edge and he agreed to go out for drinks with his buddies. I think you can figure out what happened from there.

When David was in the rehab facility and free from his daily stress, he was able to maintain a resourceful state. Making a change seemed easy to him. As soon as he returned to his life, he fell right back into his usual unresourceful state, which left alcohol as his only option.

Whenever you attempt to change something about your life—whether it's starting a diet, quitting smoking, or something as simple as improving your golf swing—certain triggers that can easily push you out of your resourceful state still exist. Additionally, our minds and bodies function primarily out of habit. We develop a normal operating procedure. The moment we change it, our bodies experience stress. As an example, fold your hands in your lap for moment. Now notice which thumb is on top. Try switching thumbs and just notice how that feels. It's a little uncomfortable, isn't it?

If you were to practice folding your hands with the opposite thumb on top for several days, your body would grow accustomed to this new habit and you would no longer feel uncomfortable. I challenge you to give it a try and see how long it takes.

What I've just asked you to do is a small change. Now can you imagine what your body must go through to recalibrate when you attempt a major change? And do you see why making a change can cause stress and tension? The good news is, I have a solution that will let you make any change you desire practically effortless.

When you are trying to improve your life, the first step must be to figure out the relationship between stress and the problem; I guarantee you, there always is one. Once you have that done, you can use the methods you learn in this book to put coping mechanisms into place. In fact, that's what this entire book is about: teaching you how to maintain resourceful states even when the stress gets intense or chronic so you can have whatever you want out of life. You will learn how to manage physical stress (the way stress affects the body), mental stress (the way it affects the mind), and emotional stress (the way stress affects the connection between body and mind).

## What Are the Everyday Stressors No One Thinks About?

While we mostly think of stress as an emotional response, environmental stressors also can impact our bodies without our even knowing it. For example, have you ever noticed how tired you feel after a long car or airplane ride? Even if you slept during the trip, you usually feel exhausted by the time you arrive at your destination. Why? Because even though it would appear that you are only sitting there in the car or on the plane, every molecule of your body is actually racing along at speeds up to 550 miles per hour. No one really knows exactly what impact this may have on our bodies.

What about electronic smog? Many scientists around the world now believe that ELFs, short for Extra Low Frequencies, may be as harmful to the human body as other types of pollution. What is electronic smog? It's the radiated energy that emanates from virtually everything that plugs into a power socket. This includes everything from televisions to refrigerators, to microwaves, washing machines, electric blankets, toasters, shavers and so on. ELFs also radiate from power lines, cell phone towers, radio frequencies, and domestic house wiring.

Electronic Smog has built gradually since the early days of the Industrial Revolution. Scientists estimate that we are now subject to two hundred times more ELFs than were present at the turn of the century. Some researchers believe that humans, animals, and plants are attuned to the natural resonant frequency of the planet, which is approximately eight hertz, but that ELFs create confusion within this system and cause cells to malfunction. In other words, the electrochemical connection becomes disorganized, and when this happens disease, stress, tension, anxiety, and many different neurological symptoms may manifest. The full affect of ELF exposure is not yet known, however, it's interesting to note that in Russia houses are not allowed to be built near high-voltage power lines because the incidence of cancer rose when families lived for many years in close range to high-voltage lines.

Think about how much time we are spend indoors these days. Most people get only a few breaths of fresh air a day as they walk from their cars into work, stroll across a grocery store parking lot, or drag their weary bodies up the driveway at the end of the day. Today we are spending the greatest portion of the day indoors, in an environment of recirculated air that is loaded with dust mites, allergens, germs, mold and bacteria, all of which strain our immune systems.

Have you ever considered how stressful even the weather can be? Try this scenario on for size: You awaken to the pitter-patter of rain on the window and want nothing more than to snuggle deeper under the covers and sleep in. Not today, though. Today you have meetings and chores and errands and kids to get off to school. So you force yourself out of bed, race around the house getting ready, and then dive out into the drenching rain. You dash from the house to the car, drive the kids to school on slick roads with crazy, rushed drivers all around you. Finally, you jump over puddles to get inside your office building and arrive dripping, wilted, and stressed to the max. And that's just a rainy day!

Have you noticed that the meteorologists now not only forecast the weather, but also warn you when your allergies will likely be at their fiercest or when fire dangers are so high your home is apt to be up in smoke before you arrive home? Forecasters now give pollution advisories and a heat index, warning people to remain indoors if at all possible. Well, how possible is that in today's demanding world? And, I suppose zero degree weather wasn't quite newsworthy enough, now we need to know that it feels fifteen degrees colder *with the wind chill*. Stress! Stress! Stress! And I haven't even touched on hurricanes, tornadoes, floods, drought, or earthquakes!

I think you get my point. The potential for emotional, mental, and physical stress surrounds us everyday, and if we don't do something about it, we become overloaded, and our health and quality of life suffers.

**Is stress silently taking its toll on you?**

The Stress Quotient Test below is your opportunity to examine the amount of stress in your life and how stress may be sabotaging your personal success. I want you to rate your agreement with each of the twenty statements by using a scale of zero to four.

## STRESS QUOTIENT TEST

Rate your agreement to the following statements by using the following criteria:
    **0=never  1=seldom  2=sometimes  3=regularly  4=always**

Below each statement, circle the number you agree with most.

1.      I work more than forty hours a week.
      0   1   2   3   4

2.      I turn to food or substances when I am feeling stressed or overwhelmed.
      0   1   2   3   (4)

3.      My job interferes with my family life.
      0   1   2   3   4

4.      I have feelings of guilt or disappointment.
      0   1   2   (3)   4

5.      I am overly concerned about what others think of me.
      0   1   2   (3)   4

6.      I feel that I have little control over my job.
      0   1   2   3   4

7.      My physician has warned me to reduce stress in my life.
      0   1   2   3   4

8.      I worry that others will discover my true level of stress or anxiety.
      0   1   2   3   4

9.      I lose my temper with family, friends, or while driving.
      0   1   (2)   3   4

10. I experience fear regarding my job security.
    0   1   2   3   4

11. I get stressed out when my workload affects my job performance.
    0   1   2   3   4

12. Changes at work and new technology overwhelm me.
    0   1   2   3   4

13. I call in sick because I just can't take it anymore.
    0   1   2   3   4

14. I hide my stress from my family.
    0   1   2   3   4

15. I have recently experienced major life traumas (death in the family, divorce, major move).
    0   1   2   3   (4)

16. I have trouble falling asleep, or wake up in the middle of the night and then struggle to get back to sleep.
    0   1   2   (3)   4

17. I wake up feeling anxious, nervous, or tired.
    0   1   2   3   (4)

18. I avoid exercise or social activities.
    0   1   2   3   4

19. I find it difficult to get motivated.
    0   1   2   3   4

20. My life feels out of balance.
    0   1   2   3   (4)

When you have finished rating each statement, add up your scores and write the total here. _____

Let me explain the scoring:

0-10 = low stress; practice the creative visualization and relaxation (CVR) techniques you learn in this book to keep your stress quotient low.

11-30 = moderate stress; you are in overdrive and on the verge of being overloaded. Schedule time to practice CVR at least once a day, practice the tension relaxation exercise as needed.

31-55 = high stress; You are overloaded. Schedule time to practice CVR twice a day, once in the morning and once again at night, preferably right after you get home from work. Practice the tension relaxation exercise as needed. If you find that practicing CVR right before bed causes you to have too much energy, then listen after work or in the late afternoon. A small percentage of people find doing CVR at night causes them to have too much energy and they can't go to sleep.

55-80 = extreme stress; Your health is at risk. See your doctor. Practice CVR at least three times a day, drink more water, practice the tension relaxation exercise daily.

No matter what you scored, you will benefit greatly from the techniques in this book, and you can get started right now by doing the exercise I've outlined below.

**Thought Experiment: Can You Identify the Stressors in Your Life?**

As I mentioned earlier, the first step in making a change involves identifying your sources of stress. Most people are oblivious to the number of decisions they face each day, the number of potential stressors they encounter, and the amount of information pushed at them. Let's take a look at the causes of stress in your life.

In a notebook or journal, write the days of the week as headings on seven separate pages, Monday through Sunday, and then divide the page into three columns. Give your columns the following headings: **Stressor, My Response, Healthier Response.** Each day, take a few minutes throughout the day to write down the **stressors** you faced.

For example, if you woke up late, that would be a stressor. Traffic, meetings, a rushed lunch, a disagreement with a co-worker, technology failures, a sick child, an argument with a spouse, a long line at the grocery store, and anything that gets you upset, frustrated, angry, or nervous should be added to your list. When you finish writing your activities and stressors for the first day, you may see, perhaps for the first time, just how much pressure you are under. At the end of the day, sit down with your list and fill in the **My Response** section. Did you get angry, frustrated, and anxious? Did you overeat or turn to another substance? Did you lose your temper with your family later in the day? Now focus on the **Healthier Response** section. This is the area that should get most of your time and attention. Was there a better way for you to handle each situation? What if you had remained in a resourceful state? What would have been the outcome if you had done so?

Repeat this exercise daily for an entire week. Do you see any patterns developing? Were you more resourceful later in the week than you were at the start?

It's important to remember that if you stayed resourceful and didn't experience stress, your blood pressure probably didn't elevate, your heart and respiratory rates most likely didn't increase, and your body didn't get a rush of insulin, cortisol, or thyroid hormones, which means you are already on your way to improved health and have reduced your risk for lifestyle disease.

*And the day came when the risk to remain*
*tight in a bud was more painful than*
*the risk it took to blossom.*
**- Anais Nin (1903 - 1977)**

Example sheet:

## Monday

I recommend that you continue this exercise indefinitely. The few minutes a day it takes could add years of quality living to your lifespan.

| Stressor | My Response | Healthier Response |
| --- | --- | --- |
| Woke up late | Frustrated | Wake earlier |
| Traffic | Angry | Breathe through the traffic |
| Meeting | Bored | Ask questions |
| Rushed Lunch | Anxious | Chew my food fully |
| Disagreed with a coworker | Frustrated | See the situation differently |
| Technology failure | Angry | Do maintenance |
| Bobby was sick | Frustrated | Be more supportive |

Day:

| Stressor | My Response | Healthier Response |
| --- | --- | --- |
|  |  |  |
|  |  |  |
|  |  |  |
|  |  |  |
|  |  |  |
|  |  |  |
|  |  |  |

## So What's the Good News?

The good news is that by learning to use the magic elixir I'll share with you in upcoming chapters, you can learn to quiet your mind, calm your body, and directly overcome the harmful effects of the fight-or-flight response—you will, in fact, gain the healthy benefits of its opposite—*the relaxation response.*

In the next chapter, you'll be introduced to the universal principles we'll use to help you regain the healthy, happy, and stress-free life you were born to live.

*"The most beautiful emotion*
*we can experience is the mysterious . . .*
*He to whom this emotion is a stranger,*
*who can no longer wonder*
*and stand rapt in awe,*
*is as good as dead,*
*a snuffed-out candle."*

**– Albert Einstein**

*"The reason most people never reach their goals is that they don't define them, or ever seriously consider them as believable or achievable. Winners can tell you where they are going, what they plan to do along the way, and who will be sharing the adventure with them."*

**- Denis Watley**

# CHAPTER
# TWO

### The Universal Laws
### That Can Change Your Life

## The Universal Laws That Can Change Your Life

We are beings of energy, and every good scientist knows that universal laws and principles govern energy. When your energy is in harmony with universal law, you feel harmonious. When your energy is out of sync with universal law, you feel disharmonious. Universal laws are what dictate the results of our thoughts and actions. It's that simple.

These universal laws govern us at each level of our being—spiritual, physical, and emotional. Stress happens when our egos try to control these laws. In other words, when we express a desire, or take an action, we attempt to direct the outcome. When you are in the flow and live in harmony with universal laws, you gain health, happiness, and prosperity. Therefore, doesn't it make good sense to ride, rather than fight, the current of energy that builds and maintains all of creation?

How much easier would life be if we simply made decisions with good conscience and then left it up to the universal principles to provide the result? I think it would feel something like a juggler, who has held dozens of balls in the air for years, finally letting them fall where they may.

Wouldn't that be a relief?

What I'm describing is the *Law of Acceptance*, which is probably the most difficult for most of us to master because we live in a society that continually tries to control us. We're all victims of a societal form of hypnosis that tells us we must have the big house with the three-car garage, an emerald green lawn, and two expensive cars in the driveway to prove our worth in this world. And so we work too hard and sleep too little. We worry and fuss and rarely have fun. We struggle, manipulate, and control and still don't get what we want. We turn to alcohol, food, and other substances for relief but wind up with more grief. Is it any wonder that our playgrounds are empty and our hospitals full?

## The Law of Acceptance

It was a hot summer evening in Phoenix, Arizona. My dad and I sat in folding chairs on his small condo patio. Our hearts felt as heavy as the stifling desert air. "We could be helping so many people," I said. "Yet here we are with only a handful of clients and barely making enough to pay the bills."

We had just relocated to Phoenix from Michigan and were beginning to realize that our prospects for opening a business were grim. Starting up an enterprise in Phoenix was much more costly than in our hometown of Battle Creek, Michigan.

"We need someone to help us get started . . . to invest in us," I said. "We're good therapists, but we need a business model."

Not an hour later the phone rang. "No, we're not interested," my dad said after a few minutes of listening to the caller. "We want to start our own business."

"Who was that?" I asked.

"Oh, that was just Dr. Adams. He's looking to set up a satellite office here in Phoenix so he can come out to visit his parents in Sun City. He wanted to know if we'd run it, but I told him we're opening our own business."

"Dad," I said, "didn't we just have a conversation about looking for someone who can help us? Dr. Adams has a great business model in Michigan. He's willing to invest in a new therapy center here, he wants us to run it, and you told him 'no'?"

"We don't need his help," he said. "We know exactly what we're doing."

But we didn't know what we were doing, and in that moment I realized that my father was unwittingly fighting the Law of Acceptance. He was unwilling to acknowledge that he needed help. Right then I decided to put the Law of Acceptance to work for me. "If you're not going to do it, I will," I said.

Dad stood his ground between the telephone and me. "You're only twenty-four years old. Dr. Adams won't be interested in doing business with you."

Not long after that I called Dr. Adams back. "If you really want to put something together here in Phoenix, give me the checklist of what you need and I'll get it done."

As Dad had predicted, Dr. Adams was dubious about my youth, but he was willing to let me try. In less than a week, I supplied him with everything he'd requested. Within a month we had a solid deal. Four short years later I was able to purchase the entire business from him. That business eventually grew into an international franchise. Today my dad and I are equally grateful that, at twenty-four years old, I had the ability to recognize that we were much more likely to get what we wanted by being in harmony with the Law of Acceptance.

Why do writers, artists, and musicians have agents? They do so because they accept the fact that, while they are incredibly talented within their area of expertise, they are lacking in business and finance skills and they don't have the networking contacts within the industry to sell their product on their own. They accept that it's okay to bring in other people to do those things they can't do. They don't try to control their entire universe. The creative people who are willing to live in harmony with the Law of Acceptance usually end up more skillful and more successful because they focus their time and attention on honing their talent.

If something in your life isn't working, chances are good you aren't accepting that you have a problem. If you don't believe you have a problem, how can the goal striving mechanism of your other-than-conscious mind go to work creating a solution? If your other-than-conscious mind doesn't know that you don't want what you're getting, why would it change anything?

Until you reach a state of acceptance by being one hundred percent honest with yourself, your mind will simply give you the status quo. In other words, if you continue to do what you've always done, you'll continue to get what you've always gotten. To make a change you must first accept that what you're doing isn't working.

This is why every twelve-step program includes the Law of Acceptance. When I was young, my Dad regularly went on drinking binges that would last several days or even weeks. He then had the uncanny ability to come out of his drunken stupor and pretend not to know how badly he'd just messed up his life and ours. Dad was such a master of denial, sometimes he even convinced us that he didn't have a drinking problem.

He spent years trying to prove that he wasn't an alcoholic when, in reality, he was such a good alcoholic that my mother had to go down to the factory where he worked to pick up his paycheck before could get his hands on it. Otherwise, he would have drunk and gambled it away in one night.

One day, after a long binge, he came to the conclusion that he needed help. He found a course on relaxation called the *Silva Method* and thought it might benefit him. As he learned to relax his mind, he realized that it was the label of alcoholic he'd fought for so many years. He began to understand what was really going on—that he was a person so stressed out that he had no better way to de-stress than to drink. From that day forward, he accepted the fact that alcohol only had power over him if he put it in his body and, therefore, he was a person who never again could consume alcohol. But it didn't matter, because now he had relaxation techniques to help him de-stress whenever he needed to do so.

### The Serenity Prayer

God grant me the serenity to accept the things
I cannot change; courage to change the things I can;
and the wisdom to know the difference.

The moment my dad used the Law of Acceptance, the unseen forces of his mind set him free from alcohol abuse. Using the techniques he learned, he decided to continue his education, and eventually he earned a Doctorate degree in psychology and Christian counseling.

When you accept where you are and accept that you need help, the next law, the *Law of Attraction*, comes into play and the universe brings the right people, the right experiences, the right seminars, the right books, and/or the right relaxation method to you. Once you accept where you are, you unconsciously send a signal to the world around you that says, I am attracting to me what I need to get me to the next level of my own growth.

**The Law of Attraction**

I finished my last bite of food and waited for Jerry. That was usually the case when we went to dinner. Jerry was a charter member of the clean plate club; he always ate every bite meticulously as if he'd be sent before a firing squad if he left one morsel of food. I was fine with that, though. It was during those times that I talked and Jerry listened.

Earlier that day, Jerry attended a class I taught for the Arizona Health Council. The purpose of the class was to demonstrate how to help second-time DUI offenders. To do that, I presented my training, *Hidden Solutions*. The problem was, the solutions seemed hidden from the doctoral and master-level psychologists I was teaching. They simply didn't understand how anyone could regard a person's thinking in the same way you might think of software in a computer.

"I need to awaken their genius," I told Jerry.

Jerry put down his fork and motioned for me to hold that thought while he finished chewing. "That's a great book title!" he exclaimed.

"What is?" I asked.

"Awaken the Genius."

Coming up with book titles was nothing new for Jerry. We often joked that he should write *The Book of Book Titles*. As I pondered his words, it hit me. I had two more days with the health council.

"Jerry," I suggested, "Let's change the topic tomorrow and videotape the session. I can transcribe the tape and write a book from it. We'll call it *Awaken the Genius*."

Jerry was a master procrastinator. He'd recently started a small publishing house in Arizona, PureLight Publishing, to self-publish his exhaustive list of book titles. His procrastination had kept him from getting the publishing business off the ground. Then there was me. English was the only class I didn't *ace* in school. I was probably the last person who should attempt to write a book.

Despite that, Jerry said, "If you write it, I'll publish it."

I scribbled a contract on a napkin and asked Jerry to sign it.

Jerry looked it over. "We need a time period on this contract," he said. "How long will it take to write the book?"

"Six months," I replied. Six months seems like a long time.

We both signed the napkin, and we had our contract.

It was a risk. I had no idea what kind of commitment I'd just made. I'd never heard of anyone writing a book in that manner. Both Jerry and I knew, though, that when I make a commitment, it will happen.

We videotaped the following two days as planned, then had the tape transcribed. It was during that time that I came to understand the term, "Writing is editing." Fortunately, I'd married the perfect editor.

I'd discovered Cynthia's talent when I was living in Denver and she lived in Phoenix. She always sent my letters back corrected with the most beautiful red pen. (Okay, she didn't really send them all back, but if you ask her, she'll tell you she wanted to!) I knew right away that she was the woman for me. Who better to edit my book? So, I wrote and Cynthia edited. Once she was done with her part, we sent review copies to friends and family members to get comments. With each piece of feedback we received, the final manuscript continued to take shape. When it was done, I placed a copy of the napkin contract on top of the completed manuscript and shipped it to Jerry.

I wish I could have been a fly on the wall the day that FedEx package arrived for Jerry. I'm sure he would have published the book even if it had taken two years to finish, but he never expected me to complete the process in six months. I wanted a bestseller, but Jerry still hadn't set up his publishing empire. What was the master procrastinator to do? Seeing the situation, Cynthia and I agreed to help him kick PureLight into high gear.

It seemed like smooth sailing at first. We found a great printer who could handle the first order and help us with everything we needed along the way. I'd pictured the perfect book cover during a visualization session—a picture of Einstein moving through space. I knew of a talented artist from Sedona, Arizona, whom I thought could design the cover I envisioned. When we received the picture, though, it was awful. I called the artist.

"For two-grand, that's what you get," he said.

I was upset, to say the least. I couldn't have my book published with that cover, but I also didn't know how to realize my vision. It seemed like an insurmountable roadblock. I went into my office, kicked back in the recliner, closed my eyes, and did an in-depth creative visualization of the cover I wanted. While I was at it, I decided to see it on the bestseller shelf at the bookstore. After I finished, I decided to go for a walk. I wandered over to a mall near my office. It was there that I met Sam.

Sam was an energetic t-shirt painter, and a darn good one. I chose a seat near his shop and watched him produce t-shirt after t-shirt, each one better than the last. After the day's rush was over, I approached Sam. I introduced myself and asked him if he did artwork besides painting t-shirts.

"Sure," he replied. "I've done some album art, and I have a studio full of paintings."

"Could you be hired to do a book cover?" I asked.

Sam's eyes lit up. "I sure can, and I—"

That's when I interrupted him and told him the story of the artist from Sedona, leaving out how much I'd paid for the disappointing artwork.

Sam assured me that I would pay him nothing if I wasn't totally happy with the finished product. "What kind of cover were you thinking of?" he asked.

I pointed at a t-shirt with a space design. "I was thinking of something like this, but with a picture of Einstein's face superimposed in the foreground—as if the ghost of Albert himself were looking at the reader."

Sam jumped up and ran to the back of the shop. What had I said that caused him to leave without a word? In a moment, he returned, grinning, and holding a sketchpad.

"You're not going to believe what I've been doing in my spare time!" he exclaimed.

"What?" I asked.

Sam flipped through the pad and revealed dozens of sketches of Albert Einstein. "I had no idea why I was drawing all these pictures of Einstein," he said. "I guess it was for your book cover."

There, on the sketchpad, was the perfect picture. "That image and that background over there," I said. "How much would that be?" I held my breath.

"Is four-hundred-fifty too much?" Sam asked. "I'll give you camera-ready art."

The rest is history. It's amazing what you can find right around the corner if you're willing to visualize it and then risk asking.

The rest of the book's production went smoothly and it was time for promotion. I quickly found out that, unless you're already a *New York Times* bestseller, no publisher wants to promote your book. It was back to the drawing board—again.

Cynthia and I visited Jerry. "Look," we said, "our business is going well, so we can commit some time to promoting the book. We'll buy a motor home and tour the country. You set up the events."

Jerry agreed, and the journey began. At long last, things were going well. As we were about to start our tour, the North American Bookdealers Exchange awarded *Awaken the Genius* "Best How-To Book of 1994." More often than not, we found the book already sold out when we arrived at a tour destination. A number of the booksellers told us that they were certain it was the unique cover that was grabbing their customers' attention. Best of all, at several locations we were told that *Awaken the Genius* had topped their bestsellers list! Everything that I had creatively visualized had been realized, with the "Best-How-To-Book" award like a cherry on the top.

I know a few skeptics who would say that it was all just coincidence, and I would agree with them; I experienced coincidental events based on what I had visualized for my book and myself. Any time you find yourself describing experiences in terms such as coincidence, serendipity, good luck, bad luck, fluke, fate, chance, good fortune, bad fortune, or destiny, you are likely on the receiving end of the Law of Attraction.

The Law of Attraction played a big role in my love life as well. Even as a young man, I felt strongly that my work was like a mission. I was certain that I had come into this life to do something important, and I realized that I needed more than a wife; I needed a life partner who would join me in my work. So one day I sat down and made a list of the qualities I sought in a wife. I meditated on the Law of Attraction for a few minutes, then tucked the sheet between the pages of one of my favorite books and forgot about it.

A few months later I overheard my dad telling my mother that he was planning on canceling an upcoming class he'd scheduled because too few people had enrolled.

"Do you mind if I do the class for practice?" I asked.

"Sure, go ahead, but don't expect much," he said, "Only a few people signed up."

Once the opportunity was mine, I decided to promote the class with a small ad in the local newspaper. The ad read something like, *Learn About the Power of Your Mind*, and gave my phone number. I was amazed (and so was my dad) when nearly thirty people registered for the class.

On that first evening, the students and I sat in a circle and, one by one, each of the participants introduced themselves. Then there she was; her name was Cynthia and I knew that one day she would be my wife.

After the class, my friend, Ray, and I went out for ice cream. "Did you see that girl, Cynthia?" I said. "I'm going to marry her."

"Yeah, right." Ray smirked. "You wish."

By the time the second class rolled around, I was convinced Cynthia and I were meant to be together—until she didn't show up. Then she didn't show up for the third class. Maybe Ray was right and being with Cynthia was more than I could wish for. I broke down and called her. It turned out she had been in a car accident and severely injured her neck. Well, that put a real crimp in the *someday this will be my wife* scenario.

Once Cynthia healed, though, she started showing up at some of the activities and functions that I was involved in.

After about a year and a half of seeing each other at events, we connected and had our first date. Later in the evening, Cynthia admitted that she'd had a crush on me ever since that first class, and that she'd been intentionally showing up in places where she might find me. She also told me that the night before that first class, she had complained to her mother about the scarcity of eligible men.

"If you want to find someone of like mind," her mother had said, "you need to go places where people of like mind might be. Do what interests you, and the right guy will show up."

The very next morning Cynthia saw my ad in the newspaper and decided the topic was of great interest to her. Was it coincidence, or the Law of Attraction, that I happened to be there as well?

But that's not the end of the story. About nine months into our marriage, Cynthia and I decided to move to Louisville, Kentucky, so we could own and manage our own practice. While packing, a small slip of paper fell out of a book and flitted to the floor. Cynthia picked it up and read it. Too late I realized that it was the list of qualities I had written more than two years earlier. I tried to grab it from her, but she wouldn't give it up. I was relieved to see that she was smiling. Finally, she handed it to me. "Read it out loud," she said.

As I read down the list, we both saw how she did, in fact, have all the qualities I had asked for.

"Wait right there," she said, as she disappeared up the stairs. A few minutes later she returned with a notebook. She flipped through the pages and then handed it to me. There was her own list of the qualities she was looking for in *her* soulmate. It had me pegged.

"The only thing you forgot to attract is a full head of hair," I joked.

We both laughed.

Our marriage has lasted nineteen amazing years. We are grateful for how the Law of Attraction brought us together and gave us both what we wanted and needed in our lives. Our confidence is strong that our marriage will last a lifetime because we were brought together by that unseen force that binds us together, and because we were both seeking a partner who could look in the same direction, and not just into each other's eyes.

## The Law of Cause and Effect

Most people have heard of the *Law of Cause and Effect,* but few truly grasp the role it plays in our lives. *What you sow, you reap.* Seems simple enough, right? Well, the Law of Cause and Effect can work in either positive or negative ways. As you read this chapter, your job is to figure out how to use the Law of Cause and Effect to create the life you want. There is no reason you can't learn to master this law in a way that will bear positive and dynamic fruit.

As I sat in the school locker room one stifling August afternoon, I had no idea how the events of that day would change my life. True, I'd been training for that moment for three years. In my mind, I had arrived. I might not realize my prediction of being team captain, but

I was finally a member of the varsity football team. No matter what position I played, it was still a tremendous achievement.

I thought back to when I'd made that bold prediction three years earlier. I weighed less than a hundred pounds. I couldn't manage even ten push-ups—and forget about running a mile. I played football, but I was known as a "thirty-second wonder." That is, with thirty seconds left in the game, the coach often looked down the bench and saw me standing there with a glazed look in my eyes.

"Porter!" he'd yell. "Are you ready to get in there?"

I'd jump to attention, scramble for my helmet, and run out to the field. Then I'd watch the clock.
30 . . . 29 . . . 28 . . .

I would watch the thirty seconds tick down to zero without ever seeing a play.

On top of my pitiful athletic ability, I was a terrible student. I'd barely passed eighth grade and, because of that, I was facing the prospect of a summer in detention.

I'd already spent two years in second grade. My dad resolved that, one way or another, he was going to motivate me to learn.

My father had just finished reading James Allen's book, *As a Man Thinketh*. He was intrigued by Allen's ideas. He decided I would be his "science experiment." So, one day in early summer, he cornered me.

"Do you have a goal for high school?" he asked.

"Yeah," I said with typical junior-high impudence. "To get out."

My dad remained patient. "What about during school?"

I thought for a moment. "I'm going to be captain of the football team."

If my dad doubted that the school's thirty-second wonder could become team captain, he didn't let it show. Without missing a beat, he reminded me, "Faith without works is dead."

"Huh?"

"We need a plan," he said. He pulled out a calendar. "Where will you start?"

I remained puzzled. "What do you mean?"

"You have to start somewhere," he said. "Unless you want to spend all summer in your room, we need a plan to get you ready for football." He started writing on the calendar. I peered over his shoulder and saw that he had written the same words on every single day: "Read *As a Man Thinketh*." He turned and looked into my eyes. "We're going to start with your head," he said. "Your body will follow."

Sitting in that locker room three years later, I realized my dad had been right. I was now one hundred eight five pounds of muscle. I could run a 4.6 forty yard dash and bench press two hundred fifty pounds. No one could catch me. I had no fear.

In fact, only one thing kept me from reaching the goal I'd reluctantly set three years before. Springfield, like all schools, had its favorite sons. Certain well-known families seemed to have the divine right of kings on their side. Coach Newton, though a good coach, upheld the status quo. I was already captain of the wrestling and track teams, but being captain of the football team seemed out of reach. My athletic ability was there, but I knew I'd never make it through that invisible social barrier.

As I sat, thinking of the past and talking with friends, in walked Mr. Ward. I liked Mr. Ward; he met me every morning during my cool-down, often handing me a glass of water. I was confused, though. What happened to Coach Newton? Then the Athletic Director, Mr. Peterson, walked in.

"Boys," he said. "I want you to meet your new coach."

When Coach Ward spoke to the team, I couldn't believe my ears. He was doing something that had never been done in the history of the school—letting every football player vote for team captain. Even the freshmen and the junior varsity team had a vote.

I had to bite my lip to hide my smile. Two years earlier, because I don't like to work out alone, I'd started a weightlifting team. Many underclassmen had joined and become my weightlifting buddies. While others in my class hazed younger students for sport, I helped make them stronger. I even started a summer running program to make them faster. I arranged a special trip to see Western Michigan play, and the underclassmen attended with enthusiasm. While doing these things, I had no idea it would lead to the realization of my goal. As I listened to Coach Ward, though, I knew. My chance had arrived!

When the votes came in, I got the result I expected. The team captain position was mine. I also learned a valuable lesson; unseen forces had conspired *with me* to accomplish my goals. The Law of Cause and Effect had worked its magic in my life. Nothing could stand in my way!

## The Law of Forgiveness

When Dorothy first came into my office I thought that helping her to relieve pain from her body was my only task. As I talked with her, however, Dorothy's intense anger toward her parents surfaced.

Dorothy was about sixty years old. I'm sure it had been a long time since her parents had done harm to her, yet her body seemed to still harbor the rage. Her joints, especially her knees, were so sore and inflexible, and the pain so excruciating, she needed a walker to get across a room.

Dorothy had heard about my work through a friend, and now asked me to help relieve her pain. She longed to walk without assistance. All my usual techniques, usually quite successful with other clients, had no impact on Dorothy. I did my best to hide my frustration, but the sessions were going nowhere.

I decided to back up a bit and just take her through a guided relaxation to see if I could get her to let go even a little. About halfway through the session, though, I got an idea. I asked her to think about the people who had caused her pain or anxiety and to forgive them one by one. At first she went along with this, until it came to her parents. Her body trembled and her lip quivered. "I can't do it," she said. "I can't forgive my parents for what they did to me."

I didn't need to know the awful things that Dorothy's parents had done. It would not be helpful to have her replay the scenes anyway; she only needed to forgive them so she could stop holding the anger in her body.

Soon Dorothy was in the throes of a complete breakdown. She wept and thrashed about for a few minutes, and then the most amazing thing happened; she sighed deeply and her body relaxed, as if she'd melted into the chair. "I forgive you," she muttered softly. She later told me that she'd had a realization that the anger she'd been holding in her body had crippled her.

By the time the session ended, Dorothy smiled in a way I'd never seen. "As I forgave my mom and dad," she said, "it started to feel as if a warm liquid flowed through my knees. It was the weirdest sensation I've ever had."

Dorothy and I discussed her experience. "My parents have both been dead for years," she said. "I feel ridiculous for holding onto that anger for so long."

"Think of your body like the hard drive to a computer," I said. " Your mind is the software and your body is the hardware. Every thought you think must be processed through your body. Negative thoughts have to manifest somewhere. The knees represent flexibility. You became inflexible due to the anger you held toward your parents. As long as you held on to that anger, there was no room for positive thoughts, or for healing."

Dorothy experienced one of the most profound transformations I've ever witnessed. A few months later, a local television station called and wanted to interview me for a news segment. "I'd rather you interview my happy clients," I said.

On the day of filming, Dorothy arrived in my office forty pounds lighter and with a smile that lit up the room. "When I first came into Dr. Porter's office I needed a walker, then I used a cane, now I don't use anything at all!" she told the reporter.

"Are you some kind of faith healer," the report asked.

"Definitely not," I answered. "Dorothy did it all herself. I gave her a map and guidebook to her own mind. She did the rest."

I had taught Dorothy to think of her body as a metaphor. As she released the anger, she was able to release the weight from her body, which in turn released the pressure on her knees. Soon Dorothy no longer needed pain medication. Through forgiveness she healed her mind and then her body.

Buddha said, "He who angers you conquers you." Medical researchers are proving this to be true. When we think negative thoughts, the brain spews out a cascade of chemicals that have the potential to destroy the body.

Transversely, if we honor whatever happened in the past as necessary for our growth, and if we forgive the people who have hurt us, then the body responds with the right elixir of hormones and brain chemicals that create health, harmony, and vitality in our bodies.

In the book *As A Man Thinketh*, James Allen says that what you think of in your heart you must become. Once Dorothy let go of her resentment and decided to love truly and deeply, appreciate, and honor her past, her body began to mirror her new beliefs; her body became the manifestation of what she held in her heart.

The word *forgive* means to give before. So as you forgive, and as you let go of the past, you will find it easier to give your body the rest and relaxation it needs so you will have the years of health that you deserve.

## The Law of Abundance

Have you ever dreamed of having a better life, radiant health, a dream home, a more fulfilling career, or owning a thriving business? Have you ever wondered how to make those things happen in your life? Beverly Nadler did and, from a young age, has been making her dreams come true using what she calls *vibrational harmony*.

"Vibrational harmony simply means that everything that comes into one's life does so as a result of what our energy field is in resonance with," Beverly says.[6] Simply put, she teaches people how to use the *Law of Abundance* and the power of thought to achieve dreams and goals in life.

Beverly appears to be living proof that her theories work. She began studying how the world works as a young child. During her studies she discovered teachings that helped her to understand the universe and her place in it. Her ravenously curious mind lead her to *Hermetic Philosophy*, a variety of spiritual teachings, modern psychology, and quantum physics. She then put into practice everything she learned. Today she is a renowned author and lecturer. She says that she has used her mind to lose weight, run her own business, become the owner of her dream home and, astonishingly, cure herself of cancer.

To understand the Law of Abundance, one must first understand that everything in the universe is connected by energy. Energy is the driving force behind all life. Therefore, the energy coming from our own minds literally directs what happens in our bodies and what we attract to ourselves. You are led to those things that fulfill a very strong, powerful positive intention, which is there even when you're not aware of it. We all have the ability to apply this principle to enhance our lives.

For example, most doctors have an innate desire to help people—to heal their hurts. That's why they go into medicine in the first place. This means a universal power flows through each doctor, helping him or her to bring about healing in the patient. Most doctors achieve abundance in their lives not because they are greedy as many people think, but because they are in harmony with their internal desires. In Chapter 9, we'll further discuss positive intention to help you understand how it can either help or hinder you in achieving your goals.

You don't have to look far to see the Law of Abundance in action. It's evident everywhere. Abundance abounds, not only in the places we experience with our senses, but trillions of light years into the cosmos as well. The universe is continually growing, expanding, and thriving in an endless cycle of plenty. For example, the Hubble Telescope has returned to earth photos of what scientists refer to as black energy, which they now know is continually expanding outward and creating new stars, planets, and solar systems. As advanced as technology has become, it is still impossible for us to fathom the vastness of infinity and comprehend the abundance that exists outside of our human awareness. Even within the earth's boundaries, new species of plant and animal life are created and discovered every day.

Even with man's disregard for the preservation of nature, through the Law of Abundance, our world continues to flourish and provide a bountiful supply of resources. Look into your own backyard at the array of wildlife you see every day. You'll discover innumerable squirrels and insects that manage to find the resources they need to survive from day to day. Birds find plenty of food and a wealth of material for building their nests. Go into any forest and lift a layer of leaves and twigs. You'll discover a cornucopia of life dwelling there. Gaze into any lake, stream, or pond and observe the abundance of life that dwells within it. This is the incredible, ceaseless, and never ending Law of Abundance in action. Our universe is based on abundance and plenty; it knows no such thing as lack and limitation.

Now, let's take a look at abundance in your personal world. Do you have the kind of abundance you desire in every area of your life? Do you have what you want financially? Is the career you have the same as the one you fantasized about as a youth? Do you own the home or car of your dreams? Is your health where you want it to be? Are your relationships happy and fulfilling? Do you have enough time to do what you want to do? Do you have enough fun? If you are lacking in any of these areas, the world has not somehow failed you. The Law of Abundance is alive and well and bountiful just as I described above.

Therefore, if you are not experiencing the kind of abundance that you desire for yourself, lack and limitation must be what you are focusing on; otherwise, the universe wouldn't provide you with lack and limitation. Having trouble with relationships? By focusing on the lack of love, the Law of Abundance delivers to you exactly what you are attracting—the lack of love. If you continually think about your lack of money and resources, the Law Of Abundance provides you with an abundance of financial lack. If you worry and fret about sickness and disease, the Law of Abundance provides illness. If you don't have enough time or fun, it's because you have chosen lack in these areas.

All of these examples are the Law of Abundance in action, which means that you will receive in abundance that which you focus your thoughts on.

I once read that if the world's wealth were divided among the people of the world, each person would get approximately seven-million dollars in cash. Sadly, though, it's believed that within a few short decades, the financial imbalance would return to the planet. Why? Because the Law of Abundance will continue to operate precisely the way it has since the beginning of time. Those who attract abundance will once again gain abundance, and those who attract lack will find ways to lose their money to the people attracting abundance.

Although you can't change the Law of Abundance, you can change yourself. You can learn to work in harmony with the laws of the universe that can provide you with whatever abundance you choose to attract into your life.

## The Law of Non-Attachment

Since the mid 80s I've been researching and using the science of light and sound frequencies for deep relaxation and creative visualization. I believed then, and still do, that a light and sound relaxation device should be in the hands of every human being, and that, if it happened, our world would be transformed instantly. This has been my goal since the day I first discovered this amazing technology.

With the advent of electronic media players, I knew what the next generation of the device should be. I regularly visualized an all-in-one light & sound MP3 player—a kind of personal achievement device. This would allow me to synchronize the lights and frequencies with each guided process I created while giving people an easy-to-use system with the fewest possible wires and plugs. During my own visualization sessions, I saw the device with my mind's eye, but at the same time reminded myself to be unattached to the *end result*.

When I sold my previous company, I decided to focus on a motivational speaking career in the high tech industry. That's when I met two Silicon Valley icons. They invited me to visit them at their magnificent home in California to discuss a program on risk.

We sat down and brainstormed. One idea led to another and then Ann asked me an intriguing question. "How are you going to protect your new message from being copied or traded?"

Ann had been a prior client at one of my franchise locations and she knew that my CDs could be easily duplicated and handed out at will. My response was, "There is no way to protect them."

She looked at Ben, then back at me, and smiled. In the next few hours we laid out a plan to build the light and sound unit I had visualized, only now it would have the added feature of encryption technology.

When we were done, I looked at them and sighed. "This is a great idea," I said, "but I've already wasted a lot of time and money trying to develop just such a machine and the experts all tell me the technology isn't yet available."

Ann smiled. "That's what everyone said back in the early 90s when we wanted to develop a phone switch. We saw the need, but everyone told us it couldn't be done. We weren't willing to accept that. It took a little time, but we found the right engineers and got exactly what we wanted."

"I remember that device," I said. "I purchased several of them for my home and offices."

The Bender's ultimately sold thousands of these devices that worked by detecting whether an incoming call was a telephone call or fax and automatically routed it to the proper equipment. "We have the experience and know-how to develop the device you want," Ben said. "And we'll make sure that it protects your content as well. In fact, I already know just the engineer to do it."

It took several months and innumerable tweaks and adjustments, but when Ben, Ann, and jason, our staff engineer, demonstrated the first working prototype, I knew in my bones that one of the biggest goals I had ever set for myself was being realized.

How does this story play into the *Law of Non-Attachment*? Well, in giving up my need to control the end result, the universe somehow brought together the group that could accomplish my goal.

Attachment to the end result of any goal causes stress. Non-attachment dissolves this stress. We are responsible for the action, but there is a power greater than all of us that takes care of the end result. In Garth Brooks' smash hit, *Unanswered Prayers*, he tells a story that demonstrates why the Law of Non-Attachment makes perfect sense. In the song, he and his wife attend a local football game where they encounter his high-school girlfriend, the woman he had prayed to God to make his for all time. As he introduces the two women, he realizes that his former sweetheart "wasn't quite the angel" he had remembered. He then looks to his wife, gives thanks for the gifts in his life, and thanks God for unanswered prayers.

Isn't it typical that we realize after the fact how this universal power knew exactly what we needed better than we did? As the Brook's song says, "I guess the Lord knows what he's doin' after all."

Another example of this law in action happens within our bodies all the time. When you cut yourself, your job is to clean the wound, put antiseptic on it, and cover it with a bandage. After that, the immune system does the rest of the work. It sends white cells to the area to protect you from infection, forms a scab, and mends the cut. You take action to aid the healing process, but you let the body do its work.

In our personal lives, it is often far more difficult for us to be unattached to the end result. Probably the greatest challenges occur within families. Many families have one member who seems to have come from another universe. This is the one person who always seems to be in trouble or has an addiction to drugs or alcohol. As a caring parent, brother, or sister, you can take every step possible to help, but you can't change another person. This is where *tough love* comes into play. Addiction experts know that, once family members are no longer attached to the outcome, once they give up trying to fix the person, they can free themselves from patterns that enable the addict's bad habits.

Of all the laws I've outlined here, the Law of Non-Attachment is the one most likely to liberate you from stress and anxiety. As you read through the stories in this book, you'll discover how other people used this law and ended up with far better outcomes than they could have imagined for themselves. Don't worry if you can't yet picture yourself living in this unattached state. The thought experiments will show you how to visualize your goals and then let go of the attachment.

*"Some of God's greatest gifts are unanswered prayers."*

Garth Brooks, *No Fences*, "Unanswered Prayers"
Written by: Pat Alger, Larry Bastian and Garth Brooks

These incredible laws of the universe form the foundation of everything else you will read in this book. They provide you with a basic understanding of how our universe operates flawlessly and with exact certainty. The following chapters offer you with the key to unlocking these principles, allowing you to attain all you ever hoped for.

In the next chapter I outline exactly what is at the heart of this magic elixir I've been talking about—*Creative Visualization and Relaxation (CVR)*. I explain precisely what creative visualization is, why it's so important to combine it with relaxation techniques, and how the two together create the ideal environment for healing, focusing, and magnetizing to yourself whatever you may want for your life.

*"Try and penetrate with our limited means the secrets of nature and you will find that, behind all the discernible laws and connections, there remains something subtle, intangible, and inexplicable."*

**–Albert Einstein**

# T H R E E

**The Stress Solution
– Creative Visualization and Relaxation**

## The Stress Solution
## – Creative Visualization and Relaxation

In the introduction I talked about a magic elixir that can change your life and the world. In this section, I'll be describing exactly what that elixir is, how it works, and why it can transform your life and the planet.

When Martin Luther King, Jr. made his famous speech, *I Have a Dream*, he used words to create visual images that would stir the emotions of everyone who heard them. Notice what happens in your mind's eye and in your body as you read the following excerpt from that speech:

> *"I have a dream that one day on the red hills of Georgia, the sons of former slaves and the sons of former slave owners will be able to sit down together at the table of brotherhood.*
>
> *I have a dream that one day even the state of Mississippi, a state sweltering with the heat of injustice, sweltering with the heat of oppression, will be transformed into an oasis of freedom and justice.*
>
> *I have a dream that my four little children will one day live in a nation where they will not be judged by the color of their skin but by the content of their character.*
>
> *I have a dream today!"*

Try this quote from George Washington on for size.

> *"If the freedom of speech is taken away then dumb and silent we may be led, like sheep to the slaughter."*

What kind of mental image do you get from the President's statement? How does it make you feel?

Here is one more from John F. Kennedy. Again, notice the

images created in your mind and the emotions those images stir:

*"Let the word go forth from this time and place, to friend and foe alike, that the torch has been passed to a new generation of Americans - born in this century, tempered by war, disciplined by a hard and bitter peace."*

George Washington, John F. Kennedy, Martin Luther King, Jr., and other great leaders like them were able to move our nation and the world to action because of their amazing ability to stir our emotions through visual images. This is the world-changing power of creative visualization.

## What is Visualization?

When we *see* with the mind's eye, we are visualizing. For example, when was the last time your mind drifted away from an activity and into a daydream? If you're honest with yourself, it probably happened within the last hour. In fact, it may have happened while you were reading this book. Daydreaming is normal; everyone does it, though some people are better at it than others, and others are more frequent visitors to their internal world. Daydreams generally happen in pictures, not words. The same is true with visualization. Visualization uses your internal perceptions to create specific visualized scenarios.

Most people habitually create negative images and think negative thoughts rather than positive ones. Dieters are often experts at this. They see themselves as fat, they fantasize about food all the time, and they focus on everything they *can't* have rather than focusing on those things can have. On top of all that, they envy the thin people in their lives. One overweight client once said to my wife, "You're so thin, I hate you!" How will she ever create a slender body for herself if she hates thin people? Conversely, naturally thin people see themselves slim and healthy, think of food as nourishment, and don't give food a thought between meals. If you are a dieter, this book will help you break that pattern so you can think and behave like a naturally thin person. Now wouldn't that be easier?

For most people, visualization is the primary component of the imagination. Albert Einstein was by no means the only great mind to use visualization. Many of history's inventors and artists attribute their success to an exceptional ability to visualize. Thomas Edison, Nikola Tesla, Henry Ford and the great composer, Chopin, all claimed to have used creative visualization to spark their imaginations.

I believe that thoughts are the most powerful force in the universe. Everything begins with the mind. All the amazing technology we take for granted today—cars, computers, cell phones, televisions, even everyday items such as cups and eating utensils—started with someone's thought.

To better understand visualization, try thinking about one of your favorite childhood experiences. Notice the images that come into your mind as you mentally relive that event.

Now remember a time when you accomplished something that made you proud of yourself. What images do you see with your mind in this experience? What feelings do you get from the experience? These are examples of *visualizing from memory.*

Now imagine an upcoming event. Perhaps you have plans to attend a wedding, birthday party, or concert. Choose one occasion and then let your mind conjure up images of what you expect to happen. What images do you see with your mind in this experience? What feelings do you get from the experience? These are examples of *visualizing from imagination,* and this is the primary type of visualization you will be using during the upcoming thought experiments.

Humanity's ability to create and innovate arises from our ability to visualize from imagination. Additionally, this kind of imagined visualization has long been the primary tool for mind/body healing. From a scientific perspective, we know that, because visualization directly impacts the body's neurological system, it can have a direct influence on us physically.

Imagine I have just handed you a large, yellow, juice-filled lemon. You slice the lemon into quarters and bring one of the quarters to your mouth and bite into it. What happened? Did your mouth begin to pucker? Did it fill with saliva? This is a naturally occurring neurological response to an imagined thought.

Have you ever watched a horror film and, in the midst of the excitement, found your palms sweating and your heart pounding? You knew it was "just a movie," though, right? This is another example of how your body is affected by what's happening in your mind. Here is another scenario that demonstrates the power of mind over body:

*You walk down a hallway toward your office. You're feeling sharp in a brand new outfit. Your shoulders are back and your head is high. A co-worker stops you to chat. "You okay?" the co-worker asks. "You look like you don't feel well."*

*"I'm fine," you say. Your shoulders slump and you return to your office. What did your co-worker mean? Maybe you're just tired. Or maybe you **are** sick. Maybe you need that facelift after all!*

*After lunch the same co-worker meets you in the hall. "Are you sure you're okay?" she asks. "You look pale today." By mid-afternoon, you're exhausted and your body aches. Work is a chore. You'd give anything for a nap. Maybe you should go home and rest.*

Most of us have had a similar experience—where one simple suggestion changes our entire mood and the way we feel physically. Of course, now that you are aware of this mind/body connection, you can change everything. If someone tells you you're not looking well, you can simply gauge the way you feel and know when the person is off base. Something as simple as bad overhead lighting may be the culprit. Just in case you haven't yet got the idea, though, let's try one more scenario:

*You're driving down the highway on a sunny Sunday*

*afternoon. You're singing along with your favorite song is on the radio. You're doing the speed limit. Suddenly you hear a siren, and flashing blue lights fill the car. What happens? Does your heart start pounding? Do your palms get sweaty? Does your breathing get shallow?*

Why does all this happen even if you know you're doing everything right? Because your mind is conditioned by past experience—or by a kind of social hypnosis—to respond to this particular stimulus with fear, your brain kicks the fight-or-flight response into high gear, and your body responds.

What I want you to understand about the mind/body connection is this: If the mind can have this kind of impact on the body, is there any reason the mind can't also be harnessed to overpower the effects of nicotine, stimulate the metabolism, trigger the immune system to eliminate unwanted cancer cells, or do away with pain?

## Why Creative Visualization?

Creative visualization, otherwise known as guided imagery, uses language to transport individuals out of their current space and into a new space of inner calm, peace, and tranquility. A natural byproduct of creative visualization occurs when the muscles go loose and limp, thereby creating the relaxation response.

## What is the Relaxation Response?

In the late 1960s, in the same room in which Harvard Medical School's Walter Cannon performed fight-or-flight experiments fifty years earlier, Herbert Benson, MD identified a counterbalancing mechanism to the stress response. In his research, he discovered that, just as stimulating an area of the hypothalamus could cause a stress response, activating other areas of the brain results in stress reduction. He termed this opposite state the relaxation response.

Once the relaxation response is triggered, the brain sends out neurochemicals that virtually neutralize the effects of the fight-or-flight response. We immediately notice the physical benefits such as a decrease in blood pressure, a lower respiratory rate, a slower pulse, relaxed muscles, and an increase in alpha brainwave activity. I'll discuss the importance of brainwaves in an upcoming chapter. For now, just know that alpha brainwaves are associated with deep relaxation and being in this state allows for greater access to what I call the *intuitive mind*, which is where healing is most likely to take place.

Because the relaxation response is hard-wired, you do not have to believe it will work for you to experience the benefits. The relaxation response happens in the body and not in the mind. As you read, you will learn in detail how to turn on the relaxation response, which naturally turns off the harmful fight-or-flight response, so you can easily transform your life and your world. The relaxation response is the perfect state for learning, healing, or focusing on goals.

> *"Repeated activation of the relaxation response can reverse sustained problems in the body and mend the internal wear and tear brought on by stress."*
> -Herbert Benson, MD
> Timeless Healing, 1996

### Why use Creative Visualization and Guided Relaxation Together?

We all have an inner critic, a part of our mind that, based on past experience, will reject new information without proper evaluation. This is known as the *critical factor*. Relaxation techniques subdue the critical factor of the mind. In other words, the part of the mind that might reject unfamiliar information is put on hold during the relaxation response.

Everyone possesses a right-brain and a left-brain. These two parts of the brain play a role in the critical factor, are essential components in the magic elixir, and perform different tasks.

### *What's the right-brain got to do with it?*

The right-brain is the creative part of our nature and is capable of visualizing incredible things for us. As a child, if you had a more active right-brain, there is a good chance your parents often had to tell you, "Stop daydreaming," or, "Come back to earth." Although the right-brain can help you fantasize what you want, it can also cause you to imagine what you don't want, which won't get you anywhere or will create excess stress in your life. Your mind needs direction.

Even though the brain receives messages from all five senses—sight, sound, smell, taste, and touch—it stores the messages as pictures or symbols. This is why people who rarely engage the right-brain often struggle with visualization or meditation techniques. It's also why I'll teach you to use images and symbols to maximize your mind's potential for giving you what you want.

We use guided visualization and relaxation techniques to create positive and appropriate ways for you to imagine your self-image, your health, or your personal goals. This helps you stay optimistic and motivated toward the changes that bring about success. Throughout the book, whenever I mention **CVR**, I am referring to this powerful combination of *creative visualization* and *relaxation*.

### *What's the Left-brain Got to Do With It?*

Let's talk about the left-brain. The left-brain is that part of our brain obsessed with control. It likes sequence and order. It is also the part of the brain that recognizes stress and responds to it. Relaxation can only happen when you release control and allow the left-brain to rest for a while. Even though it may seem counterintuitive to let go in order to gain control, this is exactly what happens during the relaxation response.

When you use many of the thought experiments within this book, you will experience specific relaxation techniques that are coordinated with creative visualization. Each helps you subdue the left-brain while stimulating the right-brain. The idea is to give you a balance, so you can reap the rewards of whole-brain thinking. The visualizations are designed to help you let go of fear, stress, and anxiety and, most importantly, to give you the power of *possibility thinking*.

Possibility thinking involves using the creativity of your other-than-conscious mind to see even the most improbable solutions that can create long-term positive effects on your life. Possibility thinking puts you in a place of choice. Most people rule out new choices based on past evidence, which is self-defeating. Possibility thinking overcomes this preconditioning and allows you to seek the best possible outcome.

On the opposite end of the spectrum is the person who has *limited thinking* and can only see the reasons why something should fail, even when there is evidence that it could succeed. Possibility thinkers can see a way to succeed even when the rest of the world says there is no way. People like Bill Gates, Steve Jobs, and Oprah Winfrey achieved outlandish success because they are possibility thinkers. They refused to settle for anything less than exceptional. For you, developing possibility thinking is at the heart of each thought experiment. Is it possible you could be the next great innovator of our generation?

**How Will CVR Help You Reduce Stress?**

CVR can help you change the way you see yourself and your life. Once you have a new image of yourself—as a healthy, happy, optimistic person—your fears and frustrations fade away, your anxiety vanishes, and you no longer let small things stress you.

In other words, CVR makes sure you are focusing on everything that makes you feel positive and optimistic. When your perception of yourself changes from *stressed* person to *easygoing person*, you no longer will have tension and doubt. If this happens, can you imagine how motivated and energetic you would feel?

I have made a more than two-decade study of people who are naturally easygoing and resilient. I knew that the key to permanent success was hidden in their underlying psychology. By talking with these people, I discovered a common thread that included a positive self-image, a relaxed, easygoing demeanor, the capacity for *seeing* the future as bright and full of opportunity, and the ability to leave the past in the past. I realized that learning how to visualize and relax the way these people do could be life changing for anyone who tried it. CVR can boost your confidence and finally let you reflect inner health and happiness. CVR can help you get back to the way you felt before stress overwhelmed your life. Every day men and women just like you discover the power of CVR, in order to lose weight, stop smoking, overcome pain, reduce stress, or otherwise enhance their lives.

People who have medical conditions worsened by stress find CVR an invaluable tool in reducing the stress-related effects of allergies, asthma, chronic pain, and arthritis, among others.

## How Can CVR Help You Unleash Your Inner Artist?

A few years ago I worked with a well-known author for overcoming writer's block. She once said to me, "I could be insanely creative if I knew no one else would ever criticize what I write." Her comment seemed odd for a published author, but it got me thinking about how much our fear of judgment holds us back.

So take a moment to ask: *If no consequences to my creation existed, if I only had to please myself, if I only had to do what I wanted (within the constraints of safety, harmony, and balance within the world) what would I create? . . . What if there was no judgment?*

Judgment is a function of the logical left-brain, which is why your left-brain needs taming—so you can unleash your inner artist and get to know the part of you that is infinitely creative, and that knows there is only an infinite number of ways to succeed from any given moment.

Imagine that deep within you there is a Leonardo da Vinci, of whom Sigmund Freud once said, *"Leonardo da Vinci was like a man who awoke too early in the darkness, while the others were all still asleep."*

## How Can You Use Logic As a Lever?

In many cases people use *idiot logic* to defend their positions. For example, a smoker, who has seen irrefutable evidence that smoking could kill her, may still say she can't stop smoking because she's smoked for twenty years. This makes no sense. If you took the wrong way to work for twenty years and then one day found a shortcut with less traffic where you could see more beautiful scenery, wouldn't you immediately stop taking the wrong way? Twenty misguided years wouldn't stop you from taking a more logical route.

Here's another form of *idiot logic* that one of my weight-loss clients once said: "I can't exercise because I've never exercised before, and now I'm sixty-years old, so it's too late."

"If I told you there was a multi-million-dollar vein of gold twenty feet beneath you, would you not dig the hole just because you're sixty and have never dug a hole before?" I asked her.

I once knew a massage therapist who leased space in my office. She and I had become friends, and we would frequently sit and chat at the end of the day.

"I have to make a decision," she said to me one day, "and it's driving me crazy. I'm thinking about going back to college to become a physical therapist, but I just can't decide."

"What's the dilemma?" I asked.

"It's going to take me four years," she said. "I'll be fifty by then."

"How old will you be in four years if you don't go back to school?" I asked.

She stared at me for a moment. "What do you mean?"

"Those four years are going to pass anyway. One way or another, you'll get to fifty. The question is, do you want to spend the next four years pursuing your dream, or do you want to arrive at fifty wishing you had?"

She gave no response.

"If you want to do something different, you've got to start making that change today. If you don't go back to school, what will you be doing?"

"The same thing I'm doing now."

"Would that satisfy you?" I asked.

"No." She shook her head, smiled, and stood up.

"Where are you going?" I asked.

"To register." She shrugged on her jacket and started for the door, then stopped and turned around. "Thanks," she said, "I can't believe I couldn't figure that out myself."

Using logic as a lever is what I did in the examples I've given above. The trick is to find out where you might be using idiot logic or where your thinking might be stopping you from making the changes you want in your life. Once you pinpoint the erroneous thinking, you'll know where you need to make the change.

## What Can Your Left-Brain Do for You?

Logical and sequential thinking, time, and control are all processed through your left-brain. When you are figuring out a math problem, or are engaged in the process of writing, you are using the left side of your brain. If you are the type of person who is analyzing every word of this book, or loves to solve puzzles or word problems, you are allowing your left-brain to do what it does best. What types of careers do you think people who are left-brain dominant are going to be attracted to?

If you were thinking of your math teachers or professors you are correct. Lawyers who are constantly analyzing the law and arguing it in court are typically left-brain dominant. You would certainly want your accountant to be left-brain dominant. I would hate to think of a tax return filed by an overly creative accountant!

Because of the nature of science, and its logical tests and rigid procedures, scientists are often left-brain dominant. Engineers, who deal with exact blueprints and create things out of nothing, need an active left-brain.

If you were a Vulcan, like Mr. Spock of Star Trek fame, you would have a dynamic left-brain. Like Spock, the left-brain seeks logic; it believes in control and precision. The left-brain is sequential; everything must make sense. Whether you are speaking with another person, working out mathematical equations, balancing your checkbook, or solving a word game, you are using the left-brain.

Also, the critical factor, which is the part of the conscious mind trained to evaluate information based upon past experience, is part of the left-brain's function. Unfortunately, that critical nature of the left-brain tends to reject new ideas before the creative right-brain has the chance to evaluate them.

The left-brain also controls your sense of time. If a meeting is scheduled for 9:00 am, a left-brain dominant person will arrive a few minutes early, whereas a right-brain dominant person may show up at ten after nine (or later), and won't understand why others get frustrated by his or her lack of punctuality. Right-brainers tend to think that time is approximate. Left-brainers are very controlled by time; everything runs on a schedule. For example, they have a specific time for lunch each day—say noon—and they eat at noon, even if they're not hungry. They eat because it's time to eat, and thus tend to eat less. Right-brain dominant people eat when they're hungry or when their appetite gets stimulated. This is why most overeaters tend to be right-brain dominant. People who are sequentially-oriented, logical thinkers are usually very controlling and are left-brain dominant.

### Here are fifteen characteristics of a left-brain thinker.
Check the ones that apply to you.

1. ☐ Do you like working with facts?
2. ☐ Are you more comfortable dealing with data in a precise and exact way?
3. ☐ Do you look at problems in a logical and rational way?
4. ☐ Do you like working with numbers?
5. ☐ Are you interested in the technical aspect of things?
6. ☐ Is performance important to you?
7. ☐ Do you prefer to analyze facts?
8. ☐ Do you prefer traditional ways of thinking?
9. ☐ Do you like facts to be organized and orderly?
10. ☐ Do you like to work with detail?
11. ☐ Do you prefer a stable and reliable work environment?
12. ☐ Do you feel comfortable with procedure?
13. ☐ Do you prefer security and safety to risk-taking?
14. ☐ Is the task at hand what's important to you? Do you do whatever it takes to complete it on time?
15. ☐ Do you prefer people who are practical?

Total: _____ out of 15 apply

## What Can Your Right-brain Do for You?

The right-brain is responsible for creativity, dreaming, and imagination. Composing or appreciating music happen in the right-brain. When you draw a picture or paint on a canvas, you are using the creative right side of the brain. Some might even argue that painting your living room is a creative endeavor. If you have struggled with poetry or creative writing, this might be because you have not allowed your right-brain creative license. Whether you are sculpting, singing, or dancing like John Travolta, you are engaged in a right-brain function. What types of careers do you think people who are right-brain dominant are going to be attracted to?

If your first thought was an artist, you are correct. Other right-brain occupations include poet, dancer, novelist, interior decorator, or musician. Although this by no means is a complete list, it gives you an idea of the type of work a right-brain dominant person would excel in.

Your right-brain is the place of free-spiritedness, dreams, visions, fantasies, fairy tales, freedom, imagination, romance and make-believe. The right-brain has no boundaries or limitations; it is the realm of pure creativity and possibility.

### Seventeen Characteristics of a Right-brain Thinker
Check the ones that apply to you.

1. ☐     Do you see the whole picture, but not the details?
2. ☐     Do you like change and trying new things?
3. ☐     Do you enjoy being busy with several things at the same time?
4. ☐     Do you have a vivid imagination?
5. ☐     Do you rarely accept "the only right answer," but look for alternatives?
6. ☐     Do you enjoy a challenge and a risk?
7. ☐     Do you get gut-feelings for new ideas?
8. ☐     Can you rearrange ideas and put them together into a new whole? (This is known as synthesizing.)

9. ☐     Do you like to vary the way you perform your routine tasks?

10. ☐     Do you like to find a connection between the present and the future?

11. ☐     Do you experience facts in an emotional way?

12. ☐     Are you sympathetic and intuitive toward other people?

13. ☐     Do you like interaction?

14. ☐     Do you make use of figurative language as well as non-verbal communication (body language, facial expressions)

15. ☐     Do you feel empathy toward others?

16. ☐     Is problem solving often an emotional, not a logical, process?

17. ☐     Do you show enthusiasm when you like a new idea?

Total: _____ out of 17 apply

**Thought Experiment: How Are You Wired?**

If you are in a place where you can safely stand up, I would like for you to do so. Support your weight on your right leg and rotate the other leg in a circle. Continue moving your leg in a circular motion and spell your name in the air with your dominant hand.

What happened when you started to write your name? Did you find it was easy to spin your leg in a circle, until you started writing your name? Did your leg stop the circular motion and begin to move back and forth? This happens when the left-brain is dominant. The circle is a right-brain function, but writing is a left-brain function. If the left-brain is dominant, it wins.

Were you able to continue spinning the circle, but forgot how to write your name? This happens when the right-brain is dominant because creating a circle is a right-brain function.

If you were able to do both at the same time, congratulations! This is a rare ability. In fact, fewer than one percent of my seminar participants have been able to do both at the same time. This ability is the domain of a fortunate few who naturally function in a whole-brain state.

Whatever you may have experienced during the process, it provides strong evidence that there is an internal power struggle going on within you. This struggle is between the left and right-brain functions. This is why, whenever you perform a new task, the dominant half of your brain automatically takes over, even though it may not be the ideal part of the brain to accomplish the task.

This internal power struggle means that when some of you walked into math or science class you felt uncomfortable. You might have felt out of place. But maybe when you walked into drama or art class you felt comfortable because that's where your brain was most productive. You felt at home. For others, the complete opposite may be true.

Our behaviors become ingrained and anything outside of our expectations often throws us for a loop.  For example, have you ever borrowed someone else's car, reached for the gear shift, only to realize it was in a different place? Or switched from driving a manual transmission to an automatic and your left foot kept stepping on a non-existent clutch? Perhaps you reached for the radio and found the knob was in a different place? Over time, you re-learn where everything is and adapt to the situation. But at first it feels awkward.

What I'm going to show you through CVR is how to live in harmony with the right and left-brain and become more whole in your thinking.

### Did You Know that You Will Almost Always Get What You Rehearse In Life, Not What You Intend?

As an example, most experts on nutrition encourage you to drink eight to ten glasses of water a day. You're used to drinking eight to ten colas a day. When you reach for the water, it feels as uncomfortable as having the wrong thumb on top. The same thing is true if you are accustomed to having stress in your life. If people conditioned by stress don't have it, they will find a way to create it because that's what feels most familiar.

Imagine the smoker who is conditioned to smoke upon awakening, after a meal, or while driving. Without the proper re-conditioning, the smoker will never become tobacco-free.

Through CVR you are going to learn how to change your neurology—to imagine your body and brain working in a different fashion. While practicing CVR, your right-brain, the creative part, sends messages to the left-brain that are processed and turned into habits. This is necessary because the left-brain is sequential, ordered, and timely. It's the control center of your habits.

With creative visualization you can let your ingenuity come out to play. Instead of reaching for a soda, you might ask yourself, "What if I enjoyed water as much as I enjoy a soda?" This gives your other-than-conscious mind another option for quenching your thirst. You now have a behavior that is just as immediate and appropriate, but that's a better alternative.

The bottom line is this: What you did in the past doesn't have to be what you do in the future.

What would happen if you were even more creative? What if you trained yourself so that every time you looked at the clock, you reminded yourself to drink a glass of water, take a deep breath, or some other positive behavior?

If you're like most people, you probably look at the clock many times a day. With the proper training, you'd condition yourself to say, "Wow, it's time for a change!" How empowering would that be? You'd really be using both sides of your brain—you'd be in a whole-brain state.

### Sample Solutions for Left-brain Dominant People: How Might You Use These Ideas to Achieve Your Goals?

Left-brain dominant people have a tendency to eat by the clock. They eat at a scheduled time rather than stopping to consider if they're really hungry. A way to engage the right-brain when the scheduled time rolls around is to ask, "Am I really hungry?" If not, perhaps the best option is to drink a glass of water.

Left-brain smokers have convinced themselves that there is only one solution to stress—have a smoke. Their logical minds have proven this to them time and time again. These same left-brainers, when busily engaged in an activity, or in a place where smoking is not an option, such as in church or on an airplane, simply don't smoke. In this case, the right-brain solution for left-brainers is to take time to do activities that relieve stress.

If you have a strong tendency to use your left-brain, try stretching your comfort zone by experimenting with right-brain creativity exercises. One method many of my clients find useful is to try a new hobby while at the same time giving themselves permission to do the activity poorly at first.

I remember teaching my son, Alex, how to play checkers. Like most children learning something new, he was not very good at first and lost almost every game. To keep him from getting discouraged, I changed the rules, suggesting that we play to lose. We both had a blast figuring out how to play to lose and, even if you lost, which meant you won, you still felt good. Alex is still highly left-brain dominant, but I think this taught him a valuable lesson that today he applies in his career as a computer technician. Look for solutions in all places. Even if you think you know the answer, make a list of possible solutions.

## Twenty Strengths of a Left-brain Thinker

As a way to get to know how much of your left-brain is dominant, circle yes or no for each and then fill in the totals below.

1.  Are you able to gather facts?
    Yes / No

2.  Do you prefer to analyze issues?
    Yes / No

3.  Are you capable of arguing rationally?
Yes / No

4.  Are you good at forming theories?
    Yes / No

5.  Do you typically measure precisely?
    Yes / No

6.  Are you a logical problem solver?
    Yes / No

7.  Are you good with financial analysis and decision making?
    Yes / No

8.  Do you have a grasp and understanding of technical elements?                Yes / No

9.  Are you good at critical analysis?
    Yes / No

10. Do you enjoy working with numbers, statistics, data, and precision?
            Yes / No

11. Are you capable of finding overlooked flaws?
            Yes / No

12. Do you approach problems practically?
    Yes / No

13. Do you stand firm on issues?
Yes / No

14. Do you maintain a standard of consistency?
    Yes / No

15. Do you have the ability to provide stable leadership and supervision?

    Yes / No

16. Do you read the fine print in documents/contracts?
    Yes / No

17. Do you organize and keep track of data?
    Yes / No

18. Are you good at developing detailed plans and procedures?
    Yes / No

19. Can you articulate plans in an orderly way?
    Yes / No

20. Are you efficient at keeping financial records straight?
    Yes / No

Total: _____ Yes / _____ No

## Sample Solutions for Right-brain Dominant People: How Might You Use These Ideas to Achieve Your Goals?

If you want to get a visual image of the right-brain, imagine a surfer kicked back on the beach without a care in the world. Someone who is totally right-brain dominant usually doesn't have problems with stress. However, he or she may be surprised to discover how many important tasks are missed or forgotten.

As mentioned earlier, right-brain dominant people have a tendency to eat when they're hungry. They are stimulated by their appetites and not true physical hunger, regardless of how recently they've eaten. They are ruled by emotion. A way for them to engage the left-brain is to ask, "Has it been four hours since my last meal? Am I mistaking hunger for thirst?" Try drinking a glass of water before eating and see if the hunger is still there. Another question to ask is, "Am I experiencing an emotional state—sadness, anxiousness, nervousness, anger, fear—that's causing me to want to eat?"

The right-brain smoker might go for hours without a cigarette until prompted by seeing another person light up. Some right-brainers use cigarettes as a meditative tool. Perhaps they smoke while planning their day. To engage the left-brain, this type of thinker needs to impose limits on their habit, perhaps by making their car or home a smoke-free environment.

## Eighteen Strengths of a Right-brain Thinker

As a way to get to know how much of your right-brain is dominant, circle yes or no for each and then fill in the totals below.

1.  Are you able to read the signs of coming change?
    Yes / No

2.  Are you capable of seeing "the big picture"?
    Yes / No

3.  Do you readily recognize new possibilities?
    Yes / No

4.  Can you easily tolerate ambiguity?
    Yes / No

5.  Are you good at integrating ideas and concepts?
    Yes / No

6.  Do you challenge established policies?
    Yes / No

7.  Can you synthesize unlike elements into a new whole?
    Yes / No

8.  Do you come up with innovative solutions to problems?
    Yes / No

9.  Do you problem solve in an intuitive way?
    Yes / No

10. Can you simultaneously process different input?
    Yes / No

11. Are you quick to recognize interpersonal difficulties?
    Yes / No

12. Are you adept at anticipating how others will feel?
    Yes / No

13. Do you have empathy for other people?
    Yes / No

14.   Do you pick up non-verbal cues of another person's stress?
      Yes / No

15.   Do you engender enthusiasm?
      Yes / No

16.   Are you persuasive and conciliatory?
      Yes / No

17.   Do you understand emotional elements?
      Yes / No

18.   Do you consider values in your decision making?
      Yes / No

                              Total: _____ Yes / _____ No

## What are the Benefits of Whole-Brain Thinking?

By accessing the whole-brain, you are able to master verbal and nonverbal communication, develop artistic ability, and process information with perfect recall. Quick and easy problem solving is also a key benefit to thinking with your whole-brain.

By using both sides of the brain, you are prompting your mind to, as Albert Einstein recommends, "Question everything." You no longer react out of habit, but engage your whole-brain to envision new responses to situations.

What comes to mind when you think about the word *learning*? Most people think of school, discipline, restrictions, rules, structure, stress, competition, boredom, tests, and feelings of panic. But this isn't what learning is about. This is what school is about. Learning and school are not synonymous. However, most people equate learning with their experiences in school, rather than with a process. Perhaps you do, too. Doing the thought experiments will help you redefine learning as a process of action and reflection.

By now you should have a pretty good idea about which side of your brain is dominant. In case you're not yet sure, the following quick quiz will help you to determine whether you're left-brain or right-brain dominant. There are twenty items and I want you to rate your agreement with each statement by using a scale of zero to three. **Three** is totally agree, **two** is sort of agree, **one** is sort of disagree, and **zero** is disagree.

**Six Major facts About Whole-Brain Thinking**

1. Learning is a mental process.
2. Intended learning occurs when specific information is retrieved from memory in a usable form.
3. Individuals have different learning styles.
4. The more flexible a person is with new information the more useful that information is.
5. Using the whole-brain may require more time in the study phase but is more efficient in the long term.
6. A whole-brain approach must be used to achieve optimum performance outcomes.

## Thought Experiment: Are you Left- or Right-brain Dominant?

Totally Agree = 3  Sort of Agree = 2  Sort of Disagree = 1  Disagree = 0

1. _____ A step-by-step method is the only way of solving problems.

2. _____ Everyone should use daydreams as a way of providing insight to solutions of important problems.

3. _____ I like people who can prove their conclusions.

4. _____ I would rather be known as a timely reliable person rather than a creative, imaginative person.

5. _____ I get my best ideas when I am doing nothing in particular.

6. _____ You should rely on hunches and a feeling of "rightness" or "wrongness" when deciding on the solution to a problem.

7. _____ Breaking the rules and doing things I'm not supposed to do is fun and everyone should try it.

8. _____ What is most important in life cannot be expressed in words.

9. _____ It is more fun to compete with others rather than compete with myself.

10. _____ Everyone needs to spend time during the day alone with their thoughts.

11. _____ I dislike things that are uncertain and unpredictable.

12. _____ It is best to work with a team rather than doing things solo.

13. _____ Everything has a place and everything in its place.

14. _____ Ideas that are out of the norm and daring concepts interest and intrigue me.

15. _____ You should give specific instructions; don't leave many details as optional.

16. _____ I want to know why something works. That is more important than knowing how something works.

17. _____ Thorough planning and organization of time are mandatory for solving difficult problems.

18. _____ You should always think through the solutions to your problems before you act.

19. _____ Always rely more on your first impressions and feelings when making judgments rather than on a careful analysis of the situation.

20. _____ Laws should be strictly enforced

Answer Key:

| | |
|---|---|
| 1-_____ | 2-_____ |
| 3-_____ | 5-_____ |
| 4-_____ | 6-_____ |
| 9-_____ | 7-_____ |
| 11-_____ | 8-_____ |
| 13-_____ | 10-_____ |
| 15-_____ | 12-_____ |
| 17-_____ | 14-_____ |
| 18-_____ | 16-_____ |
| 20-_____ | 19-_____ |

Total: _____ Left-brain    Total: _____ Right-brain

When you have finished rating each statement, add up your score and write the total in the indicated box.

## How Did You Score?

In reality, this test doesn't tell you if you are right-brain or left-brain dominant—it indicates which brain you've trained yourself to use more frequently. The reality is that you already have the ability to use both hemispheres equally if you teach yourself how.

If you found that you scored zero to ten in either section, you are weak in that brain function, which could be a serious liability. The person who is weak in left-brain functions might find it difficult to balance a checkbook or organize time for getting tasks done. Role playing or artistic activities could make you uncomfortable. If you scored this low with the right-brain functions, you might find it difficult to see the big picture, or you may get easily bogged down in details.

If you scored between eleven and twenty in either section, you are still weak but are at least experimenting with that side of your brain. Since you have a foundation, if you can get through the uncomfortable feelings, you could develop the balance needed.

If your score in either section is between twenty-one and thirty you have identified your dominant brain and are likely in your element when using that side of your brain.

If you scored a thirty-one or above and each side is balanced within five points of the other, you are a true whole-brain thinker. You have mastered both the right and left realms. If you are strongly out of balance, if the scores are more than ten points off, you have some work to do. The key is to become balanced between the right- and left-brain functions. If you are already using your whole-brain, and are capable of moving from art class to math and science without much difficulty, you are fortunate. If, like most people, you find that one side is dominant, don't worry; the key to achieving whole-brain thinking is right here in this book. By learning to use CVR and to implement the Universal Laws, you will create your new reality.

### *Thought Experiment: Using the Sphere of Influence to Get Into A Whole-Brain State*

If you are in a place where you can, please stand up. Think of the skills you will need to be successful in achieving your goals. It could be the skill of drinking eight to ten glasses of water a day. It could be the skill of thinking like a non-smoker. It could be the skill of forgetting to remember by remembering to forget stress, strain, and confusion. It could be the skill of exercising. It could be the skill of whole-brain thinking, or of creatively and logically making new choices. It could be all these skills and more.

With these skills in mind, I will to teach you the technique called the *Sphere of Influence.* Your sphere of influence includes everything you have control over: your thoughts, perceptions, beliefs, values, and behaviors. The people in your life are not a part of your sphere of influence because you have no control over them or their actions. Your sphere of influence is around you at all times; it is your personal space. Using your imagination, go ahead and put whatever skills you need into your sphere. Use your right-brain creativity to give your sphere a color and make it your favorite color. I like to tell seminar participants that this is Drama 101. So get into character and imagine the sphere is there; make it as real as possible.

Now close your eyes and imagine that the color is filling you up. Roll your shoulders back, lift your chin, and allow your imagination to take over. Breathe the way you breathe when you're confident and relaxed. Imagine that your body is an empty glass container filling with color. When you've filled yourself with this positive, energized color, open your eyes. Know that you can feel the energy in your sphere of influence at any time. Now clear away the state by shaking your body a little and looking around.

Think of your old, limited right- or left-brain dominant way of thinking. Think of how you used to respond to a situation by using the dominant part of your brain automatically.

## Jerry's Story

The year was 1979. Jerry DeShazo was considered a top salesperson in the burgeoning computer software business. To the outside world, it looked as if he had it all, but something was missing in his life. Jerry began studying Dr. Ernest Holmes's *Science of Mind* philosophy and was immediately enamored with it. Jerry became involved in the organization, and he witnessed what he says can only be described as miracles. He couldn't get enough. The problem was, the more time and energy he invested in *Science of Mind*, the less interesting his job became. Without realizing it, Jerry had become a slacker at work.

Late one Friday afternoon, Jerry was called into the office of his hard-line boss. "You'll probably no longer be here in thirty days," the boss said. "The chair you sit in has to produce to a certain level and, frankly, you're not cutting it." He handed Jerry a list of criteria that would have to be met in the following thirty days. Jerry took one look at the list and knew he was getting a pre-termination setup; accomplishing everything on that list was not impossible. It was a typical maneuver, but Jerry was shocked that it was happening to him. He went home and stewed. It seemed crazy to him. Wasn't he a top-notch salesperson?

Although he was feeling listless and angry, Jerry attended his regular *Science of Mind* service that Sunday. He later joined a group for what the organization calls a *healing treatment*. Once again he witnessed people getting healed and turning their lives around. What was wrong with him? Why was he failing at work? Discouraged and defeated, he returned home.

Sometime later, deep into that restless Sunday night, the answer came to him; he would take the *Science of Mind* philosophy to the office with him.

The next morning he went to his little cubicle, took a few deep breaths, and did a *scientific prayer*. In the *Science of Mind* tradition, *scientific prayer* involves getting into a centered place, visualizing success, and then aligning oneself with the universal principles. Jerry finished his visualization and then picked up the telephone.

In the next thirteen weeks Jerry sold three and a half years worth of business. "I don't know why I was selling so well," Jerry says. "All I knew was that I was visualizing buyers saying yes, and they'd say yes."

That hard-line boss probably thought his fear tactic was the impetus for Jerry's turnaround. He had no way of knowing that Jerry had used creative visualization to negate the fear and go to a higher level.

Jerry felt so good about the process, he started using it in all of his business dealings. He didn't have a meeting with administrators, management, or sales support people without first doing a creative visualization process. "We became this incredible team that was unbeatable," Jerry said, "and the company grew beyond anyone's dreams."

I didn't meet Jerry until the mid-80s. By then he was in his early fifties and independently wealthy. After spending a few hours with him, I knew that I wanted what he had, and not only the financial freedom, but also the kind of personal and spiritual independence he personified. Jerry became my mentor and is one of my closest friends to this day.

Now think of using your whole-brain to make a positive change. Think of the power that comes from using both sides of your brain. Recognize that many new choices are available now. Examine them. It could be as simple as asking, "Am I really hungry?" or "Is it time to eat yet?" or "Am I mistaking thirst for hunger?"

Picture this whole-brain state as a sphere that surrounds you. Use your imagination to give this sphere a color. Make it your favorite color. Close your eyes and imagine that the color is filling you up … Roll your shoulders back, lift your head, and allow your imagination to take over. Breathe the way you breathe when you're confident and relaxed. Imagine that your body is an empty glass container filling with color. Imagine that you're using your whole-brain to make positive changes. Let the energy surge throughout your body.

Allow yourself to fill up with the wonderful emotions of motivation, determination, and satisfaction that come from using your whole-brain. Let yourself feel the power. As you do this, you will find that your mind has already begun a process of creating this sphere of influence in your life, so that your sphere of influence will work for you whenever you want or need it.

Repeat the process three times, each time focusing on boosting your brain power by using your whole-brain to create a positive new reality in your life.

You now know how to use your sphere of influence to boost your brain power and activate whole-brain thinking. Your sphere of influence is always there for you whenever you need it. Notice how good it feels.

Imagine that as you go out into the world, you're bringing your sphere of influence with you. It's with you at all times and you use it whenever a challenge or opportunity arises, knowing that as you continue to use your sphere of influence you activate whole-brain thinking to design your new reality.

## What is this Magic Elixir that Can Transform Your Life and the World?

The magic elixir resides right there in your brain. It's the miraculous mixture of chemicals in your brain that cascade through your body whenever you're relaxed, or think a positive thought, or have a happy experience—or whenever you visualize these things. It's the miraculous power within each of us to eliminate the effects of stress, heal our bodies, and enjoy life to its fullest. The magic elixir is created through the power of your other-than-conscious mind and activated by CVR to bring you health, vitality, and anything and everything you desire for your life.

### *Peoople who dare to relax with CVR enjoy all of these benefits and more:*

- The Relaxation Response replaces the Fight or Flight Response.

- The right and left hemispheres of the brain become more balanced.

- Blood flow to the brain increases, resulting in clearer thinking, better concentration, improved memory, and enhanced creativity.

- Serotonin levels increase by up to twenty-one percent, which calms the mind and body and creates an overall sense of well-being.

- Endorphin levels increase by up to twenty-five percent. These are the hormones that flow through the body when we feel happy. Endorphins provide the brain with alertness, are a natural anti-depressant, provide relief from pain, and create pleasurable and loving feelings.

- Twenty minutes of CVR can be equivalent to three to four hours of sleep. Consequently, you may find yourself sleeping less, feeling more rested, accomplishing more, and basically enjoying life more fully.

- Energy levels soar.

- Relationships become more fulfilling.

- Career satisfaction improves.

- A sense of purpose develops.

- The ability to make personal changes, such as losing weight, quitting smoking, ending nail biting or other nervous habits happens faster and easier.

- And last, but certainly not least, one gains a seemingly effortless ability to handle and manage stress.

Most people would pay thousands of dollars for a magic pill that offers these kinds of benefits. With CVR, people get these results in just a few relaxing minutes a day. Are you starting to understand why CVR is the key ingredient to the magic elixir that can get you everything you want for your life?

# CHAPTER
# FOUR

**High-Tech Solutions for
High-Tech Stress**

*"In every aspect of our lives, we are always asking ourselves, How am I of value? What is my worth? Yet I believe that worthiness is our birthright."*

## - Oprah Winfrey (1954 - ), O Magazine

**High-Tech Solutions for High-Tech Stress**

In the middle of a scorching summer heat wave, I attended a convention in Las Vegas, Nevada. It was only a few months after the opening of our new enterprise in Phoenix, and I really couldn't afford to be there. My curiosity got the better of me, however, when I discovered that new mind technology would be introduced at that event.

I was rushing to my next workshop when a female voice called out to me. I glanced at the woman who smiled at me as she stood in front of her booth. I waved and smiled at her. "I don't have time," I said. "I'm late for my next workshop."

Then a strange electronic device perched on the table behind her caught my eye. I touched the machine. "What's this?"

The woman stroked the device as if it were her beloved pet. "*This* is the Sensory Input Learning System. We call it SILS for short," she said. "I'm Linnea Reid." She shook my hand then signaled to a middle-aged man sitting beside the machine. "This is my partner, Larry Gillen," she added.

"Would you like to go for a ride?" Linnea asked.

One of my early loves was electronics, so I couldn't resist giving it a try. "Sure," I replied.

Linnea told me to lie back in a reclining chair. She tucked a blanket around me and handed me a set of earphones and a pair of sunglasses equipped with small LED lights. "I'll let you go about ten minutes," she said. "Just close your eyes and have a great trip."

Not knowing what to expect, I settled into the chair and closed my eyes. Within moments my senses were awakened by the rhythm of flashing lights and tones. An immediate feeling of relaxation and well-being washed over me. Now this was something I could get into.

By the time the session ended, I was blown away. I had never before felt so relaxed. I didn't want to move. "Come on," Linnea said as she shook me, "the group is about to take a break. You need to get up."

"That was the most amazing ten minutes of my life," I said.

"Ten minutes? That was more like forty-five minutes. You seemed to be having such a good time, I decided to let you keep going."

"Wow! It seemed to go that fast," I said, snapping my fingers. "I've got to have one of these machines. How do I buy one?"

"Well, you're in luck, I happen to sell these things… and the show special is only ten-thousand dollars."

My heart sank. I was a new business owner. She might as well have said ten million dollars. Yet I had never let money stand in my way before. I simply had to own one of these amazing devices. The wheels in my mind began to turn.

As fate would have it, Linnea and Larry relocated to Mesa, Arizona, and opened their business, Light & Sound Research, a short distance from my clinic. I attended several of their demonstrations and we soon formed a friendship.

One night, we sat in a diner discussing all the possibilities the

SILS system offered. "I've got an idea," I said, "what if I sponsor your demonstrations at my clinic and, between events, you can leave the machine with me so I can research the benefits with my clients?"

"I have to admit, I'm pretty tired of hustling around to different locations," Larry said to Linnea. "Sounds like a great idea to me."

"I agree," she said. "Getting some feedback from real clients would be invaluable."

In that instant I once again had accomplished a goal without it costing me a dime. By setting no limitations on how I would possess the machine, I had visualized and realized my goal.

That was 1987. Since then almost every one of my clients, along with the clients who attended programs in my franchise system, experienced this life changing technology. To say the results were astounding would be an understatement.

**How is technology changing the way we use our brain?**

Light and sound technology, also known as *visual/auditory entrainment*, is introduced to the brain through the ears and optic nerve using computerized technology emitted through headphones and specially designed glasses equipped with light-emitting diodes (LEDs). The lights flash at predetermined frequencies and are coupled with *binaural beats*, which are heard at a low level through the headphones. The visual/auditory entrainment is typically synchronized, but can be varied depending on the desired effect.

The flickering light patterns and binaural beats reach the brain by way of the optic nerve and inner ear respectively. Within minutes the brain begins to match the frequencies of the light pulses and sound beats. The method by which this entrainment occurs is known as *frequency following response*. Unlike biofeedback, where the user attempts to consciously change brainwave activity, light and sound induced entrainment influences the brain without any conscious effort.

The frequency following response simulates the relaxed brainwave frequencies know as *alpha* and *theta*. This is the state in which the individual relaxes and the mind develops focus. Listeners experience a reduction in inner chatter and improved concentration. Because frequency following response is a learned response, the effect is cumulative. After a few weeks of regular use, users gain a sense of balance and inner calm. Most people report feeling serene, focused, and alert even when faced with high-pressure situations. Furthermore, most users report experiencing enhanced creativity and feeling more rested with less sleep.

While light and sound technology can be beneficial to most people, it is not for everyone. Persons with epilepsy, any type of seizure disorder, or any visual photosensitivity are advised against using a light and sound device. People who have a pacemaker, suffer from a heart disorder, have a history of serious head trauma, or are taking stimulants, tranquilizers, or psychotropic medications, including alcohol or drugs, should consult their physician before use. Anyone experiencing dizziness, migraine, or severe anxiety after using light and sound should discontinue using the device and consult a physician.

**How do tones create relaxation?**

In 1839, an associate professor at the University of Berlin, H. W. Dove, discovered what he termed binaural beats. His early research showed that putting a given frequency in one ear and a different tone in the other causes a person to hear a third tone, which is the difference in frequency of the two tones.

He found that the human ability to hear binaural beats appeared to be the result of evolutionary adaptation and that our brains detect and follow binaural beats because of the structure of the brain itself.

### How Binaural Beats Work

1. The binaural beat is generated from two separate tones of a slightly different pitch

2. One tone is presented to the left ear and the other to the right ear

3. Your brain combines the two tones to make a single new tone

4. The single tone pulses to match relaxed brainwave frequencies

Until a 1973 article by Gerald Oster [7] however, binaural beats were considered no more than a scientific curiosity. Oster's paper was groundbreaking not so much in presenting new laboratory findings, but rather in bringing fresh insight to the topic by identifying and connecting a variety of relevant research performed after Dove's discovery. Oster is credited with uncovering just what effect binaural beats could have on the mind and body. He viewed binaural beats as a tool for cognitive and neurological research. Moreover, he identified the auditory system's propensity for selective attention (sometimes referred to as the cocktail party effect), which is our ability to tune out distractions and focus on a single activity. Oster also found that Parkinson's sufferers and those with auditory impairments generally could not hear binaural beats. Thus, he concluded that binaural beats could be used for diagnosing certain disorders. He also discovered gender differences in the perception of beats and felt that how a woman perceived the tones could be used to gauge fluctuations of estrogen (the latter assertion rising from a study he replicated that corroborated findings of gender differences in the perception of beats). [7]

Oster's publication of "Auditory Beats in the Brain," along with his assertion that binaural beats could be created even when one of the frequencies is below the human volume threshold (which supported his hypothesis that binaural beats involved different neural pathways from those involved in our direct conscious perception), launched a wave of new research into frequency following response.

**How does light create relaxation?**

Almost since the time humans discovered fire, it's been observed that flickering light can cause alterations in consciousness and even inexplicable visual hallucinations. Throughout history, stories abound of tribal elders, healers, and shamans using this knowledge to enhance their practices.

Early scientists, also captivated by this phenomenon, explored its practical applications. Around 200 AD, Ptolemy experimented with a spinning spoked wheel placed between an observer and the sun. The flickering of the sunlight through the spokes of the spinning wheel caused patterns and colors to appear before the eyes of the observer.

## Four Brainwave Frequencies

| Brainwave Frequency | Name |
| --- | --- |
| 13–40 Hz | **Beta waves** (Reactionary Mind)<br>Active thought and concentration; associated with busyness and anxious thinking |
| 7–13 Hz | **Alpha waves** (Intuitive Mind)<br>Relaxation (while awake), daydreaming; associated with creativity |
| 4–7 Hz | **Theta waves** (Inventive Mind)<br>The place between asleep and awake; associated with deep meditation and sleep learning |
| < 4 Hz | **Delta waves** (Rejuvenating Mind)<br>Deep dreamless sleep |

Many of these observers described a feeling of euphoria after exposure to the light patterns.

Joseph Plateau, a Belgian scientist, used the flickering of light through a strobe wheel to study the diagnostic significance of the *flicker fusion phenomenon*. As he caused the light flickers to come faster and faster, he found that at a certain point the flickers seemed to "fuse" into a steady, unflickering light pattern. In 1829, Plateau dubbed this phenomenon *persistence of vision*. He noted that healthy people were able to see separate flashes of light at much higher flicker speeds than were sick people. Today Plateau is recognized as the first animator. Modern filmmakers still rely on persistence of vision to trick our brains into believing that what we are viewing is actually moving and not just a series of still images.

At the turn of the century, French physician Pierre Janet noticed that when patients at the Salpetriere Hospital in Paris were exposed to flickering lights, they experienced reductions in hysteria and increases in relaxation.

By 1990, scientists were able to measure the effect of light on serotonin and endorphin levels. In one such study, eleven patients had peridural (the outermost of the three membranes covering the brain and spinal cord) and blood analysis performed before and after participation in relaxation sessions using flash emitting goggles. An average increase of beta-endorphin levels of twenty-five percent and serotonin levels of twenty-one percent were registered. The beta-endorphin levels are comparable to those obtained by cranial electrical stimulation (CES). The researchers concluded that photic stimulation has great potential for decreasing depression-related symptoms. [9]

## Why use light and sound together?

While research has proven that both light (flickering) and sound (binaural beats) can produce relaxed states, at Light & Sound Research we found that combining the two could move the body into a more profound level of relaxation; it is the highly kinesthetic state of tranquility that is optimum for healing and accelerated learning.

When I met Linnea and Larry, it was at the dawn of the computer revolution. Microchip technology was in its infancy, and computer engineers were a rare commodity. Nevertheless, Larry and Linnea found an engineer who could program a computer chip to do the work that the therapist previously had to do. With the help of thousands of documented sessions using a *mind mirror* (EEG machine), they discovered which programs worked to optimize the frequency following response and bring about optimum states of relaxation and learning. They then designed the first portable relaxation system and called it the $MC^2$.

In the next two decades, the franchise company I founded used this light and sound technology combined with CVR to help hundreds of thousands of people facilitate life changes such as losing weight, kicking a smoking habit, or conquering an alcohol or drug addiction. Others used it to eliminate pain, have stress-free childbirth, get motivated, achieve goals, enhance sports performance, improve at sales, and other life enhancements. One gentleman found that that the light/sound/CVR combination ended a five-year battle with chronic hiccups. Another young man came to me with a habitual nose click that even surgery hadn't cured. It stopped during his first session and never came back.

What is the secret to getting these kinds of results?

One of my favorite songs is *Change Your Mind* by Sister Hazel. One of the lines in the song goes, *"If you want to be somebody else, if you're tired of fighting battles with yourself . . . change your mind . . ."* I love this song because I believe the best way, and sometimes the only way, to make changes in your life is to first change your mind. Because images, beliefs, and values are so deeply rooted in consciousness, changes must happen at the other-than-conscious level before they can manifest in your life. In my experience, the light/sound/CVR combination is the quickest and easiest way to change your mind.

If you plant a seed, and know that you are watering and caring for it, you can pretty much sit back, relax, and let it sprout. You wouldn't keep digging up the dirt to see if the seed sprouted, would you? If you did uncover the seed to see if it is sprouting, you would probably stop its growth. I believe that this is what happens when people try to make changes at the conscious level; they set a goal, but then find themselves digging up old images, beliefs, and thought patterns, and end up stopping their growth.

When you relax with light, sound, and CVR guiding your conscious mind, you are free to liberate your other-than-conscious mind. Psychologists would say that you are bypassing the critical factor and letting the other-than-conscious mind take over. In other words, you plant the seeds of change, then sit back, relax, and let them sprout.

## What are the Best Light & Sound Parameters?

A good choice for a frequency following response program that produces deep relaxation starts at a state of high cortical arousal, a beta frequency of say 15 or 16 Hz. It then ramps down by gradually changing frequency until reaching slow alpha (8 Hz). The frequency should stay there for about seven minutes of the session and then ramp up to a moderate, relaxed alpha (10 Hz). Some programs ramp down into the theta range (4 -7 Hz) in order to achieve a deep other-than-conscious experience. Light and sound combined with positive suggestion, creative visualization, deep relaxation, soothing music, nature sounds, or a combination of these, creates heightened states of awareness.

While there is a wide assortment of relaxation training systems—autogenic (self-produced) training, progressive relaxation, meditation, and biofeedback to name a few—most of these take conscious effort. With the breakthrough of light and sound technology, you don't have to "believe in" or "do" anything. Through the frequency following response, the brain "syncs" to the strobe light and binaural sounds. You are in the experience and don't have to create it.

As an example, if you and I were to go to a secluded beach on a beautiful day while the sunlight reflects off the water and the waves rhythmically pound the sand, and if, while in this environment, we discussed the life improvements you would like to make, chances are good you would enjoy the conversation and accept any advice I might offer. Because of the environment created by this seaside walk, we would be synching to an alpha state, or about ten cycles per second.

Now if we were to have this same conversation on a bustling street in downtown Manhattan with horns blowing, lights flashing, vendors yelling, and rapid footsteps all around us, we would be synching to high Beta, or about eighteen cycles per second. The results would be very different. During the city walk, you might get distracted, frustrated, or nervous. In this state, you would be much less open to a conversation about improving your life, and would probably reject any advice I may give, even if it's logical advice. Are you starting to see why brainwaves are so important to our well-being?

## What is the Benefit in Achieving the Alpha and Theta States?

As you learned in Chapter 3, getting out of the fight-or-flight response and into the relaxation response is the best step you can take to overcome the brutal effects of stress. The relaxation response can't happen as long as you generate high beta brainwave activity. Your brainwave activity must dip into alpha, which I refer to as the "intuitive mind," or theta, which I call the "inventive mind."

Because theta is the threshold of sleep, it is best known for lucid dreaming. A person in this state often cannot separate thoughts about his or her awakened state from the lucid dream state. Many believe that theta is the optimum state for creativity and that it's the only place one can make a quantum leap in consciousness. Unfortunately, the theta state is difficult to maintain. When you slip into theta (4-7 Hz), which everyone does at least twice each day (right before falling asleep and just before awakening), and when there are no beta or alpha frequencies mixed with the theta, most people lose consciousness. This is where the frequency following response comes in—it keeps your brain engaged. When people use a light and sound device, they often describe feeling as if their inner experience is more real than the outer experience, which is temporarily suspended.

Researchers might say that these people have entered stage-one sleep, sometimes called the twilight state or the *hypnogogic* (from the Greek *hypnos*, meaning sleep, and *agnogeus* meaning conductor) state. While this is a very healing state, and one that heightens the visualization experience, it was not often used for the purpose of teaching relaxation skills. I believe the results achieved by the thousands of clients who have used the light/sound/CVR combination in our franchise programs proves that when a person sees, hears, and experiences the life changes they desire in the alpha and theta states, those changes come to pass in the physical world more quickly and with far less effort.

### What are the Benefits of Light and Sound Technology?

Whenever people ask me why I'm so passionate about light and sound technology, I tell them one of my favorite jokes. It goes something like this: One evening a man in a tuxedo rushed up to a street musician and asked, "How do you get to Carnegie Hall?" Without skipping a beat the musician answered, "Practice, man, practice!"

CVR works because it involves mental practice or *spaced repetition*. In my opinion, there is no faster or easier method for achieving spaced repetition than through the synchronized rhythm of light and sound. The induction into higher brainwave states increases brain activity, while the induction of lower brainwave states reduces hyperactivity and feelings of anxiety. Brainwave entrainment within alpha states, for example, creates relaxation and a decreased stress response by providing a slower and more relaxed brainwave state. A faster brainwave state, produced by faster flickering of the LED lights, induces a higher brainwave state, and is theorized to enhance brain stimulation and increase cognitive abilities. In many cases, a faster brainwave state can decrease hyperactivity, similar to the paradoxical application of neurostimulant medications such as Ritalin and Dexedrine.

Research showing the efficacy of light and sound technology is not uncommon. Creative visualization and stimulation of brain wave activity are among the most studied areas of psychiatry and psychology. The following results have been demonstrated through numerous studies and in my own experience with thousands of clients:

- Increased long- and short-term memory
- Increased attention span and concentration
- Reduction of anxiety and depression
- Reduction of medication intake
- Increase in right-left visual-spatial integration
- Major increase in creativity idea generation
- Easier decision making and holistic problem solving
- Decrease in migraine or headache frequency and intensity
- Reduction in PMS and menopause symptoms
- Reduction in insomnia and sleep disorders
- Improvement of motivation

All of this is in addition to the benefits of deep relaxation that I outlined in Chapter 3.

***

*"The only way to discover the limits of the possible is to go beyond them into the impossible."*
–Arthur C. Clarke

# CHAPTER
# FIVE

### The Mind's Eye
### – Your Key to Focus

## What is the Power of Space and Time?

A few years ago my wife and I were involved in a civil lawsuit with a prior business associate. The woman involved was someone with whom we'd had a working relationship for several years, and she and Cynthia had become close friends. When the alliance went south, Cynthia experienced not only the emotional trauma of a lawsuit, but also the loss of a good friend.

One day, while in the midst of the lawsuit, we were in a Toronto hotel room getting ready to give a seminar to our Canadian franchisees and their employees when Cynthia received a call from our attorney. He gave Cynthia the date for her deposition and told Cynthia that her ex-friend would be attending. Cynthia closed her cell phone and started to cry. "I can't do it," she said. "I can't see her again. I'm too hurt and angry." She sobbed and started trembling.

"That's weeks away," I said. "Right now we need to do this seminar." My comment only made her cry harder.

"Okay," I said, "let's put this in proper perspective. Give me your hands and close your eyes." I had Cynthia imagine the upcoming deposition in her mind's eye. I had her see herself walking into the room with total confidence. I asked her to imagine the woman there, but that she was almost like statue in a chair, so she could take the emotion and put it behind her. She visualized herself answering the attorney's questions without fear or anxiety. Once I had her breathing the way she would be breathing on that day, relaxed and with total confidence, I had her make a mental review of every day from that future event back to this moment and see herself doing everything she needed to do with confidence and with little concern over the deposition or her ex-friend. I then asked her to imagine the upcoming seminar and to see herself in front of the group with a big smile on her face while everyone applauded her presentation. When the trembling stopped and she wore real smile, I asked her to open her eyes.

"Let's go get 'em," she said.

After that short visualization, Cynthia's attitude about the entire lawsuit was completely different. All of the fear, anger, and stress had disappeared and was replaced by an inner confidence that seemed to emanate from her. She was able to enjoy her life again. And what happened when the day of the deposition came? Well, I can only say that I have never been more proud of her.

So what was the magic that made the difference for Cynthia? She had the power of space and time on her side. You see, your mind doesn't know the difference between what's real and what you imagine. During creative visualization and relaxation, the imagination is heightened so that the other-than-conscious mind readily accepts whatever is presented as real. It's not uncommon for a person to say that a difficult time from the past is "behind me," or to say, "I'm looking forward to . . ." a future event. By using CVR, it's possible to train your mind to store negative, unhelpful experiences *behind you* so they don't filter into your perception of current events. Doesn't leaving negative emotions in the past make good common sense? You can also can train your mind to store positive experiences in your present perception as if you've just experienced them, which keeps the positive emotions current. This provides you with a strong, resourceful state from which to handle any situation. And it all works because the mind stores memories using space and time as markers, but at the other-than-conscious level, because space and time are malleable.

### *Thought Experiment: Memory Management*

**Step one:** Close your eyes and imagine a negative statement you might have thought about yourself in the past. This could be something like, "I don't read well. I'm just stupid," or "I can't lose weight. I'll always be fat and unattractive." Imagine that your mind can speed up the statement. Go ahead. No one is watching. Imagine the statement as if the Chipmunks were saying the words. Let yourself see the humor in it. Keep speeding up the statement faster and faster. Notice what happens when you speed the statement up so fast it becomes ridiculous. It can no longer hold any meaning for you.

Now, imagine you could somehow place that statement on the moon. Do this in a way that the voice is still going; you just can't hear or understand it any more. Once you have done this, open your eyes and proceed to step two.

**Step two:** Look around the room.

**Step three:** Close your eyes again. Imagine the statement in your mind's eye once again, but this time slow the statement down. In fact, imagine the statement is moving so slowly that it would take an entire year for one sentence to be completed. Now, place the slowly moving statement in the center of the earth and bury it there. Imagine it is still moving, but you can't hear it. It has no meaning for you.

**Step four:** Open your eyes and look around the room.

Step five: If you can still hear the voice, repeat steps one through four until the unwanted statement is gone from your mind.

You can do this exercise with all of your senses to remove any negative pictures, sounds, statements, feelings, tastes, or scents that may be preventing you from experiencing a natural state of joy and focus in your life. Just place them so far behind you that they no longer have any meaning for you. This is also a great example of how the mind uses the power of space—placing negative sounds on the moon or in the center of the earth—and time—speeding the statement up or slowing it down.

You will also notice that the mind has a protective mechanism that won't allow you to forget positive experiences. When you are in a positive mood, your thinking becomes clearer and is naturally more positive. Use this technique to take control of your thoughts and create the type of focus you need to accomplish any goal.

**What are "mental muscles" and how can we build them?**

It's possible to build powerful mental muscles through what I call, *Tai Chi for the mind*. Martial artists teach that one should never fight force with force. Rather, to stop an aggressor, you learn to use inner power and strength within the moves or to leverage the energy of the attacker. The same is true with creative visualization and relaxation. All memories, good and bad, have energy. That trapped energy can either be used or transformed to create the results you want in your life. You can tap into this creative energy or you can let the past energy of pain, resentment, and confusion hold you back from attaining true mental clarity. All emotions, even negative ones, are useful in the right context. The secret is to control the *e-motion*—energy in *motion*. Tai Chi for the mind means you harness that inner power and strength to achieve what you want. This can only be done by mental preparation at the other-than-conscious level of your mind. That's where CVR comes in; you are using your three-pound universe (your brain) to rehearse what you intend. By using creative visualization and relaxation techniques, you will learn to tap into that energy and use it for your benefit.

**What is Future Pacing?**

Whenever we learn a new skill or behavior, we tend to confine those changes to the environment in which they were established. *Future pacing* involves the use of creative visualization to rehearse mentally the new habits and behaviors in future scenarios. Every time you creatively visualize anything for your life, you want to future pace it into as much of your future environment as you can. This helps to ensure that the desired behaviors and responses show up at the right time and feel natural and automatic. Every time I do a CVR process, I end it with future pacing so that the new behaviors and patterns fit into the listener's future environment.

*"Man is born to live, but not prepared to live."*
Boris Paternak

**Using the Power of Procrastination**

Procrastination affects up to seventy percent of our population. According to research, forty percent of people have experienced some losses, monetary or otherwise, due to procrastination. Twenty five percent of people claim this is a chronic problem in their lives.

For those who must live with procrastinators, unfortunately, the power to change lies within the procrastinator alone. According to experts, when an employer or person in a position of power exerts pressure on the procrastinator to "try harder" or to "get more organized," the pressure has little or no effect, and often causes more problems. Friends and family also have very little power over the procrastinator's choices. Statements like, "This is a tough job so don't put it off," and "No friends or fun until this job is done," are counterproductive. Such advice only increases the pressure on the procrastinator and intensifies the unpleasant feelings associated with the task, making it seem even more impossible to accomplish. The procrastinator has to reduce the unpleasantness of the task in order to accomplish it.

## John's Story

John started smoking as a teenager. He tried to quit cold turkey dozens of times with no success. When that didn't work, John tried weaning himself off by smoking one or two fewer cigarettes each day. After about a week of this, he realized that nearly all his waking thoughts were about cigarettes. "Every time I try to quit, I have horrible mood swings and suffer intense cravings, especially around other smokers," John told me the first time we met. "It got so bad, my friends actually asked me to start smoking again. I always end up caving in, especially if I start gaining weight. I end up smoking even more than before. Now when I think about quitting, I dread it so much, I get nauseated."

John's feelings of dread are understandable considering all he had been through in his attempts to quit. The first step in helping John become tobacco-free was to do a little memory management to clear out all the negativity he associated with quitting. The next step was to use future pacing so John could experience his future not only as a non-smoker, but also with a happy mood and no cravings. Finally, I had John engage the power of procrastination so that even if he did have a desire for a cigarette, he could simply put it off for an hour, and then for another hour, and so forth.

Once John started using CVR the way I showed him, everything changed. By using CVR, John was able to kick his smoking habit without withdrawals. He not only got rid of the mood swings, but he also felt empowered. John had learned how to use CVR to become a nonsmoker for life.

In this chapter you are going to learn how to use the power of putting things off, or procrastinating, to your advantage in meeting your personal goals. We will explore together how to turn what's usually considered a negative behavior into a positive response. Just as all emotions are useful, so too are all behaviors if put in the proper context.

First let's explore just what procrastination is: ***Procrastinate***: (derived words: ***procrastination, procrastinator***):
**1. to defer an action: to procrastinate until an opportunity is lost.**
**2. from the Latin crastinus: "to belong to tomorrow."**

Procrastination is a double-edged sword. Most people want to believe that by putting something off they somehow make their lives less complicated. Who wouldn't find it easier to watch television than to do a necessary chore? Instead, procrastination creates unnecessary stress and disorganization, which we associate with failure. In this chapter we will learn how to obtain the positive benefits of procrastination without the stress and confusion usually generated when we procrastinate.

**Six Steps to Becoming a Master Procrastinator**

**Step One:** The first step is to target a task or goal that you want to achieve. It could be something just for you or something others would value or respect. Common internal statements might be:
- "I've got to start the taxes!"
- "I really need to exercise!"

**Step Two:** You delay. Your intuitive mind works with your inventive mind to think of real and imagined advantages to starting the task later. Common internal thoughts are:
- "I'll start tomorrow when I don't have as much to do."
- "I don't have all the information I need to start a weight loss program."
- "I need more schooling before I can look for a new job."

**Step Three:** You stall, becoming more and more critical of yourself and your choices. Common internal thoughts at this stage are:
- "I've put this off too long, there's no point starting now."

- "There's no way I can finish on time."

The thoughts can become self-excusing as well:

- "I can't quit my job. I'd be letting everyone down."
- "I would have gotten it done if it weren't for all this lousy housework."

Other common tactics include hiding and pretending to be too busy. Some people will even fib about other obligations. The bottom line is you made an emotional decision (to put off the task) and then justified the decision with logic.

**Step Four:** You defend your position. This causes still more delay, usually to the point where the task must be done and in a hurry. Common thoughts at this step include:

- "I'll just get it over with."
- "It doesn't have to be great."
- "If I can't do it right, I'd better not do it at all."
- "I guess it just wasn't meant to be."

**Step Five:** Self-criticism sets in. You start to believe that procrastination is part of your nature. Common thoughts here can be:

- "There must be something wrong with me."
- "I'm a better planner than a doer."

These thoughts often lead to the promise never to procrastinate again, which discounts the importance of the original task.

- "It doesn't matter if I make a change or not."
- "I guess my body just wants to weigh 180 pounds."
- "I'm never the lucky one."

**Step Six:** The procrastinator then starts to spiral downward almost immediately on all important tasks and develops a compulsion to put things off.

It makes no sense to set a goal intending not to achieve it, yet millions of people do this every day. It never helps to prolong the agony of an unwanted task. But the procrastinator still puts it off. Why? There are many possible reasons for this behavior. A few might include:

- The good feeling we get by setting a goal and declaring it to oneself or others
- The feeling that we are making a change for the better, even if it is at a future time
- To shorten the actual time spent working on a task or committing to the goal set forth

Perhaps the biggest reason people procrastinate stems from their desire to avoid the unpleasant task altogether. Surveys show that seventy-percent of all New Year's resolutions are abandoned by February 1. The average diet lasts approximately seventy-two hours. The average smoker tries quit three or four times a year.

The obvious best course of action, in most cases, would be to do the task as soon as is practical, giving ourselves enough time to do the job right and finish it completely. So why do I want you to become a master procrastinator? Let's look at procrastination from a different angle. I remember the day the lotto came out in Michigan. My coworkers and I spent hours discussing how we would spend our millions when we won. I played the lottery for several weeks hoping for my big break, until the thrill wore off.

This is similar to what happens when a dieter finds a new weight loss program. Research shows that the average woman spends thirty-one years of her life dieting. What would motivate anyone to spend thirty-one years doing something that she repeatedly fails at and that's no fun? It's that thrill of the new discovery. In the same way the lottery thrilled me for a few weeks, she believes this new diet could be the answer to her prayers. This *might* be the one.

Diets fail when the thrill wears off, just as it did with the lotto and me. The dieter is excited by the change at first, but since the average diet lasts just seventy-two hours, it would seem the excitement erodes with the realization that diets take work and discipline. By Friday it's party time. On Monday the guilt sets in and the dieter starts anew. This cycle can repeat over and over, apparently for an average of thirty-one years.

But what would happen if you could keep that Monday morning motivation all the time? What if the dieter didn't diet at all, but rather just put off eating between meals? What if she put off that piece of cake until tomorrow, and then did the same thing the next day? She's not denying herself anything; she's just putting off eating it. The same can be done to quit smoking. What if the smoker simply put off smoking, just one cigarette at a time, until he or she simply forgot about smoking? CVR is designed to do this for you using nothing more than the magic of your imagination.

All successful twelve-step programs advocate a *one day at a time* philosophy. This approach is what makes the difference between those who succeed and those who stay stuck in the vicious cycle of starting and stopping, success and failure. With CVR, you'll learn to make each new day your *motivated Monday.*

The question is, are you willing to make a lifestyle change—or as they say in the big book of AA, a *psychic change?* In other words, are you ready to change your mind? If you are won't change your mental state, you can't make a physical change. In my best-selling book *Awaken the Genius,* I wrote about Sammy who searched for the Statue of Liberty on a beach in California. His likelihood of finding the Statue of Liberty in California is about the same as trying to lose weight, quit smoking, or overcome an addiction, without changing how one thinks. It's simply not going to happen.

What state are you in right now? Are you in a negative state about whatever change you're trying to make? Is that helping or hindering you? How many times have you tried to accomplish something while in a negative and unresourceful state of mind? None of it came out right, did it? Have you ever tried to be successful while in a state of negativity? Being in a negative state of mind while trying to accomplish a goal is like trying to find the Statue of Liberty in California. It's just not there.

## Thought Experiment: Change Your State, Change Your Life

Read through all steps carefully and then proceed:

Step one: Stand up straight. Roll your shoulders back. Roll your chin up. Smile.

**Step two:** In this positive physical state I want you to try to feel depressed. Remember to keep your shoulders rolled back and your chin up. Keep a smile on your face.

**Step three:** Notice that in this physical state, you can't create the emotion of depression. You would have to change your physical state.

In seminars, whenever participants are asked to complete this exercise, we all get a good laugh. They are unable to create the state of depression while standing straight with shoulders back, chin up, and smiling. They just can't do it. What would happen if you created the habit of staying in this positive, motivated physical state?

**Step four:** If you were in an empowered state right now, a state where you take action and cast off all doubt, what could you accomplish? Take a few moments to make a list here:

_____

_____

_____

_____

_____

_____

For some of you, the answer would be to start exercising instead of just planning to exercise. Others would choose water instead of soda. Still others would go for a walk instead of falling asleep in front of the television. The options are endless. What do you want to accomplish in your life?

### What would you attempt to do if you knew you could not fail?

Imagine the possibilities. If there were no possible way for you to fail, what would you attempt? Imagine the unseen forces that would come to your aid if one-hundred percent of your being believed you could not fail. The power that would be released in that belief would help you break through any barriers on your way to success.

Now, what if you took all that energy you used to procrastinate and channeled it into action? You could stop all counterproductive behavior and use the energy to start the constructive actions that will help you accomplish your loftiest goals.

Whether you drink more water, start exercising, eat sparingly and only at mealtimes, quit smoking, stop consuming alcohol, or accomplish any other goal you set for yourself, you will do it far more easily when in the physical state of optimism. This is a scientific fact: your physiology (or your body) affects your psychology (or your mind). These two have a very powerful relationship. That's why people who exercise tend to be more positive and outgoing than those who sit back and watch life go by.

There is a law of physics at work here as well. It states: Mass at rest tends to stay at rest. Mass in motion tends to stay in motion. Albert Einstein said, *"Life is like riding a bike. You have to keep moving to keep your balance."* Thanks to great minds like Einstein's, modern psychology has discovered ways to transform the old stuck states like procrastination into mental states that stimulate motion.

I get a lot of skepticism from my clients when I say, *"What if I told you your key to success is procrastination?"* Wait. Didn't you just tell me how bad procrastination is? *The problem is, you just don't know how to use procrastination.* **Yet.** You think procrastination is a bad thing. Most people do. But when procrastination is used correctly it can be a very beneficial thing.

**What if...**
*You could put off eating between meals?*
*You could put off stress and worry?*
*You learned how to focus your attention on success instead of anticipating failure?*

Chances are you have experienced success at one time or another in your life. How did you do it? What attitude did you have? How did it feel?

We each have our own individual feelings about procrastination. These feelings are what cause us to not use procrastination appropriately. What if you could say, "Okay, I'm procrastinating now, but I know this is a great skill. How can I best use it at this moment?" You could use it to put off eating sweets, to stave off worry, or to tamper your fear about other people's opinions of you. You could put off thinking about cigarettes or food. You get the idea. The possibilities are limitless.

What can you do, right now, in this moment, to ensure your success? The key to using procrastination as motivation is to refocus your thinking by asking what you can do right now to guarantee your success. If your goal is to lose weight, ask yourself, "What can I do right now, at this meal, to make appropriate food choices?"

Harry Houdini once failed to escape from a safe even though the safe doors were unlocked. Why? Because the only thing he knew about were *locked* doors. Are you currently staying trapped, even though the door is unlocked? That's what continuing to think about procrastination in the same way is like. You're trapping yourself into one way of thinking. It doesn't take Houdini to get out of the trap. Let's explore how you can personally turn procrastination into motivation.

**Eight Steps to Turn Procrastination into Motivation**

**Step One:** Reframe your current belief about procrastination. Your new thoughts could be something like:

- "I can put off worry in the same way I put off cleaning the garage."
- "I can procrastinate sleeping in and start an exercise program."

This will get easier as you learn to play life's game like a champion instead of a victim.

**Step Two:** Think of a specific task or goal. Begin with something that has value for you alone. Later you can move on to something that has value or respect for others if you wish. Your new thoughts could be:

- "I enjoy the sense of accomplishment I get when I finish my taxes."
- "I am excited about the new body I'm building with my exercise program."

**Step Three:** When you find yourself delaying, use your intuitive mind and come up with ways to start the task or change your thinking now. New thoughts could include:

- "The more I do today, the less I have to do tomorrow."
- "I possess all the information I need to start my weight loss program. I can learn more along the way."

**Step Four:** If you become critical of your choices, stop yourself. Imagine a big red stop sign if you need to, then think a new thought.

- "Anything worth doing well is worth doing poorly at first."

Most importantly, stop self-excusing thoughts.

- Change, "If I'm not one-hundred percent into my job I am letting my co-workers down," to, "My co-workers and I deserve the best I have to offer."
- Stop thoughts like, "I just don't have the talent for this," and transform it to, "I'm excited about learning something new."

If all else fails, just be willing to *fake it 'til you make it*. Once you get busy doing something constructive you'll be amazed at what you can accomplish.

**Step Five:** If you find yourself defending your position with thoughts such as, "I just don't have time to do it," commit to being honest with yourself. You are where you are. Do the job or task to the best of your ability. Your new thoughts at this stage could be:

- "If I don't have time to do it right now, when will I have time
    to do it again?"
- "Let's do it right!"

**Step Six:** If you criticize yourself, use a key phrase such as *backspace/delete* to remind yourself you have a choice in your thoughts. If you don't like a thought, simply backspace and delete it. Then replace it with a positive thought. It's normal to have self-critical thoughts. What you do to correct these thoughts is what counts. Remind yourself:

- "There's nothing wrong with me."
- "It's okay to learn from my mistakes."

**Step Seven:** Never make a promise you don't intend to keep. As my good friend and mentor, Dr. Gil E. Gilly says, "No loss is permanent and no defeat is final." Part of life's journey is to discover how you can "improve, adapt, improvise, and overcome" negative situations. (I borrowed this line from the Marines Corps., but it certainly applies to all of us.)

One way to make commitments and stay on track is to write a to-do list. However, keep in mind that it's just that—a list. Set timelines and benchmarks and then ask yourself if they are realistic. If you do happen to set a goal that an entire army couldn't complete, don't beat yourself up for not getting it done—revise your list so that it's doable and then get started.

**Step Eight:** During your creative visualization sessions imagine your task or goal as if it is completed. Seeing the finish line while in a state of creative visualization will motivate you to complete the task and associate those good feelings of success with the process.

**What Challenges Do You Have?**

We all experience challenges that hinder us on the road to meeting goals. With practice, simply changing the way you view or think about the situation and making minor changes in your routine can alter the way you handle situations and put you in a resourceful state to help you reach your goals.

**Do you experience challenges when eating out?** Sometimes when we try to lose weight, or even if our goal simply involves maintaining a healthy lifestyle, eating out poses a challenge. We want to make good choices, but in our mind we hear our inner voice telling us, "It's a special occasion. You can indulge this one time," or, "Go ahead, get what you want," or even, "I don't want to make waves by asking for special food diet food."

**Solution:** Train yourself to think of the situation in a new way. Split a meal with someone. Ask for half your meal to be placed in a to-go carton before it's even brought out. Go off the menu and request healthier alternatives or preparation methods. In most cases restaurant staff are happy to accommodate special requests. Apply the power of procrastination to put off eating the bread or chips on the table. Better yet, practice assertiveness and ask that they not be brought to the table at all.

**Do you experience challenges when others smoke around you?** It can be very difficult to remain a non-smoker when others are smoking around you. Many ex-smokers can be persuaded to smoke by their own internal dialogue. They tell themselves, "I'll just have one to go with my drink," or, "Nicotine no longer has control over me. I can just smoke when I'm out with friends." By using the techniques taught earlier in the thought experiment portion of this chapter, you can combat this self-talk cycle and remain true to your tobacco-free goals.

**Solution:** Bring water with you and sip it while others smoke. If you have control over the environment, be assertive and ask others not to smoke. Socialize with non-smokers and observe what they do with their hands. Use the skill of procrastination to put off going outside until it's time to leave.

**Do you have trouble with boredom causing you to think negative thoughts or take negative actions?** Many people have expressed to me that it's easy to stick with their goals and plans when they're busy. They simply have other things occupying them and they don't remember to eat or smoke or engage in the behaviors they want to change. The problems show up when things quiet down and they are left with time on their hands. It's important to have a plan for these times.

**Solution:** Carry a to-do list with you. In these moments of boredom, choose to visualize your list complete. Figure out what task needs to be finished first and then do it. Commit to procrastinating boredom. I once heard it said that there is no such thing as a boring time, there are only boring people. Commit to making yourself an interesting person and put off the habit of boredom.

**Do you have trouble at parties or social events?** Social events can pose a real problem for people in many situations. Those trying to lose weight, give up smoking, or get free from alcohol or drugs all feel pressure in social settings. You may feel that you don't want to offend your host by not eating what's placed in front of you, or you may feel the need to have something to do with your hands. There are several easy solutions to combat this problem.

**Solution:** If losing weight is your goal, before leaving home have a protein shake containing ground flax to reduce hunger. Examine all the foods available and choose only the healthy ones you want. Don't sample everything merely because it's there. Use your skill of procrastination to put off eating the unhealthy foods for another time. Let everyone else enjoy them. If you feel you must have something in your hands during a party or social event, have a glass of sparkling water with lemon or lime to carry with you. It will keep your hands busy and give you the feeling that you are part of the social event.

**Do you find yourself doing for others while you do without?**

This is a big issue that many people, especially women, have to deal with. We are trained from an early age to please others. It's in our nature. But we must learn balance with this skill. We cannot take care of others if we don't take care of ourselves as well. In today's overloaded world, we must avoid overextending ourselves and adding to the stressful burden we already carry.

**Solution:** Since the people in your life already have preconceived notions of what they can expect from you, it may take a little time to retrain them. Practice saying no in front of a mirror. Use your new skills of procrastination to put off giving to those who ask for help when you are already stretched thin or have plans of your own. It's okay to say no. One tactic is to let the person know you will consider it and let them know in a day or two what your answer is. If they push the issue before your deadline, tell them you are working on your procrastination skills. That'll keep them wondering!

**Do you buy treats for your children or grandchildren?** Joyce was one of my weight loss clients. One day she showed up for her session very upset and claiming that her program wasn't working. I knew the program worked, so I needed to uncover what was preventing her from being a success in the program. "What's happening that makes you so sure the program isn't working?" I asked.

"I'm still eating Oreo cookies," she said.

"Oreo cookies?" I responded. "I didn't know we had a program for eating Oreo cookies and losing weight."

She wasn't amused.

"Where do you get the cookies?" I asked.

"I buy them for when my grandchildren visit," she said.

"How many do the grandchildren eat?"

"Well, none," she said. "I eat them up before they arrive. The weird thing is, I don't even remember eating the cookies, but I know I am. I get up in the middle of the night and bring them back to bed. My husband is very upset over the cookie crumbs in bed."

I could see how this might cause a problem. "Let me see if I have this straight," I said. "You buy cookies for your grandkids, who never get to eat them because you eat them first, but you don't remember eating them? What do you do when your grandchildren come for a visit?"

"I buy more cookies, of course," she answered.

This woman, caught in a vicious cycle, was trapped by her *idiot logic* and simply couldn't see a commonsense approach to her dilemma. I asked her if she would be willing to try an experiment for me that likely would help her lose weight. She was up to the challenge. I suggested that she go to the health food store and purchase cookies that look like Oreos. I advised her that Oreo cookies, along with most of the junk food manufactured today (yes, I said *manufactured*) have additives designed for addiction. These additives are called excitotoxins, Oreos have 23 [10] and they are added to foods to make the human body crave them. I also suggested that, since children are very susceptible to branding, she take the cookies out of the packaging so the grandkids wouldn't know they had been switched.

A week later the same woman stopped by my office. "I'm astonished," she said. "I haven't eaten any Oreos all week and my grandkids like the health food store cookies just as well."

"Amazing how if you don't buy them, you don't eat them, huh?" I said.

What a concept. Not only had she cured her problem, but she was making a healthier choice for her grandchildren as well.

**Solution:** If you feel you must have treats for your children or grandchildren, make sure to have healthy ones—perhaps those purchased at a health food store. Keep in mind that the food choices you make influence your children and grandchildren's eating behaviors now. Isn't it far better to teach them about healthy choices rather than having them suffer through dieting later in life?

**Do you let stress, frustration and worry control your life?** Stress is a part of our daily lives. It's unavoidable. As I outlined in earlier chapters, we can control and manage stress and worry. It's important not to let stress, frustration, and worry take control of your life. Stress is unhealthy and can cause a variety of social and emotional problems.

**Solution:** Practice creative visualization and relaxation. Take time out for deep breathing and self-relaxation. Practice isolated moments when you visualize upcoming positive scenarios about current events. Use the techniques I share in this book. By practicing CVR, you will learn how to combat everyday stress and frustration. By rehearsing positive results, you will achieve positive results. By seeing yourself as a successful person, you can become a successful person. By seeing yourself as relaxed and stress-free, you will become relaxed and stress-free.

What does it really take to transform procrastination into motivation? The simple answer is discipline. Legendary basketball coach, Bobby Knight, has four steps to discipline:

1. Do what has to be done,
2. when it has to be done,
3. as well as it can be done,
4. and do it that way every time.

Following these steps seems simple—and it is for those who are disciplined. Unfortunately, the mental program of procrastination is already in place in many people's minds. If you are a good procrastinator, even when you want to do something, you will find ways not to accomplish your task. But what if you could accomplish any task even when you really didn't want to? That's what happens when you practice using procrastination the CVR way. You put off your bad habits and put energy into your new habits or goals. Keep in mind one simple rule: You get what you rehearse in life, not necessarily what you intend. It does no good to intend to clean your garage if you don't actually practice the steps needed to get it done!

**Recommendations for the reformed procrastinator**

Reduce any fear of failing by reframing your fear. Your worth is not determined by an assignment at work or by a certain grade. Use the future pacing you are doing in the thought experiments and the CVR processes to develop plans for success. Use positive self-talk to change your inner state.

**Use your inner language to stop the procrastination cycle:**

Say things such as "There is no such thing as failure, only feedback. I have just found one way that will not work."

When my daughter was young, we joked about her having great excuses. In fact, we started keeping an excuse journal for her. This opened her eyes and changed her outlook on what she could or could not do.

What excuses are you using? What thoughts and feelings do you have when making excuses? What did you do instead of accomplishing your task? What was the outcome? What were your thoughts and feelings on that outcome?

At this point, I think congratulations are in order. You made the choice to purchase this book and are learning ways to change your old thoughts and habits. You are reducing the dread of the past. You can say, "I can enjoy smart, responsible work. It's part of a good life." Taking responsibility for where you are frees you to create a path for where you want to go.

**Use your inner language to stop the procrastination cycle:**

| Procrastinating Language | Motivating Language |
|---|---|
| I must...(or) I have to...(or something awful will happen) | I choose to; I can; Only good things happen to me. |
| I have to finish... | I enjoy getting started on projects. |
| This task is too big. | First things first, I can enjoy the journey |
| I *have to* do well, I *have to* be fantastic, I *need to* be perfect. | My best is good enough; I'll do okay; I'll give it time. Anything worth doing well is worth doing poorly at first. |
| I can't take time out to play. | Rest, play, and enjoyment are important to my health. |
| My life and work is a grind. | Life and work can be fun. It's okay to enjoy myself. |
| I don't have what it takes to succeed. | I have a better chance of succeeding if I take action. |

## You are an Overachiever, Workaholic, or Perfectionist. Are You Still a Procrastinator?

If you are an overachiever, workaholic, or an ambitious perfectionist, you are likely a master procrastinator. How can that be? You work so hard? The overachieving procrastinator tends to live in the future. These perfectionists say things like, "It'll be great when my business makes it big," or, "When I become a millionaire . . ." or, "When I make the honor roll . . .." These people are busy spinning their wheels. They don't live in the now because future events consume them. The overachieving procrastinator either works too much or feels guilty about not working enough. If you're this type of person, you must learn to *love* each day as if it's your mission in life. Pretend you are already that lucky person you see yourself to be in the future. Say, "I love my work, my life. My *present* is so bright, I've gotta wear shades." Productive people take vacations—without guilt. Insist on having fun now and again.

Turn worry and self-doubt into assets by asking yourself, "What is the worst possible outcome?" Having prepared yourself in this way can help your other-than-conscious mind plan what to do if the absolute worst happens. You will also discover that you can use your worries to help you become stronger and more capable. Once you plan, you no longer need to worry and you're free to let go of self-doubt.

One of the most popular business books of all time is the *Seven Habits of Highly Successful People* by Steven Covey. In this resourceful book, Dr. Covey has devised an ingenious program for organizing tasks by putting them into quadrants. This is one method of time management. There are many. If you do a little research, you'll find the one that fits best for you. Managing your time is an effective way to avoid procrastination and eliminate doubt and worry about whatever task you want or need to accomplish.

Now that you have seen what procrastination is, learned how to *eliminate* it in situations where it's harmful, and *utilize it* where it is beneficial, let's participate in a thought experiment to solidify the lesson.

## Thought Experiment: Self-Discovery Visualization

For best results, record the following in your own voice. Speak slowly and allow yourself time to follow each instruction.

*With your eyes comfortably closed, go ahead and take in a deep, cleansing breath. Let it out with a sigh. Notice how with each exhalation you go deeper and deeper into a state of creativity and relaxation.*

*With this in mind, imagine what you have planned for today. Today you choose to be open to all that is good and healthy. Today you can enjoy getting started on projects. You enjoy doing first things first. Today you enjoy the journey of life.*

*Think of a task that you need to complete. As you visualize yourself completing the task, allow the following thoughts to play in your mind: Your best is more than good enough. You'll do okay. It's natural to give it time to get results. Anything worth doing well is worth doing poorly at first.*

*(Pause for forty-five seconds)*

*Imagine something you really enjoy. While you visualize having fun, allow the following thoughts to move into your mind: "Rest, play, and enjoyment are important to my health. I am finding creative ways to find balance in my life. Life and work can be fun. It's okay to enjoy myself. I have a better chance of succeeding when I take action."*

*From here allow yourself to take a mental vacation. Just let yourself go. Take time to enjoy the journey, and when you are ready to take action and accomplish your daily goals your eyes will open and you will be wide awake... wide awake.*

***

> **"Put your hand on a hot stove for a minute, and it seems like an hour. Sit with a girl for an hour, and it seems like a minute. THAT'S relativity."**
> **- Albert Einstein**

# CHAPTER
# S    I    X

**The Physiology of Transformation**

## The Physiology of Transformation

In my book, *Awaken the Genius*, I talk about fear being the biggest block people face when utilizing their *genius*—their talents and skills. The same is true with change and self-transformation. When fear traps you, your body locks up and freezes you out of any resourceful responses you could draw on to make a change. In this chapter, you will explore how to train your brain to use the relaxation response to stay in a resourceful state and accomplish your goals.

It's important to note that **FEAR** is essentially just an acronym meaning: False Evidence Appearing Real. Most things feared never come to pass as imagined. Fear is a necessary part of human nature and serves us in most situations. For example, as children we are born with an innate fear of heights. This fear is an innate part of our nature. This natural fear of heights is not necessarily a bad fear to have when you are small and can happen upon dangerous situations. Fear only becomes a problem when it inhibits your personal growth or your joy in living.

### What are Conditioned Responses?

Roman Emperor and Philosopher Marcus Aurelius once said, "If you are distressed by anything external, the pain is not due to the thing itself, but to your estimate of it; and this you have the power to revoke at any moment."

What Marcus Aurelius is talking about is false evidence appearing real. Once you learn to revoke it, any power that f.e.a.r. had over you will vanish. The challenge comes in overriding the mind's natural inclinations. Our minds are accustomed to categorizing and organizing information for recall, but the mind also predicts the future based on information gathered in the past. This process of the mind is what's at play when we awaken each morning with a sense of what the day will be like. This is also the part of the mind that brings fear into the equation.

Your brain is the hardware, your mind is the software, and

your senses are the keyboard of the hundred-billion neurobit computer that organizes your life. If you allow your mind to be programmed by television, advertising, family, friends, and society, you end up with unhealthy triggers, like eating when you are stressed or drinking when you are depressed.

These triggers take residence in your neuro-computer while you surf along the tide of life. In other words, if you don't pay attention to what floods into your mind, you get what you get by default. Soon the triggers become conditioned responses over which you seem to have little control. These automatic responses have some sort of payoff for you. Let's use the example of eating when you are overwhelmed.

When your body is in a stressed, eating can be used to instantly change your state. One minute you are in a trance called stress. The next minute you are eating a bowl of ice cream. Now you are in a trance of happiness, or at least immediate gratification. However, once that bowl of ice cream is gone, what happens? The stress returns and is compounded by guilt.

## What is Distorted Thinking?

The input our brains receive from the outside world can often create thoughts that are distorted and harmful. For example, when a mother strikes a child in anger for bad behavior, the child's brain links improper conduct and anger with hitting. When children at preschool anger the child, he or she responds by striking the other children.

### *What are Some Examples of Distorted Thinking*

Distorted thinking can happen in countless ways and is usually subtler than the scenario I just outlined. No matter the distortion, it can harm you or your relationships.

**Catastrophizing**: You are certain that a catastrophe is just around the corner. You hear about tragedies and fear they will happen to you. You engage in *What if* scenarios. "What if my husband also dies in a plane crash?" (What if your husband makes it home safely? Realistically speaking, which is more probable?)

**Personalizing**: Thinking that what other people say or do is always about you. For example, your boss spends little or no time with you, which must mean he doesn't like you. (Maybe he's just busy, or perhaps it means he trusts you to get the job done on your own.)

**Discounting the Positive**: You reject positive experiences or statements by insisting they don't count. A co-worker says, "You did a great job on that presentation," and you think, He's just saying that to get on my good side.

**Idiot Logic:** You make self-excusing assumptions based on past beliefs and experiences or outdated concepts. "I struggled with math in high school, therefore I can't pass it in college." Or, "Everyone knows smoking is the toughest addiction; Quitting is impossible."

**Emotional Logic:** You believe that what you feel must be true. If you feel dumb and boring you must be dumb and boring. People who smoke will say, "I'm a smoker." Each time they say it, they own it. I remind them that they cannot be a behavior. Therefore, they are a person who chooses to smoke, not a smoker.

**Polarized Thinking:** You see things as black or white, good or bad; there are no shades of gray here. If you're not perfect, you're a failure. (With this kind of thinking, isn't it easier not to start a task at all?)

**The Blame Game:** This one can go two ways. (1) You blame other people for your hurts and struggles; or (2) You blame yourself for every problem or loss and then feel guilty for your failures.

Distorted thinking comes in many forms, but I think you get the idea from those listed here. For this example, think of states of mind as different trances. Are you in the trance of catastrophizing, personalizing, or discounting the positive? Does your trance involve idiot logic, emotional logic, or polarized thinking? Is blame the name of the game for you? In creative visualization, the objective is to do away with distorted thinking and put together a series of new trances that get you the results you want. The idea is to create a set of triggers that form the trances for achieving your objectives instead of continuing to get what you get by default. In other words, you get transformation—a formation of trances or states—that help you accomplish your personal goals.

### The Worry Tree

A carpenter I hired to help me restore on old farmhouse had just finished a rough first day on the job. A flat tire made him lose an hour of work, his electric saw quit, and now his ancient pick-up truck refused to start. He sat in stony silence as I drove him home, yet he invited me into his home to meet his family. He paused briefly at a small tree and touched the tips of the branches with both hands. He opened the front door and was transformed. His face glowed as he smiled and hugged his wife and two small children.

Afterward, he walked me to the car. We passed the tree and my curiosity got the better of me. I asked him about the tree.

"Oh, that's my worry tree," he replied. "I know I can't help having worries on the job, but one thing's for sure, troubles don't belong in the house with my wife and children. So I just hang them on the tree every night. Then in the morning I pick them up again." He paused and smiled. "Funny thing is, when I come out in the morning to pick 'em up, there ain't nearly as many as I remember hanging up the night before."

Author Unknown

## How Can I S.T.O.P. the Triggers I Don't Want?

The best way to stop unwanted triggers is to avoid all conflict and live in a place where peace and calm are the norm. Unfortunately, this utopian place exists only in fairy tales. In today's world, over fifty thousand messages hammer us every day. These come from billboards, TV, radio, family, friends, and our own internal messages. Many of these messages elicit negative triggers for us.

My goal is to teach you how to control the internal and external messages and make the right choices. You may find that it's easy to control your internal state if you are well rested and having a great day. But if you find yourself in a situation where you're **S**tressed, **T**ired,

**O**verreacting, or **P**rocrastinating, it's time to STOP whatever you're doing. This is the time to regroup. If you are in a state of STOP—stressed, tired, overreacting or procrastinating—chances are, stress and tension control your life and your body in ways you don't even realize. You may find yourself eating (or overeating) to deal with the tension. You may find yourself smoking more. Some people end up treating other people poorly—even those they love. Others abuse alcohol or drugs. These behaviors may make you feel better—but keep in mind, the benefit is temporary. These fleeting fixes almost always cause more stress. To best deal with these triggers, you must recognize them as they occur, then take action to rid yourself of them. This is where creative visualization comes in.

Let's use athletes as an example. Can you imagine a professional athlete neglecting to practice situations he or she might encounter in a game? Of course not. Athletes practice every conceivable situation. That's how they perfect their skills and become good at what they do. Golfers might imagine they are sinking a putt for their club championship. A basketball player imagines shooting a game-winning buzzer shot. A tennis player mentally rehearses the perfect serve.

If creative visualization works for professional athletes to enhance their game, is there any reason it can't work for you in your everyday life?

**What Result Can I Expect from CVR?**

Life itself is a stressful event. And you now know that stress suppresses the immune system. The key benefit to CVR is the reduction of anxiety and stress, which results in better health due to an optimized immune system. Therefore, you are learning skills that will serve you well for the rest of your life.

CVR also helps you let go of the fear, stress, and anxiety associated with difficult life choices and, most importantly, gives you the power of possibility thinking. Possibility thinking means that you see solutions no matter what problems confront you, resulting in the ability to manage whatever stressors life doles out.

## Mitzi's Story

Mitzi Lynton stood in the middle of her bedroom, a half-packed suitcase in front of her and six cats at her feet. She was preparing to leave her Arizona home for a weeklong conference in California. As she tucked her cosmetic bag into the suitcase and zipped it shut, she mused about how the conference might change her life. The trip turned out to be the start of a big transformation in her life, but not in the way she expected.

No sooner had Mitzi arrived at the lake house where she would spend the week when she was overwhelmed by an intense migraine and nausea. The headache returned every day that week with increasing intensity until she could do no more than lie in a dark room with a cool cloth over her eyes.

Mitzi returned to Phoenix hoping that the headaches were somehow related to the California lake house and would subside. The pain continued to return almost daily with relentless intensity.

Mitzi's husband, Ron, suggested that perhaps it was her eyes and scheduled an appointment with an optometrist. Sure enough, Mitzi was in need of reading glasses. Would that be the end of it? Mitzi and Ron both prayed that their nightmare was over. Mitzi was working for the Governor's office at the time, assisting Hurricane Katrina victims. She was also a part-time minister and a seminar leader. The reading glasses were no help, and the headaches continued to rage on. She couldn't work. She was nauseated. She was frightened.

She went to her medical doctor, who thought it might be related to change-of-life issues. Mitzi left the doctor's office with prescriptions for the migraines and nausea. Neither did much to alleviate her suffering.

She next decided to try for a natural cure. At her local health food store she picked up a few herbal remedies for migraines. After having a severe reaction to the herbal concoctions, she threw them in the trash.

The next day at work her entire left side went numb. Was

she having a stroke?

Ron took her directly to the Arizona Heart Hospital where they did an MRI and a CT scan, both of which came back negative.

Next Mitzi went to a naturopathic doctor who told her that her adrenals were shot and she needed to get off of caffeine immediately. He also gave her hormone cream.

Once Mitzi stopped caffeine, she started to get relief from the headaches and nausea. She also decided to release some other commitments that were causing undue stress. The headaches slowly subsided.

Mitzi put the headache trauma behind her and took a vacation to Colorado. One morning she looked in the mirror and noticed that one of her eyes was bloodshot. Over the next few days the redness intensified. Did she have an allergy? Had she somehow scratched her cornea?

She purchased eye drops and allergy medication at the drug store but saw no improvement. By the time she returned home, the eye had started to bulge, blurring her vision. She returned to the optician who referred her to an ophthalmologist who sent her to Barrow's Neurological Institute. "We believe you have a carotid sinus fistula," the doctor said. "We need to do an angiogram to be sure. If we find the fistula, we will need your permission to put a stint in your head right away."

"What percentage of people with this condition will heal up on their own?" Mitzi asked.

"Less than five percent," the doctor answered. "You need to have this procedure."

"So if I have the stint put in, then I'm done, right?"

"Oh, no, the doctor answered, "You have to come back in six months for another angiogram."

"Then am I done?"

No, you'll have to come back in another year and then another year," he said.

In that moment, Mitzi felt divinely guided. This wasn't the

path she was supposed to take. "I think I can be in that five percent," Mitzi said, "I'm making my mind up right now to be in that five percent."

The doctor looked at her as if she were out of her mind, but agreed to let her give it a try. Mitzi and Ron scheduled the procedure for a couple of months out and went home confident that she would be healed before the appointed day ever arrived.

Mitzi had previously taught classes on the Law of Attraction. Healing the body by using the mind was a concept with which she was familiar. From that day forward she gave thanks for her healing. She gave thanks for her perfect and healthy body. She incorporated this gratitude blessing into everything she did and all the food and supplements she put into her body.

Ron recorded a visualization process for Mitzi that she used several times a day. The visualization started with soothing harp music and a guided relaxation. Mitzi loved fairies, so Ron had Mitzi imagine beautiful healing fairies with little golden threads in their hands hovering around her face. She would take a deep breath in and the tiny fairies would go up through her nose and into her headspace. The fairies would use their little golden cords to mend the carotid sinus fistula. After doing their magical work, they would sprinkle fairy dust throughout every cell until her entire body vibrated in harmony.

Mitzi had a large group of people attending her Law of Attraction course at the time. When people in the class would comment on her eye, she would affirm, "It's being healed right now as we speak. I'm having a health opportunity and right now, as we speak, it is being healed."

Mitzi's appointment for the procedure was scheduled for early December. By the beginning of November the fistula was gone. With a smile, she called and canceled the appointment. When people would ask, "How is your eye doing?" she'd answer, "It's perfectly healed right now." And so it was.

## What Are the Six Emotional States Associated with Change?

One or more of the following emotional states is almost always the root cause of failure. Here we will explore what those states are and how they can impact your life.

**1) Denial.** The emotional state of denial can cause people to smoke, drink alcohol, or consume large quantities of unhealthy food. These same people may continue to stress themselves by overworking or taking on tasks they are not physically capable of handling. The person is doing all of this with the hope that by hiding in these activities somehow, magically, the stress will go away, but they never take into account the harmful effects on the body. *Do you identify with the emotional state of denial?*

**2) Fear.** Although fear is a normal emotion, if left unchecked it can become more than one can bear.  It also can escalate into the kind of debilitating fear that harms the body. Fear is also one of the biggest contributors to procrastination. *Are you letting fear stand in the way of your success?*

**3) Anxiety.** Anxiety is similar to fear, but can manifest in the body as restlessness, sleeplessness, nervousness, and tension. Living in a high anxiety state places extreme stress on the body and certainly is not conducive to leading a positive and fulfilled life. *How much anxiety do you feel every day?*

**4) Anger.** When facing a personal change, going through short lapses of anger is natural. Anger left unchecked, however, may cause one to treat family and friends poorly or even harm oneself. *Is anger negatively impacting your life?*

**5) Frustration.** Getting overly frustrated can make you want to just give up. It may cause you to stop listening to your creative visualization processes. Creative visualization and relaxation can help you overcome frustration and practice solution thinking. *Does frustration hinder your ability to get things done and be a success?*

**6) Negative Thinking.** Walking around in a cloud of negative thoughts can compel you to push away your support system and to view the world as a negative place, continuing the cycle of negativity. My goal is to teach you new ways to handle the negative thoughts.

### *How many negative thoughts have come into your mind today?*

How much would it be worth to you to rid yourself of these negative emotions that stand in the way of your success? How much better would your life be without denial, fear, anxiety, anger, frustration, and negativity?

Are you starting to see the dramatic impact that relaxation and creative visualization can have on your life? Just wait until you discover all of the side-benefits you'll gain by relaxing and visualizing your future. Here are just a few:

- An increase in energy, confidence and stamina
- More fulfilling relationships
- Better job satisfaction and/or a more successful career
- A sense of purpose
- A peaceful state of mind
- And last, but certainly not least, an enhanced ability to handle and manage stress.

Now that you know all the ways stress, tension, and fear can stop you from achieving your goals, let's get started transforming your emotional states to positive, active trances that can help you get whatever you desire in life.

### *Thought Experiment: Taming the Tension Tiger (Part I)*

For this exercise, you're going to count down from three to one. On the count of three, I want you to tighten your hands and make them into a fist. Squeeze tightly, as tightly as you can. Notice the tension in your hands and forearms.

Now, on the count of two, take a deep breath. Hold the breath. Continue to study the tension in your hands and forearms. Feel the strain and pressure.

On the count of one, let go of the breath; exhale all the air out of your body. Relax your hands and release the tension. Let it go. Do you feel that tingling sensation in your fingers? That's blood flow returning to the ends of the fingers.

When you're under stress you restrict the flow of blood and oxygen to the cells of the body. But when you're relaxed, the blood flows easily to all organs, especially to the brain. This allows you to make better choices and decisions.

You can practice this tension/relaxation exercise anywhere and anytime. It can instantly take you from fight-or-flight to the relaxation response, which is, as you now know, your most resourceful state. You can do this by first noticing where you are feeling tension. As you count the number **three**, you will increase the tension in that area. Then you will study the tension as you count the number **two** and take a deep breath. Then at the count of **one**, you will let it go with a sigh. This relaxation is going to represent your best possible trance.

It is best to practice this technique by starting with the feet and moving up through the body to the top of your head. Use your imagination to give this tension and relaxation time to work for you. Picture a stressful event in your mind now, so that you can imagine letting it go at the count of one. While in that event, you are going to study the relaxation and imagine that all the new skills or abilities you need are present. These new skills could be listening to a recorded CVR process. It could be feelings of happiness. It could be hitting that long straight drive, or the desire to exercise, or an urge to eat fruits and veggies instead of junk food. It could be confidence, more energy, or being relaxed around difficult people. It could be all those things and more. Use your imagination to the best of your ability to imagine where and when you would need the relaxation response the most.

As you build the stress and tension throughout your body, study it. Then you will learn to let it go by rolling you shoulders back, lifting your head, and allowing your imagination to take over. You will imagine breathing the way you would breathe when you're happy and proud.

Take a moment to try that now. Roll you shoulders back, lift your chin, and breathe the way you breathe when you're happy and proud. Imagine how that happy and proud feeling begins in your body. Isn't it amazing how this simple change in your physiology so quickly changes everything about the way you feel?

Another effective visualization is to imagine your body as an

### Jennifer's Story

When I first met Jennifer Severo, she was a twenty-something singer in an alternative rock band. Appearing before live audiences was relatively new to her. She knew she needed to exude confidence on stage if she wanted to be taken seriously. She also knew that being able to connect with audiences was vital to her success. Yet she couldn't relax no matter how hard she tried. While on stage, she stayed safely behind her keyboards and avoided looking out into the audience. Her voice, often too soft and hesitant, was usually drowned out by the instrumentals. Soon the effects of stage fright spilled over into other aspects of her life. As an artist, she was no longer able to find joy in painting. Her relationship with her boyfriend, a member of the band, became strained. "It's as if anxiety and depression have overtaken me," Jennifer told me at our first meeting. "Why is it I can pull out all the stops in rehearsals, but totally lose it on stage?"

When Jennifer learned to practice CVR before and between shows, her life changed dramatically. While using CVR, Jennifer created a stage image that personified her true spirit—one that made her comfortable in her own skin. A few weeks later, Jennifer invited Cynthia and me to one of her band's performances. We were blown away. When Jennifer walked onto stage, it was as if she was illuminated from the inside. The stage had been re-set so that Jennifer was front and center—and she wowed us. At the end of the show, the crowd roared and begged for more. "Now I practice CVR every day," Jennifer says. "My self-esteem is sky high and my confidence is soaring. I even sing better than ever before—I know, because I get dozens of compliments after every show."

empty glass container filling with relaxation. Some people find it helpful to imagine this as a specific color.

With each creative visualization process, the goal is to build long-term thinking. This is the ability to think beyond what is currently happening to what the consequences of those actions will be. With this mental exercise you are going to think of future times when you might become anxious about a stressful event.

When you think of that stressful event, practice getting into the physiology of the event and feel the tension. After just a little practice of CVR, you will find it easy to trigger your relaxation response. Once you're in the right trance, you can easily imagine all the skills and abilities you will need and all the best choices you can make.

With just a little practice, you'll be amazed by how easily the tension and stress can leave your body—and it all happens because you have mentally rehearsed a different response. This is how you tame the tension tiger. With practice, you will learn to let go instantly of the unneeded stress and tension.

### *Thought Experiment: Taming the Tension Tiger (Part II)*

After practicing taming your tension tiger, you can take it another step by imagining living the next day of your life with a positive upbeat attitude. As you walk out into your life, roll your shoulders back, raise your chin, and take a deep, refreshing breath. Imagine yourself filling up with the positive feelings from your mental training—relaxation, peace, balance, a positive frame of mind—and then dream of all the positive changes awaiting you in your future.

### Thought Experiment: Taming the Tension Tiger Visualization

For best results, record the following in your own voice. Speak slowly and allow yourself time to follow each instruction.

*With your eyes comfortably closed, take in a deep breath and let it out with a sigh. Today you are going to tame the tension tiger. To do this, you are going to practice the three-to-one method of relaxing. When I say the number three, tighten an area of your body. When I say two, take a deep breath and study the tension in that part of the body. It is important that you hold the tension and the breath until you hear the number one. When you hear the number one, let the tension and the breath go, and study the relaxation. As your body learns the difference between tension and relaxation, you will learn the relaxation response.*

*Let's begin by tightening the hands into a fist, and then tighten from the hands to the shoulders. Three. Hold it just as tight as you can. Study the tension. Two. Take in a deep breath and experience only the tension. Hold it... (Pause five seconds) One. Let it go with a sigh. Study the feeling of relaxation. Does it come as lightness? Or heaviness? Or a tingling feeling? Just enjoy that feeling and become aware of what relaxation feels like.* (Pause ten seconds.)

*Now, once again tighten the hands into a fist. Now tighten the feet and legs all the way to the hips, while at the same time tightening the hands to the shoulders. Three. Just as tight as you can. Study the tension. Two. Take in a deep breath and study the tension. Hold it...* (Pause five seconds). *One. Let it go with a sigh. Study the feeling of relaxation. Just enjoy that feeling and become fully aware of what relaxation feels like. Soon you will be able to trigger relaxation and rid your body of stress at will. Notice how it is easier than the time before.* (Pause ten seconds.)

*Next tighten the hands into a fist. Now tighten the feet and legs all the way to the hips. Tighten the hands to the shoulders, then the chest, back, and stomach, all the way to the neck area. Three. Just as tight as you can. Study the tension. Two. Take in a deep breath and study the tension. Hold it...* (Pause five seconds.) *One. Let it go with a sigh. Study the feeling of relaxation. Notice how each time it is getting easier than the time before. Feel the stress draining from your body.* (Pause ten seconds.)

*Now you are ready to tighten your whole body. Three. Tighten every part now, even your face. Just as tight as you can. Study the tension. Two. Take in a deep breath and study the tension. Hold it...* (Pause five seconds.) *One. Let it go with a sigh. Study the feeling of relaxation. Feel the stress draining out of your body. With relaxation in mind, create your special place. This is a place where you can relax, let go, and unwind. This is a space between the tick and tock of the clock. From this creative place you can imagine how your life will improve as you tame the tension tiger.* (Pause one minute.)

*Now you know how to create the relaxation response. So when you start to feel stress in the body, you can count three and study the tension, count two and take in a deep breath, then count one and let it go. With time it will be as easy as taking a deep breath and letting it go.*

*It's time to return to fully awake consciousness. Mentally count yourself back by counting from one to five. At the count of five, say to yourself wide awake, wide awake, feeling fine and in perfect health. Everyday in every way I am getting better, better, and better. And this is so.*

*"The written word can be erased*
*- not so with the spoken word."*

**- Author Unknown**

# C H A P T E R
# S E V E N

## Name It and Claim It!

## Name It and Claim It!

As I mentioned in Chapter 3, your other-than-conscious mind is the key ingredient to the magic elixir that can transform your life. One of the benefits of the other-than-conscious mind is its ability to evaluate the environment to prove why we are either right or wrong. This behavior is hardwired into our brains. Science calls this part of our brain the *reticular activating system*. The reticular activating system is designed to continuously scan for things that are congruent, potentially dangerous, and familiar.

I'll discuss the reticular activating system in more detail in Chapter 9. For now, know that what is most extraordinary about our brain's reticular activating system is that it is set in motion by the experiences we have and the beliefs we form throughout our lifetime. From birth, we use our conscious and unconscious minds to process information, and this affects our beliefs later in life. This was demonstrated in research done with third-generation welfare families. Starting in early childhood, members of this group witnessed the welfare way of life through the behaviors and lifestyles of two previous generations. They saw no other standard of living. As a result, this third generation, in general, did not develop a belief system that prompted them to change their situation by finding work, getting an education, or learning a trade. They were conditioned to believe that having a career wasn't possible and, even if it were possible, their circumstances wouldn't change; therefore, why waste the energy?

In contrast, when billionaire real estate mogul Donald Trump teetered on the brink of bankruptcy, he did not consider his situation hopeless. He took immediate and focused steps to change his circumstances by brokering the purchase of a building in Florida worth millions. Without putting up any of his own money, he rebuilt his fortune and ultimately became the celebrity he is today. His success resulted from his belief that he could change his situation. By refusing to limit himself, he found a turning point in his life against devastating odds.

## Can You Afford to Risk Negative Thoughts?

Cynthia and I pulled our big Penske truck into Louisville, Kentucky, anticipation high. We had waited months for this day. Finally, I was going to have my own practice in a holistic hospital. Our new partners had told us they were finalizing construction and that the facility would be ready in a week or two. Unable to contain our excitement, we decided to drive by the building. As we rounded the corner, our jaws dropped.

Where was the hospital?

Instead of the shiny, new building we'd been expecting, we saw an abandoned shack with boarded up windows. By the looks of the structure before us, we'd be lucky to be up and running in a year. Our son, Alex, played in the back of the truck, unaware that his parents had just made the biggest mistake of their lives.

Six months earlier I was in San Francisco giving a talk for Light & Sound Research. After my speech on the benefits of light and sound, a man named Dwight met me at our display booth. There, he told me of a holistic hospital he was building in Louisville. It sounded like the opportunity of a lifetime. I'd always dreamed of helping patients use the power of their minds to overcome pain and accelerate healing.

I was cautious, though. I asked Dwight dozens of questions, and he responded with all the right answers.

"What are your plans right now?" he then asked.

I told him I was recently married and that my wife and I were looking for a place to set up our own practice.

"Why don't you set up in Louisville?" he suggested.

Dwight went on to assure me that, if we made the decision to join his team, he and his partner, Charlie, would take care of everything. They would even see that we lived rent-free for the first year if we committed to take space in the new hospital. I couldn't resist the offer.

As we sat in front of that forsaken building, it seemed everything had gone wrong. We drove in silence to the Denny's where we were to meet our new partners. As we waited in the restaurant, I couldn't eat. My life, my work, everything I'd built was in the back of that Penske truck. It appeared there was nowhere to unload. A sense of numbness set in.

When our would-be partners finally arrived, they had a young woman with them. "I want you to meet Gayle," Dwight said. "She's the love of my love and the most amazing hair dresser." He squeezed her shoulders and smiled.

Dwight and Charlie assured as that we had no reason to worry. They had a plan. "The hospital didn't work out like we hoped," Dwight said, "but we're building a beauty shop. You can rent space there."

*A beauty shop?* I glanced at Gayle's beaming face. *Ah, a beauty shop.* Not knowing what else to do, I agreed to look at the space. We squeezed into one car and drove by the shop. It was nice enough, but it was no hospital, was situated in a poor location, and was weeks, if not months, away from opening.

I took stock of our situation. We had loaded everything we owned in a truck and driven cross-country to start a business in a place we had not researched with people we didn't know. It looked like a dead end. Fortunately, Dwight let us move our belongings into a tiny one-bedroom apartment above the beauty shop. We weren't destitute.

A few days later the phone rang and my world fell apart. It was my younger sister, Sarah. "Patrick," she said, "Mom has cancer. They say she only has six weeks to live."

As I hung up, my body went numb. My mother? If the call had been about my alcoholic father, I would have believed it—but my mother? She was the health nut. She was the one who convinced the rest of the family to be health nuts. It was she who eliminated white sugar and white flour from our house. She was the woman always looking for that special health food or supplement to cure every illness. I would not accept that my vibrant, health-conscious mother could be dying.

I dropped everything and flew to Phoenix. My mother seemed fine on the surface. She was normal . . . until you looked at the brain scans. She had not one, but three large tumors in her head. One had grown into her brain's pain center. Because of that tumor, she was physically numb to any pain the cancer may have otherwise caused. Had she felt the pain at the onset of the tumor, treatment may have saved her. As it was, the cancer had filled her body. "Six weeks at best," was all the doctor had to say.

That was when it hit me. Throughout the years, during my father's drunken episodes, my mother had said over and over, "I'm numb to it all." She lived her life in a state of numbness, and it manifested in her body.

Just as the doctors predicted, in six weeks to the day, my mother lay down after a three-mile walk and never woke up.

I returned to Louisville with a fresh sense of purpose. My mother had been only forty-seven years old. Life is short; I didn't have time to be numb to it all. My circumstances weren't Dwight's fault or Charlie's fault. It was my fault I was in Louisville without a building in which to open my practice.

That's when I became a reverse paranoid. I believed that all seen and unseen forces would work for me, and not against me, for my success. Cynthia and I sat down in a local restaurant and tried to think up a game plan. We could go back to Phoenix with our tails between our legs, or we could make the best of the situation. We stared at our plates in silence, until Cynthia let out a big sneeze. "Geez," she said as she gazed around the room, "everybody's smoking in here."

"Yeah," I said. "I noticed that at Denny's too."

We looked at each other and, in that instant, knew what to do. We started making plans to open a stop-smoking clinic. We agreed to use the little money we had to open our practice. Louisville, Kentucky was the best place to open a stop-smoking clinic. At that time, fifty-six percent of the adults in Kentucky tobacco-country smoked. We were busy from the moment we opened our doors. Cynthia and I grew our business to seven locations until we sold the centers and moved to Virginia Beach, Virginia, where we expanded the concept and created an entire franchise system based on our methods.

Had I not allowed the Law of Acceptance to play out, had I instead chosen to wallow in numbness, negative thinking, or blame, had I not made up my mind to be a reverse paranoid, I never would have risked starting that first stop-smoking clinic. I never would have been motivated to franchise centers across the United States and throughout Canada.

The secret of risk is to risk for the right reasons, to listen to feedback, to be willing to experience a little pain, and to learn and grow from it. Being numb to your circumstances can kill your dreams. It could even cost you your life.

As children, we are influenced by and learn from family members, friends, neighbors, teachers and acquaintances. In most cases this is a good thing and brings with it a series of important learning experiences. While most of these are positive and support our growth, there are negative experiences that get stored in our minds and act as a filter for future experiences.

Let me give you an example that is a common occurrence in school. It's art class and you are asked to draw a picture of a tree. Without further instruction you get busy drawing what you believe a tree to be. You are proud of what you have drawn, but the teacher has a different idea. Your tree is too skinny. You don't have enough leaves. Your teacher tells you to draw your tree again, specifying what her idea of a tree should be. You do what you are asked but are confused by the teacher's request. You begin to doubt your abilities.

This same thing happens when you are asked to draw a dog and a cat. By the time you are asked to draw a house, you freeze up. You are unable to draw the house because you doubt your ability to draw. The teacher comes by your table and your paper is empty. You have learned from the past that whatever you do, this teacher is going to find fault with it, so you are going to wait for instruction. Your teacher is confused and asks you why you haven't drawn your house. You listen as your teacher explains in detail what he or she wants. Only then do you feel comfortable with following through and drawing the house.

In this scenario you are zapped of your creativity and resourcefulness because of someone else's idea of how something should be done. The mind will use this example as a template or filter for all other tasks. A one-time event doesn't carry much weight, but if, over time, that incident is supported by other negative experiences or your own self-talk, you will build in negative triggers and set up programs that can be counterproductive the rest of your life.

This is why you must learn to eliminate negative thinking and negative thoughts at all costs. Envision them as weeds in the garden of your mind. Weeds aren't much fun to pull out, but in the end your garden is healthy and beautiful, and left with plenty of room for you to sow new seeds. So, too, your thinking will be healthy and vibrant once you pull the weeds of negative thinking and acting from your other-than-conscious mind.

> *"At the moment of commitment,*
> *the universe conspires to assist you."*
> –Goethe

## Why is There Power in Thinking Big?

Unlike negative thinking, *expanded thinking* carries with it enormous power. An important saying to remember is: *Shoot for the moon. If you miss, you'll still land among the stars.* This is exactly what I am teaching you with the creative visualization process—to expand your thinking. Once you see, hear, and experience a world of success and abundance in your mind, then you can have it in the world. If you can't see it, hear it, or experience it in your mind, you will never accomplish it.

Be willing, when using these visualization processes, to stretch your mind and build a belief that you can have it all. Dr. Wayne Dyer says, "Consciousness is like running shorts. When the old ones don't stay up, you will stop wearing them." When you start thinking big, the old outdated beliefs of fear, frustration, and lack will be like the old running shorts you are too embarrassed to wear. You will discontinue using the old beliefs and replace them with a bigger expanded view of your future where the unseen forces of your mind go to work creating your success.

## Why Concentration is King

My good friend, Dr. Bob Harris, is fond of saying, "We either have results in our lives or excuses why we don't." In my experience, the ability to concentrate and focus is what separates people who succeed from people who fail. Why? Because you will always get what you focus on all day long; it's the Law of Cause and Effect in action.

In life, generally two kinds of people exist—pessimists and optimists. Pessimists are so busy finding reasons why things won't work that they have a hard time succeeding in anything they try. Polar opposites, optimists stay busy finding ways to make things work. The possibility of failure is rarely enters their thoughts. In the world of psychology we would call the pessimist *away from motivated* and the optimist is *toward motivated*. This means that the pessimist generally takes action when motivated to *get away from* something uncomfortable, painful, or frightening. The optimist generally takes action to move *toward* something pleasurable or positive. Both motivational strategies can be appropriate in the right context.

I believe it is healthier for me to be a pessimist. Of course this is based on the fact that I am a reverse paranoid. Again, as a reverse paranoid, I tend to believe that everything seen and unseen conspires *with me* for my success. Adding a little pessimism to the mix helps to keep me in balance. Obviously, this philosophy isn't the answer for everyone. The true secret to personal success involves knowing when to be pessimistic and when to be optimistic. For this reason, I have dedicated a whole process to this in my *Life-Mastery* CVR series called the "Optimal Risk Zone."

Now that you understand a little bit about pessimists and optimists and how they get motivated, I'll describe in detail the characteristics of each. As I explain them, think about your own life. Do you display any of these traits? Are they serving you? Would your life improve if you made changes in any of these areas?

## The Nine Characteristics of the Pessimist

### Characteristic 1: *Do you believe negative events are normal?*

Fred was a realtor—or at least he said he wanted to be. He came to see me as a referral from a successful client. During my interview with him, he spent the entire time explaining why his decision to get into real estate was the wrong one. He said the timing for the venture was bad and he was convinced the market was about to fall apart. "This happens all the time. I was a car salesperson just before gas prices went up," Fred whined. The real clincher for me was when he said, "I'm like Bad Luck Schleprock from the Flintstones. Bad luck follows me wherever I go." He had gone into the decision to become a realtor expecting it to be a mistake, therefore his brain had set about finding all the reasons it was a mistake.

Are you, like Fred, always waiting for the other shoe to drop? Do you assume that negative situations will last a long time? Do you blame yourself whenever negative events do take place? If so, you might be a pessimist. Not to worry. At this point we are just taking an inventory. The goal is to help you develop a healthy optimism for your life.

**Characteristic 2:** *Do you believe you have nothing but bad luck?*

I still remember the day Rachael came into the office looking so frazzled even her hair seemed to stand on end. She was a weight-loss client and we had scheduled her for a ten o'clock appointment. She arrived at our office at ten-thirty and was adamant that the timing mistake was ours. The point was not to place blame, but to help the client, so we moved on with the session.

As Rachael and I talked, her story of blame continued. She explained how all the traffic lights were red, and she almost got into an accident, and on and on it went. Then at the end of it all, she said, "Well, that's a typical day. It happens to everyone." Then she added, "I don't even know why I'm here. I'm destined to be overweight anyway. All the women in my family are fat." Rachel believed that she was cursed with bad luck, and the events in her life convinced her it was true.

I am always amazed by how often I hear clients say, "If it weren't for bad luck, I'd have no luck at all." Luck, in any form, is a meta-physical concept. In other words, it places all the power outside of you. I like the way motivational speaker Anthony Robbins describes luck as an acronym: L.U.C.K. – Laboring Under Correct Knowledge.

With that definition, you can see why it isn't luck at all, but the steady movement toward your goal that produces results. Naturally, as in Rachael's case, the steady movement away from a goal produced what she called bad luck.

**Characteristic 3:** *Do you take no responsibly for failure and all the credit for success?*

Caroline was a business owner who came to see me with an interest in communicating better with her staff. Caroline consistently referred to her staff as stupid and complained that they never listened to her. She lamented the fact that she couldn't find intelligent people to work for her. It's not hard to figure out why Caroline had staffing problems, is it?

I explained that her communication with employees is only as good as the response she elicits. Her staff's inability to communicate was actually her doing. She stared at me with wide eyes. "The only reason my company is successful is because of my communication skills," she said with a huff.

"That may be true," I said, "However, your failure to communicate with your staff must be costing you time and energy as well as creating a high turnover rate, or you wouldn't be here."

This is a common trait of pessimists. When things don't go their way, they are quick to blame something or someone else—genetics, the economy, Congress, their boss, spouse, or some other external source. They refuse to accept responsibility for any problem but are quick to take credit for successes. I remember something my father once told me that applies to these situations: "If you are at the center of all your problems, look inside yourself. You might be creating them."

**Characteristic 4:** *Do you feel more comfortable operating within negative emotions such as fear and doubt?*

During my first year as an assistant track coach, the head coach decided to use a special tactic on my younger sister. One day I found

Sarah, who was normally happy and optimistic before a competition, sitting on a bench at the sideline, red-faced and crying. "The coach won't let me compete in the long-jump," Sarah said.

The long-jump was Sarah's favorite and best event. I asked the coach why she had made such an unusual decision.

"Don't worry," the coach said as she patted my arm. "I plan on telling Sarah just before the event that she can compete after all. That'll get her all charged up and motivate her to win."

Did this coach really believe her old-school approach to coaching would work on Sarah, who had developed her own system of motivation, and had won every long-jump competition thus far?

Too often coaches use the tactic of yelling at their team and telling them what bad players they are in a misguided attempt to motivate the team to prove him wrong. This type of motivation works well for the person who tries to get *away from* pain, but has the opposite effect for people like Sarah who run *toward* a goal.

Fortunately, I had uncovered the coach's plot with enough time to help Sarah get on her usual game face. She won the event and broke her previous record.

Some of us have unwittingly learned this negative motivational strategy and use it on ourselves all the time. Are you the type of person who wonders why you feel drained at the end of the day? It may be your negative motivation strategy. It takes a great deal of energy to worry about things that may never happen, and this can drain your energy reserves. One study done in the late 80s found that over ninety percent of the things we worry about never happen. When they do take place, they are rarely as bad as the pessimist imagines.

**Characteristic 5:** *Do you make your problems universal?*

My client, Richard, wanted to learn to speak Spanish. He believed, however, that no one over a certain age could learn a language.

According to Richard, you had to be born into the language or start studying at an early age to master it. He was busy trying to prove his point when I interrupted him. "Are you trying to convince me or yourself?" I asked. I was really asking Richard if he was trying to talk himself into his belief to avoid the work involved and have an excuse for not succeeding at his goal.

I told him that anyone can learn anything if properly motivated. In fact, the co-creator of Neuro-linguistic Programming, John Grinder, was a master at learning languages. He modeled his strategy after children. Instead of trying to memorize foreign words and all the rules and laws that went with the language, he immersed himself in the language. As a professor of linguistics, he went where young people spoke the language and communicated with them. John Grinder is an optimist. He realized that everyone at one time had the problem of needing to learn a language. Most of us solved it as children. As an adult, he applied that knowledge to his own goal and became a master at it.

Are you a Richard or a John? If you didn't get good grades in school, do you believe it was because you were not smart enough? Do you blame the teachers or are you convinced they had conceived a diabolical plot to hide the information from you? If you don't get along with a certain person, do you assume that you can't get along with people in general? Do you believe it's difficult for everyone to lose weight, stop smoking, or make a change in life? If you answered yes to any of these questions, you need to practice possibility thinking.

### Characteristic 6: *Do you make successes specific?*

Ralph, a superstar athlete, was at a turning point in his life. His goal was to become as successful in the business world as he was at athletics. His initial attempts at entrepreneurship were ineffective at best. The setbacks he suffered had him convinced that some people are wired for business and others are not. By the time he came to see me, he was certain that he was not wired for the corporate world. Ralph was used to being physical and was accustomed to handling problems in somewhat unrefined ways. He realized that his skill set didn't fit into the business realm, and he didn't feel equipped to gain the knowledge he needed.

I explained to Ralph that he had limited himself by making his success specific only to athletics. "You can take the same attitude you used to be successful in sports and apply it in business," I told him. "You just needed to be shown how to do it."

Do you limit your successes the way Ralph did? Maybe your issue is school. If you are good at math, do you limit your thinking by saying, "I'm good at math," as opposed to saying, "I'm a smart person," or "I'm a good student"? When you think about your relationships with others, do you pick a specific person to like? Do you say, "I get along with Charlie Johnson," instead of expanding your horizons and saying, "I get along with people"?

While practicing creative visualization, we will expand your definition of success and learn to harvest past skills so you can apply them into new areas of your life.

## Characteristic 7: *Do you internalize your problems?*

Our local lottery uses the slogan, You Can't Win If You Don't Play. I think a more accurate statement would be you can't lose if you don't play! The reality is that you have a better chance of getting hit by lightning than winning the lottery. Does that make me sound like a pessimist? Not really, because I believe you win the moment you pay your dollar. I'll explain in moment.

For now, imagine that you bought a lottery ticket and, like several million other people, you lost. How do you feel? What do you say to yourself? Instead of acknowledging the slim chance you have of winning the lottery and playing for fun, do you internalize the loss telling yourself, *I'm a loser. I never win anything?*

The first time I bought a lottery ticket, I was with a friend and we made a commitment that if either of us won we would split the winnings. We started talking about all the things we would do with our windfall. Before you knew it, we were in a whole new dimension of unlimited wealth. We enjoyed our imaginary winnings in our minds just as naturally as we breathed. We were in the moment. I later understood that my brain had dumped thousands of dollars worth of positive neuro-chemicals into my system.

So when I say you get your winnings just as soon as you buy the ticket, I mean it. You don't have to win a million dollars to get the "high" from the neuro-chemicals that pour out of your own brain whenever you think a positive thought. You win every time you are optimistic. Now doesn't that feel better than telling yourself you're a loser?

**Characteristic 8:** *Do you believe that good events happen because of external causes?*

When Becky came into my office and told me she had low self-esteem, I found it hard to believe. She was a tall, beautiful, and quick-witted woman. "I'm only successful because of my looks," she said, "no one really takes me seriously." She believed that, when it came to her beauty and success, she just drew a lucky number in the crapshoot of life. "I didn't do anything to earn what I've got," she said. "I get uncomfortable when people compliment me because I don't feel worthy of their praise. Even if they're admiring something I've accomplished, I know they're just flattering me because of my appearance."

Becky had so externalized her self-worth, she could no longer recognize her abilities. She was blinded by her perception of how she believed other people saw her, which had no basis in reality.

Do you ever do this? Do you undermine your own confidence based on external influences? For example, if you win at a sporting event, is the first thing out of your mouth, "I only won because my opponent had a bad day"? Do you downplay your own achievements? If you receive praise for doing well on a test do you say, "Well, it was an easy test," and shrug off the compliment? "If you've fallen into these kinds of bad habits, don't worry, you'll soon learn how to own your successes so you can enjoy a healthy self-esteem and savor your achievements.

**Characteristic 9:** *Do you get stressed out during the ordinary ups and downs in your life?*

This characteristic is last but certainly not least. In fact, humanity's uncanny ability to get stressed out is the main reason we are even discussing optimism. I know many people who don't need a good reason to be stressed. They can be sitting on a beautiful beach with nothing to do but relax. The next thing you know, they get stressed and upset about some trivial detail such as the way the neighbors put out their garbage can that week. They are upset about an event that has nothing to do with the current situation.

One of the biggest secrets to a stress-free life is to learn that at times we must give up control over things that we have no control over so that we can gain control over what we can.

Before moving on to the characteristics of an optimist, let's review the pessimist's nine attributes. Don't worry if you identify with any of these. You're reading this book so you can change them.

You're likely a pessimist if you:

1. *Believe negative events are normal*
2. *Believe that if it weren't for bad luck, you'd have no luck at all*
3. *Take no responsibly for failure and all the credit for success*
4. *Feel more comfortable operating within negative emotions such as fear and doubt*
5. *Make your problems universal*
6. *Make successes specific*
7. *Internalize your problems*
8. *Believe that good events happen because of external causes*
9. *Get stressed out during the ordinary ups and downs in life*

## The Eleven Characteristics of the Optimist

Now let's take a look at the eleven characteristics of the optimist. Once again, think about your own life. Do you display any of these traits?

**Characteristic 1: *Do you think of negative events as temporary setbacks?***

One day while talking to my friend, Jerry, he referred to himself as an "angel investor," a term I had never heard. Jerry seeks out companies that show great promise but lack the funding to realize their full potential. When he finds the right company, he steps in (like an angel) and makes a substantial investment. Being an angel investor is a risky proposition and is not for the weak at heart. More than seventy-five percent of the time the investor will lose all or some of the investment. But the other twenty-five percent of the time, when everything falls into place, it can be like winning the lottery. If Jerry didn't understand how to properly organize his risk, he would have stopped being an angel investor after his first loss.

I consider Jerry a successful optimist. He never dwells on negative situations nor does he seek pity from others when he doesn't succeed. He, along with other optimists, believes that tomorrow is the start of a brand new day and the solution to the problem is right around the corner. Jerry is fond of saying, "There's gold in every pan. You just have to know how to find it."

**Characteristic 2: *Do you believe that the natural order of the world is positive?***

It's common knowledge that I grew up the son of an alcoholic. As a child, when I saw my father laid out in a drunken stupor, I never believed that what I was experiencing could be positive. I had to grow into adulthood to realize that it was one of the best things that could have happened to me. In fact, without the upbringing I had, I wouldn't have developed into the person I am today, nor would I have the insight to write this book. In *Awaken the Genius*, I dedicated a chapter to how I was *blessed* to be the son of an alcoholic. As I have grown in my understanding, I realize that everything happens in perfect order for what we need, even though that may not always be what we want.

As a reverse paranoid, I genuinely believe that life is grand and only getting better. Even when something negative happens, I always can connect a positive learning experience to that negative event. Winston Churchill said, "Those who fail to learn from history are doomed to repeat it."

## Characteristic 3: *Do you see challenges as opportunities?*

In rock climbing there is an expression: *If you can, you can't. If you can't, you must.* Rock climbers are in it for the challenge. A dedicated climber never takes the easy way out.

What do you think might happen if someone who wanted to lose weight developed this same attitude? Since the average diet lasts seventy-two hours and the average woman spends thirty-one years of her life on a diet and, in spite of that, an alarming number of people in this country still suffer from obesity, it seems obvious that a change is needed. That change, of course, must be of the mind. Diets don't work. If they did, everyone would be slim and healthy. If there isn't a mental change, there is no chance for permanent weight loss. If people can change their minds so that lifestyle changes are seen as new opportunities instead of insurmountable challenges, perhaps we can begin to tackle this obesity epidemic.

Optimists seek out ways to triumph over challenges and believe that overcoming obstacles makes them stronger. Like the Marines, they believe the saying, *That which does not kill me makes me stronger.*

## Characteristic 4: *Do you believe that all seen and unseen forces are conspiring to help you succeed?*

This characteristic is the one that a pessimist has the most trouble overcoming. You see, optimists have a sense that when the telephone rings it is a friend on the other end simply because he or she thought about that person. The pessimist assumes it is a bill collector or telemarketer. An optimist believes the radio station is playing the sound track to his or her life. Optimists wake up every morning as if they are royalty, assuming that all of creation is helping them in unseen ways throughout the day. The pessimist has a tendency toward paranoia. Pessimists believe each new day is full of challenges to be overcome and that the seen and unseen forces will conspire against them in order to make them fail.

**Characteristic 5:** *Do you operate on positive emotions such as happiness, joy, and a sense of well-being?*

It's difficult for an optimist to believe that anyone would waste time on negative emotions such as anger, fear, or resentment. Buddha articulated the truth of the matter over five thousand years ago saying, "He who angers you conquers you!" Medical science has proven this statement correct.

Medical visionaries like Dr. Deepak Chopra demonstrated that when people think negative thoughts, their bodies produce neuro-chemicals that break down and destroy the body. When they think a positive thought, their bodies produce neuro-chemicals that strengthen the body and cause them to feel good. Ah, there's that magical elixir again.

**Characteristic 6:** *Do you have an emotional buffer to handle crisis situations as lessons to be learned?*

Because optimists run on positive emotion, they seem to have a hidden reservoir of joy that helps them through the lows of the day. This is really where the daily practice of creative visualization comes in.

As mentioned earlier, our bodies work like a capacitor. During the day, by the experiences we go through, we build up a charge (negative emotions) and then discharge when it is maxed out. This discharge often comes in the form of lashing out in anger, fear, or frustration. Unfortunately, without proper mental training, such as creative visualization, we discharge on family members and friends. We do this because we understand that, in most cases, no matter what we do or say, our loved ones will take us back.

The optimist uses natural ways of relaxing such as exercise and healthy eating to rid the body of stress. While some people are blessed with this natural ability, the majority of people need training in this process, or they will seek unhealthy ways of de-stressing such as drinking, smoking, or overeating.

**Characteristic 7: *Do you make your problem areas specific?***

When speaking or thinking about a personal relationship, an optimist may make a statement like, "I don't get along with Charlie Johnson." This is a specific problem area. An optimist doesn't generalize by saying, "I don't get along with people." This has to do with the way you sort information. When it comes to healthy behaviors, it's best to sort negative experiences out of our personal experience and sort positive experiences back into our lives.

**Characteristic 8: *Do you make your successes universal?***

On the flip side of this, as an optimist you want to make your successes universal and expand them beyond the specific. For example, do you make comments like, "I'm smart," or "I get along well with other people" instead of limiting your successes like the pessimist does? If you do, then you could be an optimist!

**Characteristic 9: *Are you the type of person who externalizes problems?***

Would you tell a friend, "My family may have had some problems, but I'm moving forward with my life," or "My high school education was limited, but I'm overcoming that obstacle"? If so, you're probably an optimist. An optimist doesn't play the blame game the way pessimists do. A pessimist likely would say, "My family ruined my life," or "My high school education was so bad, I can't go to college or get a good job." Optimists refuse to identify with negative traits or past history, choosing instead to leap over obstacles in constant pursuit of their dreams.

**Characteristic 10: *Do you internalize good events?***

In school, when you perform well on a test, do you make the comment, "All my studying was worthwhile"? When something good happens at work, do you pat yourself on the back and say, "My hard work paid off." If you do, chances are good that you are an optimist. An optimist believes that he or she is worthy of praise and worthy to receive the benefits of hard work. In opposition, the pessimist says, "Oh, it was just an easy test," or "My boss gave me a break."

**Characteristic 11:** *Do you function with far less stress than many of the people you know?*

The most beneficial of all the optimist's characteristics, functioning without stress allows you to be unaffected by life's ordinary ups and downs. The optimist focuses on the positive and remembers to forget the negative. This commonsense way of thinking allows them to sleep deeply, experience profound, positive dreams, and awaken refreshed in the morning.

Before moving on to the steps that will help you build these positive traits, let's review the the optimist's eleven attributes. Don't worry if you don't identify with these characteristics. This book is going to help you acquire them. You are likely an optimist if you:

1. *Think of negative events as temporary setbacks*
2. *Believe that the natural order of the world is positive*
3. *See challenges as opportunities*
4. *Believe that all seen and unseen forces are conspiring to help you succeed*
5. *Operate on positive emotions such as happiness, joy and a sense of well-being*
6. *Have an emotional buffer to handle crisis situations as lessons to be learned*
7. *Make your problem areas specific*
8. *Make your successes universal*
9. *Externalize problems*
10. *Internalize good events*
11. *Function with far less stress than many of the people you know*

Now that you know the difference between a pessimist and an optimist, I will explain how to build optimism, the key component for thriving in overdrive.

First, let me share a story that made a profound impact on the way I think about optimism. My dad once told me about working with a Native American in his office in Phoenix, Arizona. This gentleman told him that he had once felt as if two dogs were raging a battle in his head. One dog was white and the other red. At times the fighting was so bad it disturbed his sleep. One day, the man said, he had a spiritual awakening and, low and behold, the fighting stopped.

At that point he stopped talking and simply stared at my father.

"Okay, you got me. Which dog won?" My father asked after a moment of silence.

"The white one, of course," the man said with a chuckle.

"What do you mean?" my father asked. "How did it win?"

The Native American grinned. "The white dog won because it was the only one I fed."

Which dog are you feeding—the dog of pessimism or the dog of optimism? I hope that with your use of creative visualization you will start feeding your true optimistic nature and starve your pessimistic inside.

**What are the Seven Simple Steps to Building Optimism?**

**Step #1:** *Make a list of past successes and use them as a resource generator.*

The successes you've experienced in the past carry with them the memories in feelings, pictures, and words that can help you recall the patterns you use for success. Once your other-than-conscious mind knows the pattern, it can engage it as needed to maximize your success each day.

**Step #2:** *Find a mentor who is optimistic.*

Almost everyone knows someone who is optimistic and successful. In the past you may have envied people like this. Now you know better. All you have to do is imagine what it would be like to be as upbeat and optimistic as these role models. During a creative visualization session, imagine following an optimist, observing how he or she operates, and then allowing your mind to install the optimistic characteristics into your own experience.

**Step #3:** *Take inventory of the things you do well and put them to good use in your community.*

A candle burning under a basket casts no light. But if you take the basket away, the candle's can shine bright for all to see. Imagine the good you could do by helping out in your community. During my training days, a group of fellow classmates and I visited a homeless shelter and practiced using the new self-help strategies we were learning with those who couldn't afford the help. It was amazing to see the transformation in these homeless men and women as they became open to the possibility that they had other possibilities besides staying stuck in a shelter.

**Step #4:** *Read or listen to self-help books to feed the right dog.*

Think of the white and red dogs as good and bad thoughts. Which are you feeding? Think about all the time you have driving in your car. If you travel a half-hour every day, that equals three and a half hours of potential learning time each week—or over fifteen hours a month. Spend this time feeding the right dog instead of allowing your local radio station, with its loud music and obnoxious commercials, to toss scraps to your red dog. Nearly every self-help book is available on audio. Commit today to creating your self-improvement college on wheels. You will be amazed at the breakthroughs you can have while sitting in traffic.

**Step #5:** *Reframe your beliefs about past failures.*

Set a goal to be your own angel investor—and the enterprise you're investing in is your future. Reframing is the same as finding the gold in every pan. Reframing is the ability to look at something differently. As an example, if you lose your job, don't think of yourself as having been fired; think of it, instead, as an opportunity of infinite employment. In other words, being fired opened a whole new world of options and opportunities. Perhaps it is the freedom to work toward a dream career or to start a new business. You can reframe the ending of a relationship as well. Rather than think of it is a painful break up, recognize that you've just been handed the opportunity to find the true love of your life and to explore your ability to forgive, forget, and move on.

**Step #6:** *Become a life-long learner by attending training with local experts in the areas you need to strengthen or that hold interest for you.*

You may wish to attend adult community education courses or enroll in a college course. It's never too late to learn something new. An inspiring example is Grandma Moses, whose greatest accomplishments happened after she turned seventy.

Anna Mary (Grandma) Moses had only sporadic periods of schooling during her childhood and spent nearly all her adult life on a farm raising five children. After her children were grown and her husband passed away, she decided to paint for her own enjoyment. She placed her paintings in a drugstore window, and the first person to buy them was an art collector from New York. Today she is known as one of America's most beloved artists. When Grandma Moses was in her nineties, she painted on television. When she turned one hundred, she danced a jig at her birthday party.

People are like fruit on a tree. They are either learning and growing or aging and dying. Don't allow your mind to shrivel from disuse. Challenge yourself to learn something new. Who knows what you might accomplish.

**Step #7:** *Just say "no" to the people in your life who rob you of enthusiasm and joy.*

Life is too short to waste time and energy on the kind of people I call "energy vampires." Surround yourself with your support team. Find family members or friends who encourage you to grow as a person. Seek out the optimists in your world.

**Here is a quick review of the seven steps to creating an optimistic mind set:**

1. *Make a list of past successes and use them as a resource generator*
2. *Find a mentor who is optimistic*
3. *Take inventory of the things you do well and put them to good use in your community*
4. *Read or listen to self-help books like the Life Mastery series in order to feed the right dog*
5. *Reframe your beliefs about past failures*
6. *Become a life-long learner by attending training with local experts in the areas you need to strengthen or that hold interest for you*
7. *Just say "no" to the people in your life who rob you of enthusiasm and joy*

*"I would rather be ashes than dust! I would rather that my spark should burn out in a brilliant blaze than it should be stifled by dry-rot. I would rather be a superb meteor, every atom of me in magnificent glow, than a sleepy and permanent planet. The function of man is to live, not to exist. I shall not waste my days trying to prolong them. I shall use my time."*
—**Jack London**

### Resilience—Your Key to Transforming Negative Patterns

It was the week before Christmas and I had finished a book tour at a Barnes & Noble in Southern California. We were heading for Phoenix where we would spend the holidays with family. Jerry, our publisher, stopped by for a visit before we left. Tucked under his arm was a small holiday-wrapped gift. We sat down in a restaurant to discuss our future plans for my book.

"Business can wait," he said. "I found the perfect Christmas present for you. Here . . ." He handed the package to me. "Open it now."

"But Christmas is more than a week away," I said.

"I don't care. I want you to open it right now."

"Okay, okay," I couldn't imagine what was so special about his gift.

When I got the present unwrapped, I held in my hand a small Energizer Bunny (battery operated, of course).

"Thanks, Jerry," I said, trying to hide my disbelief.

"You don't get it, do you?" he said.

"Alright, no, I don't . . . I'm sorry."

"He took the bunny from my hand, flipped the switch, and then set it on the table. The little pink creature in blue sandals and sunglasses, marched across the table, beating its toy drum. "Look," Jerry said, "That's you!"

My eyebrows shot up.

Cynthia, who had been sitting quietly at my side, laughed. "I get it," she said. "You're like that. No matter how many times you get set back or knocked down, you just keep going and going and going."

I think being one of six boys helped me to build the resilience to keep going in the face of adversity. Also, for me, sports played a big roll in turning negative experiences into positive life lessons. Don't worry if you weren't one of six boys or have no interest in sports, you still can learn to reframe past experiences and build that can-do attitude—even if you have never had to overcome an obstacle in the past.

**What are the Four Keys to Building Lifelong Resilience?**

**Key 1:** *Use your creative mind to give life to your goals.*

During your creative visualization sessions, daydream about your goals. Imagine them in full living color. Place your favorite music into the scene. Then step into it. Feel the way you would feel in that situation. Give yourself permission to enjoy your goals from the perspective that they are already accomplished.

### Key 2: *Practice using the "What if" frame.*

When pessimistic thoughts come up in your mind, play a little mind game with yourself that will reduce the negative to the ridiculous. Start by thinking about the polar opposite of the negative experience you're having. For example, *what if* you were to get a new job that fulfilled your every dream? *What if* you found that ideal relationship? *What if* you were to feel so good, you couldn't help but smile? *What if* smiling for no reason became a habit?

### Key 3: *Use the stop sign metaphor to interrupt negative thought patterns.*

If your mind starts playing out a doomsday scenario, visualize a stop sign. Say to yourself, "STOP! Stop giving it life. Stop giving it energy." Then, imagine the *What if* frame again. *What if* the positive changes you want for your life were already made? How would your life be different? *What if* you accomplished the most important goal you've set for yourself? What would you be doing? What would it feel to accomplish that goal? As you hone your creative visualization and relaxation skills, you will master this key.

### Key 4: *Create a back-up scenario.*

Prepare for the worst and plan for the best. Successful business people write business plans that have contingencies for what they will do if things go south. I believe each of us could use this same strategy in our personal lives.

### When is it Better to be a Bit of a Pessimist?

As compelling as it sounds, the notion that you could and should be an optimist all the time isn't realistic. There are situations when it's best to be a bit of a pessimist, or at least neutral. What are the three times when it is best to put off being optimistic?

1. If your goal is too risky, choose a little pessimism. Optimism is not a good mindset if you are planning to leave everything behind and start a new life. It is best to look at this type of scenario with careful consideration of the downside as well as the upside.

2. Don't sing songs of optimism to someone who has a dim future. If a friend lost a loved one, a job, or has recently divorced, he or she needs a strong shoulder more than a cheerleader. Making a friend in need angry by using overtly cheerful behavior at the wrong time will only escalate his or her negative feelings.

3. Finally, it's best to rein in your optimism if you want to show your support or lend a sympathetic ear while listening to the troubles of others. Pace their emotions before slowly guiding them into a more positive way to look at their situation.

Now that you know how to be discerning about optimism, let's run through the basics for building optimistic thinking in your life.

## What are the ABCs of Stimulating Optimistic Thinking?

### Attend to every thought

No one can afford the luxury of a negative thought. Medical research proves that positive thoughts heal and negative thoughts harm the body. Practice opening your mind to infinite possibilities. At first this might be scary, but with practice you'll find it easy to emphasize what you enjoy and spend time on what's constructive. Start today by taking personal responsibility. You are the sum total of your thoughts, actions, and beliefs. Imagine a life where you add value to yourself and others.

### Beliefs are not truths

Be willing to change the pictures, sounds, or emotions that hold negative beliefs in place. With practice, you can dispel the hold negative thoughts have on you. Base your assumptions on reality, not fantasy. Use possibility thinking to plant the seeds of greatness and you will build your self-confidence. Acknowledge that you are worth the time, energy, and effort by taking the time to practice your creative visualization sessions.

## Commit to changing your thoughts

Have you ever envied wealthy people? Do you assume that those who have more material wealth are somehow luckier than you? Challenge that assumption by creating a sense of abundance for yourself and others. Imagine the world full of opportunity for everyone. Picture yourself, your life, and most importantly, your future as moving forward in a positive light. Notice how life supports you at every turn. Reframe your thoughts from complaining to planning. Avoid pointless whining and come to terms with the reality that life isn't always fair. Life gives to you in direct proportion to what you give to life.

Those are the ABC's for stimulating optimism, but here are a few more for good measure:

## De-catastrophize

Stop your fears by coming up with a realistic alternatives. Use the stop sign technique discussed earlier. Use humor. The healthiest people find it easy to laugh at themselves. Reframe your shortcomings and think like a great inventor. Thomas Edison once joked that he had found 999 ways in which he could not create a light bulb before he found the one way that worked!

## Evolve

Question your limits. Are you really using every skill, ability, or resource to its fullest? Take advantage of constructive skepticism from the people you trust. Imagine life as a game and make change part of that game. Experiment with fresh approaches to problem areas of your life. It is possible to change at any age. If Grandma Moses could become a renowned artist in her seventies, what could you do? Use your newfound creative visualization skills to design a new life for yourself; create a life that is magnificent and worth your efforts. Be honest with yourself. Recognize that you are a work in progress, that you are your own artist, that you, and only you, have the final say on your evolution. Decide today that you are green and growing. Creating optimism sometimes takes more than changing your attitude; you may need to develop new friends, excise old ones, create new hobbies, or learn new skills.

Now that you know the characteristics of the pessimist and optimist, you can begin transforming your life through optimistic thinking today. Follow the seven simple steps to building optimism, engage the keys to resilience, and then implement the ABCs for stimulating optimistic thinking.

### John's Story

Bravado is not a word anyone would use to describe John Shoecraft. No one would call him a daredevil or risk-taker. John is a pretty ordinary guy. But this ordinary guy did something so extraordinary, it earned him a spot in the *Guinness Book of World Records*, and he says that he owes his success to creative visualization.

John's story starts in the spring of 1980 in Phoenix, Arizona, when he attempted to set an altitude record in a helium balloon. He and his partner ascended to 21,000 feet where they caught a jet stream that swooped them away at a hundred miles an hour. They landed thirty minutes later in Apache Junction, a small desert town fifty miles from Phoenix. He had never ridden a balloon at such a fast clip and found it exhilarating. "None of the chase vehicles could keep up with us," John says.

Three ballooning enthusiasts had recently made the news as the first team to fly a balloon, the Double Eagle, across the Atlantic. This gave him an idea. Why not fly his helium balloon across the United States of America? No one had ever done it. And with the rugged terrain and unpredictable weather patterns that could come from either Canada or the Gulf of Mexico, this feat would be a more dramatic one than flying across the Atlantic.

John couldn't get the idea out of his head. After convincing his partner to join him, he set about working out the details, and the pair paid a visit to the Double Eagle team to get their advice. They dubbed their helium balloon adventure **Super Chicken Across America**. The name came partly because the balloon was supposed to look like a Phoenix bird, but actually resembled a comical chicken, and partly because there was something *super* about what they were preparing to do, but they were still *chickens* at heart. John received permission from the FAA to lift off in September of 1980. They would launch from a ballfield at Orange Coast College in California.

When the day arrived, John was focused on getting the balloon off the ground and on the right path, a feat they accomplished without a hitch. They rode the wind all the way to Texas when a voice on the scratchy radio system warned of a weather pattern developing in St. Louis. The air stream they were following would take the Super Chicken right into the storm. However, there was a chance they could get through before the storm came together—enough chance that the pair decided to go for it.

A few hours later the duo faced a wall of black, lightning-streaked thunderclouds, a force of nature far more powerful than the Super Chicken. They had to put the craft down. John radioed for help and within minutes helicopters surrounded them. It started raining and the Super Chicken thrashed in the wind. John's partner escaped by parachute while John brought the gondola as close to the ground as possible. He then jumped for his life. Moments after he tumbled out, the Super Chicken was swept up in the storm. It was discovered the next day, a mangled mess, in Harrisburg, Pennsylvania.

"It was a hair-raising sixty-six and a half hours," John says, "but in less than a month we were ready to try again." The pair launched their spare balloon in late October. They had gone over every detail of the last trip, mapped out what went wrong with the weather pattern they'd been caught in, certain now that they had covered every contingency.

The second Super Chicken had made it over the Sandia Mountains in New Mexico when it got caught in an updraft that lifted them from 20,000 to 30,000 feet in a few short minutes. At that altitude, the balloon started to lose its helium gas and began dropping too quickly. The team spent the night throwing off ballast (a sand and rock mixture balloonists use to maintain weight balance) to keep the gondola from falling too fast. By the time a rosy sun peaked over the horizon, they had run out of ballast. They had no choice but to land. They had been in the air only twenty-nine hours and came down in Liberty, Kansas.

After the second failure, John's partner decided he'd had enough of transcontinental ballooning. John, more determined than ever, convinced his former flight instructor to take the trip with him. This time, though, John knew he had to do something radically different. He decided to view his previous failures as learning experiences. There was more to it than weather and wind. He didn't believe in bad luck. So what was missing from those first two trips? John pondered this question for days until the answer finally dawned on him. He had been focused on all the wrong things. He had started each trip focused on take off and the flight, but never with the end in mind.

John closed his eyes and creatively visualized the attainment of his goal. What hadn't they done on the first two trips? Well, they hadn't landed on a beach. So John visualized the gondola gliding onto golden sands with waves lapping at the eastern shore. He saw himself sticking a flag in the ground like the lunar landing team. He imagined sitting in a lawn chair on the beach, his partner beside him, the Super Chicken behind them. "A toast," John says as he raises his glass of champagne, "to a couple of chickens with a great spirit of adventure."

And that's what happened. Taking only fifty-five hours of flight, the third Super Chicken soared across America, from California to Blackbeard Island off the coast of Georgia, and alighted on a sandy beach. "Once I did that creative visualization, there was never a time that I wavered from my end goal," John says. "I never once bothered to concern myself with anything else. I knew we would make it, and we did. It was a perfect day. I now use creative visualization for every goal I set. It's become a way of life for me."

## Thought Experiment: Optimism and Resiliency Visualization

For best results, record the following in your own voice. Speak slowly and allow yourself time to follow each instruction.

*Your eyes should be comfortably closed. Today you are going to use this thought experiment to build your optimism and resiliency. In the past, you did the best you could with the information you had at hand. Today* you are using new information . . . information that will change the way you see, hear, and experience the world within you and around you. Today, and from this day forward, negative thoughts, concepts, and beliefs will have no control of you, at this or at any level of consciousness.

With this thought in mind, plan your day. Imagine the people you will see and the conversations you will have. Notice how you are attending to every thought. Positive thoughts lead to positive actions. Take a moment to plan on success today. If a negative thought comes into your mind, mentally say the word STOP. Visualize a big, red stop sign and say to yourself, "Stop giving this thought energy. Stop bringing it into my mind. Stop giving it time."

Now replay the day in your mind and visualize how you would like the day to go without any of those negative thoughts. Imagine you are evolving your thinking to the point where you consider negative thoughts as weeds in the garden of your mind. Negative thoughts may be natural, but you keep them out of your mental garden. You choose to fill your mental garden with beautiful flowers that give off the sweet scent of success.

Each time you practice this visualization, it will get easier to transform the negative programming of the past and replace it with the new thoughts and new actions of your bright and compelling future. Today you know the truth. You are far greater than you have been led to believe, and far more powerful than you have yet allowed yourself to be. Today you are committed to excellence in execution. Today you will improve and take action.

From here imagine how this evolved attitude will help you accomplish the goals you have set for yourself. When you are done and you know that you will succeed, go ahead and count yourself back into the room by counting from one to five. Wide awake, wide awake, feeling fine and in perfect health, everyday in every way you are getting better, better, and better than the day before. And this is so.

\*\*\*

"Men acquire a particular quality by constantly acting a particular way... you become just by performing just actions, temperate by performing temperate actions, brave by performing brave actions."

- **Aristotle (384 BC - 322 BC)**

# CHAPTER
# EIGHT

**Step into the Spotlight of Your Life**

## Step Into the Spotlight of Your Life

William Shakespeare wrote, "All the world is a stage and all the men and women merely players." How might each of our lives change if we thought of life the way Shakespeare did? First of all, we wouldn't take our lives so seriously. The dramas we create in our lives— the problems, challenges, and crises—would become something over which we have control.

I think that when Shakespeare made this now famous statement, he realized that we are all not only acting in a huge play, it's a play with no script—an improvisation. We make up the storyline and the dialogue as we go. We also make up the roles we play. One minute we may play the role of lover and the next minute mother. The next day we may be cast as stressed-out boss, supportive friend, or helpful neighbor. Another time we play kind, helpful characters and, in different circumstances, we play the bully or villain. Sometimes we are joyful, and other times we are sad. We may portray a cautious, uncaring character on one day and then turn around and play the maudlin victim the next. At yet another time we are the happy-go-lucky sidekick.

In improvisation, each actor is free to make up his or her role as the play unfolds. A new bit of dialogue may cause the play to meander in different directions, which is something that makes improvisation so interesting. And isn't that quite a lot like life? One off-hand remark from your spouse or boss can send your day careening in a different direction from where you started. Maybe you woke up that day feeling happy and confident and then, POW, a few wrong words from a character in your life, and you're thrust into the role of wounded victim, angry lover, disgruntled employee, or whatever.

Actors don't believe they're the character they play. Even the audience is aware of the actor being separate from the role he or she portrays. This gives us some distance from the Law of Cause and Effect. In our real life roles, however, we become so entrenched in the characters we play that we struggle to maintain a distance from the emotions involved.

Perhaps if we could see our daily lives as something akin to participation in improvisational theater, we might become less mired in reactions, habits, and attitudes. This would put each of us in a place of choice. After all, we're only playing a role, right? Even when other people anger, insult, or hurt our feelings, we can respond in whatever way we choose—we can choose to be angry or not, we can be hurt or not, we can throw an insult back or not.

With the power of choice we can decide the roles we play and how to play them. We have the choice to say yes to one role and no to another. You could tell the director of the play (which is also you by the way), *I'm done with this role. I don't want to play this character anymore. I'm tired of being the victim. I'm going to play the hero. I'm rewriting the script and changing my role.*

If the whole world's a stage, there is an unlimited number of roles you can play. Even if you choose to sit in the audience and watch, you're playing a role—that of the uninvolved, which means you get whatever you get by default.

Assuming your goal is to make a difference in your life and the world, then you have a responsibility to choose your roles with care and good conscience.

That said, I am going to help you discover a simple yet powerful tool called *modeling*. Modeling enhances your ability to think, act, and respond to life with an attitude of success. With modeling you are going to choose other characters to assist you—each character will play the role of *mentor*.

Modeling was an important part of your internal system when you were a child. It's the art of imitation. As a child, you learned by imitating others—your parents, brothers and sisters, other family members, friends, your doctor, your neighbors, even the check-out person at the grocery store. At times you were conscious of your modeling choices, but most of the time it happened at the other-than-conscious level of your mind.

If you've been married you know what I mean. Has your spouse ever said, "You're acting just like your mother," or, "just like your father"? Do you wonder how that's possible when you swore you would never be like your parents?

## Writing the Script of Your Life

Growing up, you may have felt like other people controlled everything. Most parents never sit their children down and explain that we each have control over our own lives. Parents tend to teach children few, if any, life skills, and most school systems are parsimonious with life education. At school we were taught *what* to think, not *how* to think. Therefore, we learn life skills at the school of hard knocks. Our other-than-conscious minds assess the world around us and, like a sponge soaking up water, we absorb the morals and beliefs of others. This is called *social hypnosis,* and it happens whenever we passively learn what to think. Social hypnosis affects every aspect of our lives including religion, politics, career, fashion, diet, lifestyle—even which sports team we root for.

In this chapter I will help you take back control of the script for your life. I'm going to teach you how to think. Instead of playing a bit part in life, it's time to become the central character—the hero of your life story.

## Why Do You Need to Write a Script for Your Life?

It's important to write your own script for your life so that you can have and maintain creative control. If you don't, you might be stuck being the victim—or worse yet, the villain. As an example, your parents and loved ones had the best intentions, but when they told you to clean your plate because there were starving children in China, and you wrote that into your character at meal time, they didn't realize that later in life the habit of plate cleaning would cause you to gain two to three pounds a year. Now you are twenty to thirty pounds overweight.

The subconscious mind doesn't work on logic; it learns by imitation. In this regard, the subconscious is no more intelligent than a fourth grader. Consequently, people develop habits that are robotic and irrational; but remember, they didn't write that script for themselves.

Actors who play the same or similar roles over and over again are called *character actors*. Perhaps you've watched an action movie and noticed that the same actor you saw in two other action films plays the bad guy. Character actors tend to rehearse to perfection a specific way of acting that fits an archetypal character such as villain, side-kick, or mentor. That's what makes them believable. Like a character actor, the subconscious mind acts out what it has rehearsed. Once it discovers a way of doing something, the subconscious will, by nature, eliminate other options. Like most children, the other-than-conscious mind takes the path of least resistance.

With these facts in mind, I hope you agree it's time for a casting call. Can you say "movie star"?

## How Do You Develop Your Story?

Imagine you're getting ready to audition at an open casting call. What would you have to do first? Of course, you would need to learn the role for which you are auditioning. What information would be important?

1) You would need to know the part into which you would be cast.
2) You would need background information on the character.
3) You would need to know the skill set needed to play the part.
4) You would need to know the desired outcome for the performance.

Once you had the answers to these four questions, you could begin your research.

You did know that actors do extensive research on the characters they play, right? They learn to *be* the character they portray. Let's pretend you are a famous Hollywood actor. How would you research your character?

You might start by reading books about the subject. You could attend lectures on the topic. A major drawback to this option involves time. Actors that play doctors don't have time to get medical degrees. So what do they do?

They find a role model—a mentor, if you will.

An actress readying herself to play the role of a hardworking doctor in an emergency room setting might spend a few weeks at an emergency room. She'd watch what happens and would notice how the doctors respond in certain situations.

The actor then might interview the staff at the hospital for the inside scoop. She might ask questions such as, "What goes through your mind when you receive a call that a gunshot victim has just been admitted? What would the steps be in saving the victim's life?" She may ask female doctors, "How does dealing with all these emergencies affect your personal life and your family?" Big budget films often pay real doctors to be on the set to watch the shots and confirm the accuracy of the performance.

With this concept it mind, let's take a look at how you can apply modeling to your own life.

**Change, Like the Movies, is a Process**

*Step One: As the writer of your life, decide who you want your character to be.*

Some people may want to be a naturally thin person, others a non-smoker, and still others a scratch golfer, a great speaker, or a top-notch salesperson. In the space provided, write down your main goal for using CVR. Make sure it's written in the positive. Don't write what you don't want. In other words, if you want to be a scratch golfer you wouldn't say, "I don't want to score above 90," you would say, "I am playing the role of a scratch golfer." If your goal is to lose weight you wouldn't say, "I don't want to be overweight." You would say, "I am playing the role of a naturally thin person."

**Who is your Character?**

_____

_____

_____.

When accessing your other-than-conscious mind, it's imperative that all the information is stated in the positive and uses pictures and words of success. This brings about the feelings of success.

### Step Two: As the director, decide what needs to happen to convince others that you are staying in character.

This step consists of listing the behaviors or actions the actor will demonstrate to convince the audience that he or she is a believable character. As an example, if golfers wish to advance from a bogie golfer to a scratch golfer, they might first employ a swing coach and practice using CVR to hardwire the new information. They might rehearse a strong, consistent drive and work on improving their short game. And this step might end with them winning their club's member tournament.

Of course, a good director will work with the writer to confirm that the integrity of the character is maintained.

### What Behaviors Will Your Character Demonstrate?

_____

_____

_____

_____ .


### Step Three: As the actor, figure out how you will know everything you need to know.

List three people who possess the skills and have demonstrated the outcome you want. These are your mentors. After listing those people, either real or imagined, you can move forward. Don't worry, you don't need to know everything about the people you choose because it's only your perception that matters anyway.

Keeping with the golf example, as a woman golfer you might choose Annika Sorenstam as your role model. After all, she is one of the top LPGA golfers. As a man you might choose Tiger Woods.

Of course, if you are not into golf, these names won't mean a whole lot to you. You have to make your list from your own heroes. If you want to be naturally thin, you might have a sister in-law or a friend who demonstrates the skill you need. If you wish to be a public speaker, you may consider a presenter you admire.

Once you have this information, you are ready to do your research as an actor.

## Who are Your Mentors?

_____

_____

_____

_____.

## Are You a Hero or Victim?

The only difference between heroes and victims is the choices they make. If you reflect on your life experience and you think of yourself as a victim, this book will give you the time and resources to make a change. If you are already a hero, congratulations are in order. Now, are you willing to take it to the next level?

Armed with information from your inner writer, director, and character, it's time for you to step into the role you designed for yourself. Think of this as Drama 101—which means we need to get you into character.

## How do you get into Character?

The first step is to imagine yourself watching one of your mentors demonstrate the success you have chosen. For this example let's imagine you have chosen a female friend to demonstrate the skills of a naturally thin person. Imagine that you are following her as she goes through a typical day. From a distance notice how she interacts with people, food, and situations.

From this disassociated perspective, imagine yourself watching her non-verbal communication. Notice how food never becomes all that important to her—how she looks at a a plate full of food, a dessert, and a drink, and how she makes decisions to eat when eating is appropriate and to say no when it's not appropriate..

The next step is to imagine the same scenario again, but this time place yourself in her experience just as if you are seeing through her eyes, hearing through her ears, and experiencing everything she feels. Imagine you have access to her self-dialogue. In other words, you listen to what she says to herself when she makes the right decisions. This part of modeling gives you the inside view. Don't worry; imagining these things will be easier during the actual CVR process.

Now that you're getting to know your character, the thought experiment exercise will help you continue to practice getting into this personality so it's easy to stay in character in challenging situations or around difficult people.

An important point when using modeling is to think from the perspective of your mentor. For instance, imagine that one of your mentors is a thin person who used to be overweight. What might be her internal dialogue when she sees a piece of chocolate cake? Can you imagine her saying something like, "That cake won't get me what I want. If I eat it, I know I'll feel bloated and uncomfortable. The guilt and shame are not worth my time."

This is quite different from the response of an overweight person who might think of the immediate gustatory gratification. She might say, "Mmm, that cake is going to taste good!" Later, after the cake is eaten, she feels guilty and shameful and angry with herself. In this example, because the thin person thinks of the end result of her actions before making decisions, she remains thin.

When naturally thin people think about exercise, they think of the long-term benefits. They think of how it improves their health, boosts their stamina, and gives them an appealing body. Overweight people tend to think of exercise as punishment. It makes them sweat and pant and hurt. They forget to think of the long-term benefits.

## Making the Mind/Body Connection

Now let's talk about physiology and the way it affects your thinking. In other words, how does physiology affect your psychology? Most people are aware of how their emotional state affects their physiology. For example, if you're depressed, you tend to slouch and hang your head. But most people aren't aware that their physiology also affects their psychology. A brief exercise illustrates this point.

*If you just won a million dollars in the state lottery would you:*

a) Drop your chin, slump your shoulders, breathe shallow, and frown, or
b) Roll your shoulders back, lift your chin, hold your body in a proud posture, and then smile?

If you're like most of my seminar attendees, the answer is obvious. In fact, just thinking about it made many participants roll their shoulders back, lift their chin, and smile. Their brains didn't know the difference between a real and an imagined scenario. If this happened for you, it means that, in a very real sense, you won the lottery of life. With a simple thought you released powerful, positive brain chemicals that made you feel good. And the truth is, if you had to buy these chemicals in the form of a drug, it would cost you hundreds of dollars, would probably be illegal, and all you would get is a fleeting moment of joy, one that you can create simply by adjusting your physiology.

Let's go back to drama class. If I were to ask you to display non-verbally that you are in a state of exhilaration, how would you do it?

What about achievement? Elation? Happiness? Excitement? Enthusiasm?

If you found that you had to adjust your physiology to get to these states of psychology, you are not alone. The two, physiology and psychology, are symbiotic—they exist together in human nature. Now try something else. Roll your shoulders forward, drop your head, shallow your breathing, and try to demonstrate a feeling of triumph or victory.

What about pleasure? Satisfaction? Delight?

Did you find this impossible without changing your body posture?

Are you aware that your body has its own memory? For example, think about the front door of your home. Which way do you have to turn the doorknob for your door to open?

To answer this, did you imagine yourself standing at the front door and turning the knob? Did you, like many seminar participants, reach out and turn an imaginary doorknob? Turning a doorknob isn't a left-brain decision. Because you have opened thousands of doors, you do it out of habit, without conscious thought.

You may be surprised to know that you turn doorknobs in different directions depending on whether the door is hung from the left or right. Yet you don't have to think about it. You just turn it. This is called *unconscious competence*. You demonstrate mastery of something without knowing how you know to do it.

Is it any wonder that repeating old habits is easy and learning new habits is hard? For example, if you can't seem to pass a cookie jar without reaching inside, you're experiencing unconscious competence. You don't think about the action, it just happens. Next thing you know, you're munching a cookie that you didn't want. Some people are so unconsciously competent, they forget to taste the cookie!

What if you could have this same kind of unconscious competence for what you want? How easy would it be to lose weight if you had unconscious competence for eating right? How quickly could you master golf if you had unconscious competence of the perfect swing? What if you had unconscious competence as a non-smoker?

Well, get ready, because that's just what the next thought experiment is designed to do for you. With the power of modeling, I'm going to ask you to step into the spotlight of your life. This happens as you train your body to overcome old memorized habits. Instead of your body leading your mind, as your own *software engineer for the human mind* you are going to train your mind to lead your body.

This new software will help you re-program your body and mind to behave as the person you desire to be. This will work with any outcome, and that's the real purpose of this process—to learn the skills, abilities, and resources of the successful people in the world around you, and then emulate those things.

*Let's go over the three steps for the thought experiment.*

**Step 1: Imagine you are watching an expert at the skill you have chosen.**

For this example, let's imagine you have chosen a male family friend to demonstrate the skills of a non-smoker. Imagine that you are following him as he moves through a typical day. Notice from a distance how he interacts with people, how he acts after a meal and in other situations. From this disassociated perspective, imagine you are watching his non-verbal communications. Notice how the thought of a cigarette never enters his mind—how he can look at a cigarette, how he can watch others smoke, and not give smoking a second thought.

**Step 2: Imagine the same scenario again but this time as if you are seeing through his eyes, hearing through his ears, and experiencing everything he feels.**

This will be easier during the actual creative visualization process. This part of modeling gives you the inside view. Imagine you have access to his self-dialogue and you can listen to what he says to himself when he makes all the right decisions.

**Step 3: Imagine three places in the next day you would like to have this skill.**

If your goal is to be a public speaker or to improve your golf game, then you would think of the specific place in the future where you could demonstrate the new skill. As mentioned earlier, this is called future pacing. We know that the future will arrive. With mental practice you can pace the future with new skills, abilities, and resources so that you can live your dreams.

**How long will it take to master the new skills?**

There are four levels to learning and unconscious competence is only one of them. Timing may depend on where you are on those levels with the change you want to make in your life.

The first level is *unconscious incompetence.* This means you don't know what you don't know. This is a place of frustration for those trying to improve. *Unconscious incompetence* is probably the reason you're reading this book, and it's why you'll be mentally rehearsing your new skills through the thought experiments and CVR processes.

Here's an example: If you want to improve in golf, yet you are visualizing the wrong swing, you won't improve much. You have *unconscious incompetence* about your golf swing—you don't know what you're doing wrong. If you seek out a pro to train you, however, and use creative visualization to gain *conscious competence*, your improvement will be greatly accelerated.

The Second level is *conscious incompetence.* This is when you know what to do, but have not yet mastered the new behavior. One weight loss client put it this way, "I knew what I needed to do, but I had no idea how to get motivated to do it." This client eventually took off forty pounds, which she couldn't do on her own because she needed the *unconscious competence* to make it easy and automatic.

### Reverend Michele's Story

The first time Michele Whittington walked into the First Church of Religious Science in 1989, she felt at home. The church itself, a lovely building on Seventh Street in Phoenix, Arizona, seemed like a sanctuary to her. She attended services there until, for reasons she chooses not to discuss, she and her husband decided to leave the congregation.

In the year that followed, Michele often thought of the church. She missed the serenity and spiritual inspiration she had experienced there. One day, while feeling somewhat spiritually disenfranchised, she received a call from a member of the congregation. "We're thinking about spinning off and creating a new place of worship," the woman said. "We just want you to know about it in case you and your husband would like to join us."

Michele made a mental note of the name of the new church—Creative Living Fellowship. Once the group got organized, she and her husband started attending services and became comfortable within their new spiritual family. Through what Michele calls "a series of incredible miracles," she eventually became the minister of the new church; she had finally answered the call that had been in her heart for years.

The group settled into a small rented space in a thrift shopping center. After five years of trying to make the space work, the congregation decided they wanted to own their own building. They decided to do a *visioning* session to determine whether or not the idea was right for them. Visioning is like a precursor to creative visualization. It's what you do before you have conceived what you want to creatively visualize. The board gathered about forty congregants who sat together, closed their eyes, and asked questions of each other such as: What is the path for our church over the next ten years? Who do we each need to become in order for this vision to come forth? Each person then shared his or her vision and together they created a ten-year vision for the church—a vision that included owning a building. "It was uncanny how similar the visions were," says Reverend Michele. "As each person read their vision, others would say, oh my gosh, I saw that too, or I felt that too."

So while the congregation creatively visualized a beautiful new church, focusing on the size, shape, atmosphere, and location of a building, Reverend Michele and her board took action. They held fundraisers and hired a realtor to start the search. At one point they thought they had found their perfect location, but the governing body of the existing parish decided not to sell after all. Even through the disappointment, though, the congregation of Creative Living Fellowship kept creatively visualizing their dream.

Reverend Michele decided it was time to ask the Universal Intelligence that was guiding her for the next step. If they could have any building, anywhere, without regard to cost or availability, where would that perfect match be? "I got a full-bodied response," Michele says, "chills, tears, butterflies in my stomach." The answer was Michele's beloved little church on Seventh Street.

At first glance, the answer seemed absurd. About seven or eight years earlier, the original Religious Science church had folded and sold the building to a Polish-Catholic congregation. Even if the building was for sale, which it wasn't, they couldn't afford it. They had raised about four hundred thousand dollars, and had been doing some work with lenders. In total they had about a million dollars with which to buy a property. "It felt so right, like all of the creative visualization we had done over those four years was taking us to that particular church, and yet my logical brain said there's no way we could ever have it," says Michele. "So I did another visioning, and I asked what would I do next if I didn't think it was impossible to own that church? The immediate answer was, find out if it *could* be available."

Michele contacted the realtor and discovered that, about five years earlier, he had made the sale to the existing congregation. He knew them well. The realtor placed the call and was surprised to hear that the Polish-Catholic congregation had been thinking about calling him to start looking for a new facility; they had outgrown the Seventh Street church and were in need of a much larger space. It happened that the realtor had a property for sale a couple miles north that they fell in love with. Unfortunately, the Catholic Diocese, who actually owned the property, said no to both transactions. Once again Michele asked the question, what would I do next if I didn't think this was impossible? The answer was, raise more money and look for other lending options.

At one point in the next five months, Michele, having grown despondent, had a conversation with a minister at her college. Let's do some creative visualization right now," the woman said. "I want you to physically put yourself in that church, on the front stage. See yourself as the minister of this church. Look out at the full sanctuary. Feel the enthusiasm and the excitement that your congregation has for being in this new space." Michele finished that session knowing that all the obstacles could be resolved. Five months later the diocese finally said yes, but when they listed the property it was for $2.4 million, more than twice what Michele's congregation had available. Again Michele asked the question, what would we do if we didn't think this was impossible? They were ultimately directed to a company that could get the deal done for them. In the month it took to put the financing together, the realtor kept warning them to hurry. "This is a hot building," he said, "somebody's going to snatch up this property." Michele and her congregation just kept holding to their vision. Even though dozens of groups had looked and expressed interest, no one else made an offer. Michele's congregation, on the other hand, offered what they considered a reasonable amount of money—the amount they could afford. It was significantly less than the diocese had asked for. "I've worked with the Catholic Diocese," the realtor said. "They never come off their price,"

"Well," Michele replied, "they've never had an offer from the Creative Living Fellowship before." And that's how Reverend Michele's congregation bought the charming Seventh Street church, a facility that wasn't for sale and that they couldn't afford—and the one place where Michele felt most at home.

It pays to remember this: Anything worth doing well is worth doing poorly at first. CVR accelerates your learning at the other-than-conscious level—so reaching *unconscious competence* feels easy and effortless. Knowing the right way to do something and rehearsing it in your mind accelerates your learning and you demonstrate the behaviors quickly and, for many, automatically.

**The third level is *conscious competence*.** This is where you know what to do and you know that you are doing it. A good example of this is when you first start taking care of your health and you start reading labels. Soon you will know which products aren't even worth your time. You consciously make changes until it becomes automatic.

The fourth level is _unconscious_ competence, which, of course, is your goal. This is when you are demonstrating the new skills without even thinking about it—and this is where creative visualization really excels. Each time you go to the other-than-conscious level, you are storing the memories of success in your mind. Each time you practice eliminating negative thoughts, concepts, and beliefs, the new habits become unconscious and automatic, allowing you to be positive and optimistic and capable of accomplishing any goal you set for yourself.

It's now time to record and listen to your thought experiment process, "Step Into the Spotlight of Your Life," where you will become the writer, director, and actor for producing all the positive changes you want for your life.

## Thought Experiment: Step Into the Spotlight

For best results, record the following in your own voice. Speak slowly and allow yourself time to follow each instruction.

_Go ahead and close your eyes and take a deep breath. Imagine your creativity improving each and every time you listen to these thought experiments. In your mind's eye, imagine the mentors you know who have the skills or abilities you would like to have._

_Imagine you are thanking them for being a part of your life and for being someone you can model. Imagine they are thanking you for picking them as a mental mentor. From here, imagine that, one at a time, you are watching them move through the amount of their day. As you watch, notice the way they interact with people. Notice the way they communicate and carry themselves. You are doing all of this from a distance. (Not Spoken: Pause for a minute and let your imagination discover the skills, abilities and resources they are using.)_

_Take a few deep breaths and notice your level of relaxation. Scan your body and notice that you are relaxing to the next logical level. Soon you will become unaware of your body and totally aware of your mind and_ *all the power and resources you have there.*

*Next, imagine you have access to their minds. Imagine you can hear what they hear, see what they see, even feel what they are feeling. Then imagine their day is starting again. This time you can even hear their internal dialogue. It is like you are on a ride at Disneyland. You are just along for the ride, recording their skills, abilities and resources. Take a few deep breaths and let the day begin. (Not Spoken: Pause for a minute and let your imagination discover the internal skills, abilities and the resources they are using.)*

*Again, take a few deep breaths and notice your level of relaxation. Scan your body and notice that you are relaxing to the next logical level. Soon you will become unaware of your body and totally aware of your mind and all the power and resources you have just seen, heard and experienced.*

*With these positive thoughts in mind, imagine that you are integrating these new thoughts, ideas and concepts into your daily life. Imagine where and when you will be using these skills. Take your time and imagine using them with family members, friends and coworkers. Let your imagination flow through the next day, the next week, and into the months yet to come. Take all the time you need to explore the infinite number of possibilities from each moment in time. Each time you use this thought experiment you will make a mental breakthrough using the laboratory of your mind to improve the quality of your everyday life, knowing if there is a problem in your life you are going to find a solution. (Not to be recorded: pause for one minute to visualize.)*

*Go ahead and notice your level of relaxation, knowing that each time you will become less and less concerned with your body and more and more concerned with your mind. Exploring your mind's potential is fun, and each time it gets easier and easier. Each time you get better at seeing, hearing, and experiencing in your imagination.*

*From here imagine your personal place of relaxation. Let yourself go. When you feel rested, relaxed, revitalized and renewed, go ahead and return back into the room. But first, imagine three places where you would use this new modeling skill to improve the quality of your life. When you have done that say to yourself wide-awake, wide-awake and return fully back into the room.*

*All the world's a stage,*
*And all the men and women merely Players;*
*They have their Exits and their Entrances,*
*And one man in his time plays many parts...*

**–Shakespeare**

# CHAPTER

# NINE

**Life Lessons – Reframing Your Life**

## Life Lessons - Reframimg Your Life

*"You cannot go around and keep score. If you keep score on the good things and the bad things, you'll find out that you're a very miserable person. God gave man the ability to forget, which is one of the greatest attributes you have. Because if you remember everything that's happened to you, you generally remember that which is the most unfortunate."*
*–Hubert H. Humphrey*

In the above quote, Hubert Humphrey sounds more like a psychologist than the thirty-eighth vice president of the United States. His statement is as true today as it was when he wrote it, and the wisdom within it is the essence of this chapter.

### Why is it Important to Reframe Your Life?

As was discussed earlier, reframing is the ability to look at something from a new perspective so that you can become the type of person who finds gold in every pan and forgets "that which is unfortunate." It's possible to reframe our lives because, as human beings, we tend to clearly remember only the very good or the very bad in our lives anyway. Our other-than-conscious minds keep the everyday humdrum events buried so that our conscious minds don't get bogged down. Can you imagine trying to function from day to day with every memory sitting up close and personal in your conscious mind? It would be impossible.

Wouldn't it be nice if we could use that same mechanism of the mind to lock away, or bury, those habits and patterns that we no longer want? Well, you're in luck, because you can, and it's really quite simple. I'm going to teach you a technique we call a *compulsion blowout*. A compulsion is something that even though you don't want to do it, you do it anyway. The technique does exactly what it says; it blows out your compulsions and locks them away, so you can be rid of them once and for all. In order to learn to do this, I first need to teach you how to use the photo center in your own mind.

## What is the Photo Center in Your Mind?

A few years ago my wife, Cynthia, lost her beloved sister, Christa, to lung cancer. Christa battled the disease for over two years and Cynthia was at her side throughout a good portion of the ordeal. During that time, Cynthia discovered a dark side to memories that she'd never experienced before; a side that's ugly and painful and, to her, felt nearly impossible to forget.

For weeks after Christa's passing Cynthia agonized over the suffering her sister had endured. Cynthia described the experience like this:

*"After Christa died, my brain seemed to idle on the most awful moments of her battle against the vile disease. Images raged through my mind—Christa coughing, vomiting, or dropping to the floor like a rag doll, lumps of brown hair left on her pillow, bruised veins, a bulging tumor on her neck, her precious arm purple and bloated from a botched transfusion. I could no more stop these memories than I could stop a raging hurricane."*

I knew that Cynthia had to work through her grief in her own way, so I did my best to be supportive and let her be. Then one day, after a particularly intense bout of tears, she came to me and took my hand. "This isn't working for me," she said. "I want to remember Christa's beautiful face, her gentle nature, and the fun we had together, not the horrible months that took her away from me."

"You can do that," I said. "All it takes is for you take control of the memories and store them the way you want instead of letting negative images run rampant in your mind."

"I'm ready for that," she said.

I then took Cynthia through the process you're going to learn here. I helped her to store the awful negative images of her sister's illness behind her, in black and white, with no sound or emotion. I then had her focus on the good times she'd had with her sister and remember them in color, with all the sights, sounds, smells, and tastes present. I had her place these good emotions into her future. Here is how Cynthia described it:

*"Once all the dark memories were behind me, tears of joy and relief streamed down my cheeks. I let open the floodgates to the happy memories of the life Christa and I had shared: The two of us hiked in the desert and chatted about nothing. We held newborn kittens and laughed at the silly names we'd given them. We walked to the park with our sons, took them trick-or-treating, then tucked them into Ninja Turtle sleeping bags. We played with splash bombs in her pool, giggled until our sides ached, and sat side by side in her backyard watching an Arizona sunset. A warmth and peacefulness filled me for the first time in months."*

How did Cynthia make such a dramatic transformation so quickly? By using the photo center of her mind. It works because our minds are hardwired with the ability to store everything we take in through our senses. Someone who is happy-go-lucky stores positive memories in color. They remember them with sound. They can even get into those experiences and relive them. This would be called *association*.

This same happy-go-lucky person also stores negative experiences offline. The negative memories are vague, fuzzy, or actually gone from their minds. Like an old movie, they are outdated and black and white. They might even be still pictures. You have probably said to yourself, "I'm over that experience." This is a form of *disassociation*.

The reverse of the happy-go-lucky person is someone who has had a very traumatic experience and chooses to hold tightly to that memory. These people tend to continually replay the scene in their minds and store the negative events in color and with sound. This is what Cynthia was doing in the weeks immediately following her sister's death, and the result was sadness, depression, anxiety, and a feeling that she had lost the good memories of her sister.

Today's psychologists recognize this phenomenon and are changing to a more positive approach to psychotherapy. They realize that talking about a problem or past event simply can't bring about a release from negative symptoms. Every time the person speaks about the event, he or she is reliving the experience and bringing it back into the present along with all the negative emotions. This does nothing to solve the underlying problem.

This same person, because his or her focus is on the negative, tends to block positive memories by making them black and white, like silent movies with no emotion. These memories aren't real to them. Soon the positive experiences can feel like dreams that are so far in the past they will never surface again.

To use the photo center in your mind, I'm going to ask you to think of something you are compelled to do that you no longer wish to do. Write down the behavior, attitude, or belief that is your compulsion. Don't let this challenge you. Simply write down whatever you want to change today.

In fact, if you can, think of the top seven compulsions that you would change.

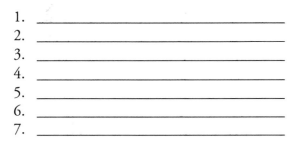

1. _____
2. _____
3. _____
4. _____
5. _____
6. _____
7. _____

Don't worry if you don't have seven. Write whatever comes to you. For you overachievers, you don't have to make up compulsions just to fill in every blank. In case you're having trouble, though, I'll give you some examples of typical compulsions.

**As an example, let's consider seven behaviors that many overweight people are compelled to do.**

1. They have to open the refrigerator whenever they walk into the kitchen.
2. If a co-worker has candy on the desk, they have to grab a piece every time they pass by.
3. They have to continue eating until their plate is clean.
4. When they see candy at the checkout, they have to buy

something.
5. When someone offers them food, they eat it, even if they're not hungry.
6. When they are stressed out they believe eating calms them down.
7. Even if good water is available they choose soft drinks or iced tea.

**For a second example, let's consider seven behaviors that people who smoke are compelled to do.**

1. They have to smoke a cigarette when they wake up.
2. If someone lights up around them, they have an urge for a smoke.
3. When they walk out of a smoke-free building, they have to light up.
4. When they are done eating, they have to have a cigarette or the meal isn't complete.
5. When someone says let's go have a smoke, they go even if they don't really want to.
6. When they are stressed, the only thing that calms them down is a cigarette.
7. Even after exercise, they need a smoke.

Even if you don't have a weight problem or have never smoked, these fourteen examples can give you a starting point in discovering your specific compulsions. We'll use these compulsions in the thought experiment at the end of this chapter.

**What is Selective Memory and the Reticular Activating System?**

Your other-than-conscious mind picks and chooses what you focus on. This is called *selective memory*. Habits, like those I mentioned above, have to do with a trigger in our brain called the reticular activating system. The reticular activating system is an organic part of the brain that works outside of our awareness and is the mechanism behind selective memory. Imagine this reticular activating system like a super-efficient librarian who instantly brings you all the information you need on a specific topic, sometimes even before you know you need it.

**Why is it Essential that You Learn to Forgive, Forget, and Move On?**

If you don't train your brain, the automatic functions take over. There are three outside influences for which the reticular activating system is always scanning the environment. These are called *reticular activators*. They are:

1. That which is *congruent*
2. That which is *dangerous* or *threatening*
3. That which is *familiar*

I'll explain each of these one at a time.

**1. That which is congruent.** Your reticular activating system is always checking the past records stored in your mind against what is presently happening in the world around you. In other words, it is seeking congruency with past behaviors and beliefs.

For instance, a person might find this system is triggered when he or she passes by a certain doughnut shop when the light is on. The doughnut shop and light are reticular activators. If stopping for a doughnut when the light is on was a behavior this individual displayed in the past, he or she may feel compelled to stop.

Should this person attempt to drive by the doughnut shop without stopping, the reticular activating system will likely trigger an uncomfortable feeling, or perhaps even a craving for a doughnut, without the person knowing why. Some people may even feel nervous or get agitated.

This all happens because the reticular activating system is designed to keep everything status quo and is designed to signal the conscious mind when something is out of order.

**2. That which is dangerous or threatening.** The second important function of the reticular activating system is to tell your conscious mind if you are being threatened or are in danger.

Let's use a primitive man as an example. When this particular man was a boy, he had witnessed a saber-tooth tiger attacking and devouring his friend. The next time he saw a saber-tooth tiger, what do you think happened? Naturally, that past memory instantly triggered a fight-or-flight response. This is exactly how the mind associates experiences. The other-than-conscious mind doesn't discern between good or bad. Its only function is to store information for recall.

With this kind of trauma, our caveman would likely start anticipating where the tiger might attack. The primitive man might even develop a phobia of the dark or of loud noises for fear a tiger is lurking about.

Since you and I will rarely, if ever, have life threatening events such as encountering a saber-tooth tiger, this part of our mind is used in other areas. In adapting to our environment, our modern minds learned to use this danger trigger for emotional issues as well as physical threats. As an example, you might know someone who seems incapable of love. After getting to know this person, you may discover that as a child she was physically and mentally abused. Perhaps a parent abused the child while at the same time saying, "I love you."

This set up a trigger in her mind. The individual might now think that love means pain. Even though this may seem illogical at a conscious level, at the other-than-conscious level, it makes perfect sense. The primary job of the other-than-conscious mind is to protect and preserve the body. In the case of this abused person, therefore, the other-than-conscious will continually sabotage loving relationships so she doesn't get physically abused.

**3. That which is familiar.** The final responsibility of the reticular activating system is to let you know if something is familiar. In CVR, we call this function of the mind the critical factor. As mentioned earlier, the critical factor is the part of your mind that is highly skeptical and rules out information because it's foreign to what it knows.

In the underground blockbuster documentary, *What the Bleep Do We Know* they demonstrated how Native Americans probably could not even see the ships of the Colonial Fleet in the harbor because they didn't have the consciousness to conceptualize ships of that enormity. For those Native Americans the ships simply weren't there. There is additional research that shows there are certain colors that are common today, but were not seen by man during the time of Christ. If this is true, what could be out there on the horizon of your life that your limited beliefs are stopping you from seeing?

The inclination of the reticular activating system to seek that which is familiar can play a role in the development of addictions such as alcohol or drugs. When people first start drinking, the self-medicating nature of alcohol usually works quite well for a while. Unfortunately for the unsuspecting alcoholic, the reticular activating system starts writing a program that this intoxicated state is "normal." The sensation of intoxication becomes familiar, and so the reticular activator causes the desire or craving for alcohol. It can even go so far as to condition your conscious mind to believe that you can't function without alcohol.

Please keep in mind this is all happens at a *meta-level*, which is a level of mind far beyond the conscious level. The other-than-conscious mind only knows what it has been told and responds accordingly—something like a computer. This part of the mind can be likened to a well-trained government employee who is conditioned to believe, *"This is the way we have always done it, so this is the way we will continue doing it."*

While the three qualities of the reticular activating system are beneficial when your survival depends on them, they can be a problem when you have programmed this part of your brain with habits that are counter-productive to your goals—such as reaching for the refrigerator door even when you're not hungry, or smoking a cigarette just because someone else lights up. Worse yet, you may have conditioned your mind to be so negative because of past experiences that you can't imagine yourself with a winner's attitude.

**Can You Improve Your Memory at Any Age?**

Yes! It is possible to improve your memory at any age. It's been proven that the physical brain is far more capable of healing than once thought and evidence now shows it can even repair itself. The concept is called *plasticity*, which is the brain's innate capacity to reshape itself and even increase its complexity throughout a lifetime.

In a recent issue of *Discover Magazine* [11], neuroscientist Michael Merzenich, PhD says that you can tone the mind and stave off memory loss. He says all it takes is time in his mental gym—Dr. Merzenich's computer program that helps stimulate and keep the brain active. This means that, unlike old dogs, we can teach our brains new tricks. Since I'm a gadget/technology lover, I would sure like to try out Dr. Merzenich's software. At the time of this writing, however, it is still in its research phase. In the meantime, I believe you can build your own mental fitness the same way Albert Einstein and other great inventors did in the past—through CVR. This is what the thought experiments in this book are all about.

I believe we can also train our brains to enhance not only cognitive abilities, but also improve our emotional states by working with our memories and how our brains store information. The key lies in knowing how to store good times, and how to store bad times. In this next thought experiment, we will explore how to conquer negative experiences and think like a winner.

**Thought Experiment: Compulsion Blowout**

**Step 1: Choose one of the compulsions from your list.** Consider how useful it would be if you could reprogram your mind like reprogramming a computer. This means stepping out of your comfort zone. Keep in mind that if your current best thinking could help you, this problem or negative experience would not be a problem. You would have easily solved the situation. So we are going to work with the reticular activating system to help you create new thinking and become comfortable with change.

**Step 2: Acquire Definiteness of Purpose.** I think Napoleon Hill, author of *Think and Grow Rich* and the grandfather of the positive thinking movement, best explains this step. He is quoted as saying "There is one quality that one must possess to win, and that is definiteness of purpose, the knowledge of what one wants, and a burning desire to possess it."

With this thought, ask yourself the following: What, specifically, do you want out of the change you're making? In other words, what is the specific benefit you'll get by ridding yourself of the compulsion? Now, how can you translate that into a burning desire to possess it?

**Step 3: Think of your negative trigger.** What is the negative thought, attitude, or experience that is causing your compulsion or stopping you from achieving your goal? This exercise works best if you think specifically of the negative experience as a trigger that stops you from thinking like a winner.

**Step 4: Place the image in a picture frame.** I'm going to ask you to join me in drama class. Role play reaching out with your hands as if you are grabbing an imaginary picture frame. Push it straight out and away from you. Inside the frame could be the cigarette you want to smoke, or the cookies you want to eat, the strong desire to finish all the food on your plate, or whatever typically triggers you.

Imagine an invisible force behind you that is drawing that image out of your range. Use your imagination to really feel the pull, as if your arms are tied to powerful rubber bands that are pulling this image behind you. Continue holding on, but know that this force is fueled by your burning desire to put the image behind you.

**Step 5: Feel this desire burning inside.** Feel the tension building. Imagine that you really want it behind you. Continue to build the tension.

**Step 6: Feel the tension building even more.** Imagine an invisible force that is 200-300 feet behind you. As the tension builds, your desire builds. Once the pressure builds to a point you can't hold it back, let your hands go and move them quickly past the side of your head. Some people find it helpful to make the sound "whoosh" at the same time they move their hands behind their head.

**Step 7: Let the image go.** Pretend that the image is moving so quickly and easily past you that the pictures, images, sounds, and feelings about the event are all so far behind you that they are gone from your mind, gone from your thoughts, and gone from your awareness. Become aware of the quiet calm as the past negative trigger is eliminated from your awareness. Soak up this calm, peaceful feeling and dwell on the result.

Now let's future pace what you want. For example, if your goal is to be naturally thin, imagine yourself in front of a mirror one year from today and you have done it. Your shoulders are rolled back, your chin is rolled upward, and you are smiling. You are at your natural and ideal weight—healthy, whole and complete.

If your goal is to organize your life so you are debt free, imagine you are there with your financial advisor and you're smiling. You're smiling because you have the money to do the things that you need and want to do. You've paid off your bills and are free to accomplish your next financial goal. Whatever your goal, simply imagine what it will be like when you've made it, and then live it fully with the power of your imagination.

As I mentioned at the beginning of the chapter, this technique is called a compulsion blowout because it works best with things that you feel a compulsion to do—those things that you really don't want to do, or know you shouldn't do, but you find yourself doing anyway.

Like all thought experiments, you will need to reinforce this with practice. The compulsion blowout works best if you practice this visualization exercise at least three times a day until the old negative trigger creates little or no response in your life.

**Can you answer either of these two questions?**

**1. What if you forget to remember any negative triggers and just start thinking like a winner?**

Or...

**2. What if you remember to forget any negative triggers and just start thinking like a winner?**

You see, it really doesn't matter as long as you get the result you want. The reticular activating system can work equally well to give you either *selective memory* or *selective amnesia*. Selective amnesia simply means that we can choose what we forget. If my wife could do it with the negative memories of her sister's illness, is there any reason you can't do it with unwanted habits or behaviors? Imagine how useful it would be if you simply forgot your negative habits? Well, that is exactly what I will be reinforcing with this next thought experiment "Thinking Like a Winner."

Imagine using your powerful reticular activating system as a peaceful weapon against negative thoughts, attitudes, and beliefs. Then imagine how all kinds of wonderful positive thoughts will fill up those places in your mind that used to hold the negative. Let your mind dream of the result—how your life changes . . . and how reaching your goal is suddenly so much easier. Notice how happy you feel . . . and how well you treat others . . . and how you're getting better and better each day . . .

And now, get ready to live this life of your dreams!

## Thought Experiment: Thinking Like A Winner

For best results, record the following in your own voice. Speak slowly and allow yourself time to follow each instruction.

*Go ahead and close your eyes. Take in a deep breath and let your mind settle on how you remember the room looking just before you closed your eyes. Remember the colors of the room, the furniture, and let your body go loose and limp...totally relaxed.*

*Now, take a moment to hear any sounds in the room. Let the sounds guide you deeper and deeper inside your mind where you can move to the photo center in your mind. In this space, this place, between the tick and tock of the clock you can learn new ways to store information— information about your past, present or future.*

*In your space, your inner place, imagine right there in front of you is a picture frame. Go ahead and place your hands straight out in front of you as if you are holding that frame back. Imagine the tension building by imagining a strong rubber band stretching from the picture frame to a point 200-300 feet behind you. Feel the tension building. Imagine the pressure.*

*Now, place into that picture frame something you feel compelled to do. Something that, even when you don't want to do it, you do it anyway.*

*With this picture in mind, let your desire for putting it behind you build. Really imagine the tension from the giant rubber band pulling the image, trying to snap it behind you. Once you feel the tension and you can't hold it back at all, let go of the picture frame. Feel it move quickly behind you—gone from your mind... gone from your thoughts... gone from your awareness. Let it go.*

*Notice how your body feels. Then take a deep breath, let it out with a sigh, and let yourself go deeper into relaxation.*

*Now, imagine three places where you might encounter that old behavior. Notice how just as you thought of it, the picture frame and the tension pull the image and place it far behind you.*

*From here, imagine going on a mental vacation. Take a few minutes to enjoy the journey and when you are ready, return fully from the photo center in your mind.*

*"Any idea, plan, or purpose may be placed in the mind through repetition of thought."*

## - Napoleon Hill

The Rolaids Effect

## The Rolaids Effect

I have a friend who once told me about a childhood spelling bee in which he was an unwilling participant. Given that spelling was probably the least of his talents, he was gratefully disqualified early in the competition. However, the entire student body was required to sit still and watch the remaining contenders. My friend said he was bored silly until one boy was asked to spell relief. Without missing a beat the kid answered, "R-O-L-A-I-D-S." The adults in the room and few of the kids started laughing. My friend was confused. He didn't get the joke. Wasn't that right? Then he heard the jingle in his head and realized the boy had repeated the spelling from the Rolaids commercial and had not spelled relief at all.

Those of us who grew up in the 60s and 70s were the first to learn reading through advertising. Our introduction to spelling was through the brand advertising we saw on television. As toddlers we couldn't yet put two sentences together, but we could sure spell J-E-L-L-O, and we knew that our *boloney had a first name*, and that was O-S-C-A-R. These jingles would roll off our tongues well before we were able to recognize or grasp the alphabet. Today these early spelling lessons are as engrained in our consciousness as the ABC song.

Why is this important to you and what is the Rolaids Effect? The effect is a process in our minds that links information. Your mind is always searching your environment consciously and unconsciously to find the best, fastest, and most efficient way to bring you information from the world around you. The marketers of the Rolaids brand simply linked their product with *relief.* Jello and Oscar Meyer linked their foods with *fun.*

Here's another example. On one of our family vacations my son, Alex, begged us to take him to a go-cart track. He had talked his sister, Cheree, into the idea as well. Cynthia and I finally agreed that the two of them were old enough to drive go-carts. However, that's where our agreement on the story ends. Here is how each of us vividly remembers the event:

Patrick: *After paying five dollars each for the kid's tickets, Cynthia and I stood at the sideline to watch. We were in Arizona and there was a crystal blue sky. Alex took off first and made the initial round with no problem. Cheree had a little more trouble. For some unknown reason, she floored it right out of the gate and crashed into the wall on the first turn. The front tire popped off her go-cart and rolled across the track. Cheree got out of the cart, tears streaming down her cheeks, and walked over to us. The attendant handed her a five-dollar bill and told her to try again when she got a little older.*

Cynthia: *We were on a Canadian cross-country trip when the go-cart incident took place. Before we started the trip, Patrick had committed to doing a training session with a group of therapists in British Columbia. While Patrick did the training, I took the kids to the go-cart track to keep them entertained. I paid the five-dollar fee for each of us to ride the carts. Alex got in the first cart, Cheree was behind him, and I was in the cart behind her. Alex took off and rounded the corner with ease. I remember sitting in my little cart, knees in the air, thinking that Alex would make a good driver someday. Cheree took off next. She floored the gas pedal right out of the gate and crashed into the retaining wall. The front tire flew off and rolled across the track. She turned around and looked at me, big tears welling in her eyes. I hopped out of my cart and ran over to her. As I walked her to the sideline the attendant approached us. "Here," he said, handing Cheree a five-dollar bill. "You might want to wait 'til you get a little older." That evening, when we met up with Patrick, we told him the story. Cheree was the only one who didn't think it was funny.*

How is it that Cynthia and I have such completely different memories of the same event? I remember being in Arizona, she recalls Canada. I remember her standing next to me and she recalls being in a cart behind Cheree. And, what's really strange, is she insists that I wasn't even there! This is where the disagreement always ensues.

"How is it that I remember standing on the sidelines watching the whole event if I wasn't even there?" I ask her.

"I think you've just told the story so many times, you've created your own version in your head," she responds.

"No way," I say, "I *remember* being there and you were standing next to me!"

"And I remember that you *weren't* there and I was in the cart behind Cheree!"

And the argument goes on.

Most long-term couples have at least one story similar to ours. A family reunion is also a great place where disagreements abound as childhood stories are told from each person's perspective. I believe this happens because we each store our memories based on links to our past experiences, beliefs, and values. Therefore, no two people will store a memory in the same way. The key, as advertisers well know, is *repetition*. They know that the more often you hear a message the more likely you'll be to remember and believe it. The good news is, the adage, "The more you hear it, the more you believe it," is effective not only for advertising, but for positive affirmations as well. In other words, if memories are malleable anyway, why not change them so they benefit us?

In this chapter we're going to explore how, through the Rolaids Effect, you have linked behaviors and experiences so well that they've turned into the tough-to-break habits you may be struggling to kick today. I will then teach you how to reconnect to *resource states* that will help you to visualize and accomplish your loftiest goals.

**Are You an Emotional Hostage?**

German language's greatest 20th century poet, Rainer Maria Rilke, once said, "All emotions are pure which gather you and lift you up; that emotion is unpure which seizes only one side of your being and so distorts you."

In this section, you are going to learn how to reconcile feuding parts of your mind that may be sabotaging your personal success. In other words, you'll be coming to terms with the *unpure emotions* that may be hindering you. I'll explain this in more detail in a moment, but first I would like to discuss the power of intention. Over the years I've helped thousands of people improve their lives by learning to use their own minds. In that time, I came to realize that all behaviors have an underlying *positive intention*.

For many, this can be a difficult concept to grasp. How can smoking have a positive side when it's so harmful? How can overeating be positive when it causes weight gain and health problems? How can procrastination be positive when it keeps you from living life to the fullest? I'm not saying that the behaviors are necessarily positive. I'm saying that underlying the behavior is a true and positive intent for the person demonstrating it.

For example, a person who gets angry at another driver when he gets cut off isn't getting angry so he can release a cascade of harmful neurochemicals and hormones into his body. He is probably channeling the emotion of fear out of his body, but is doing so by expressing his wrath. Getting angry isn't a positive behavior, but it may be the only behavior he knows in that instant. With creative visualization, a person can learn to interact with a situation instead of *reacting* to it.

With the road rage example, there is a part of the person that fears he will be injured by another driver and responds with a flare of temper. However, there is another part of that person that knows a better way to handle the situation. This is where the concept of *bridging the gap* comes in. The key with this technique is to learn a new behavior that is equally as immediate and appropriate without the negative impact.

**What is the Gap and How Do You Bridge It?**

With weight loss clients, I often hear people say that even though they're committed to losing weight there's still a part of them that craves certain foods. There's a part that still wants chocolate, ice cream, or cola, or that still wants to snack on a bag of chips at ten o'clock at night—and then there's another part that knows better.

This constant battle can be like having an angel on one shoulder and a devil on the other. I'm going to show you how both these parts truly have a *positive intention*. The part of you that enjoys chocolate isn't trying to make you fat. It's simply seeking gratification. And the part of you that wants to be naturally thin doesn't want to deprive you of the pleasure you get from eating chocolate. It just doesn't know another way to get that kind of pleasure. Therefore the purpose behind bridging the gap is to help you build choices.

The following is a sample exercise used by a client to discover the positive intention behind a negative behavior. At the end of the chapter you'll have the opportunity to complete this thought experiment for yourself.

## Sample Thought Experiment: Finding Your Positive Intention Pattern

**Step One:** Uncovering the problem.

- What is your negative behavior
  *Answer) Eating snacks*
- Where are you having the problem?
  *Answer) Between meals*
- What challenge has the unproductive behavior created?
  *Answer) Being overweight and uncomfortable.*
- What evidence in the world proves to you that it is <u>not</u> useful for you to behave that way?
  *Answer) Gained 50 pounds over the past 10 years*

**Step Two:** What Part's Responsible?
  *Answer) The part of me that feels like it needs energy.*

**Step Three:** Finding another way to meet the secondary gain with new behaviors.

- What if your positive intention or secondary gain could be met in another way?
  *Answer) I would lose weight and have more energy.*
- What would that other way be?
  *Answer) Eat healthier, more high-energy foods at mealtimes, exercise, and use my creative visualization processes.*
- When would it be most useful?
  *Answer) Every day*
- How would you know it was a positive habit?
  *Answer) I would have more energy and lose weight.*
- When would you start using it?
  *Answer) Today*
- Is there any downside to the new behavior?
  *Answer) Only that I would lose the immediate gratification of snacking.*

## With This New Information Let's Explore the Underlying Positive Intention

As I mentioned earlier, it's important to acknowledge that both parts of your mind have a positive intention. Even though the concept can be difficult to grasp, all negative behaviors are motivated by some *positive intention*. For example, a dieter may make an unwise food choice because he or she fears not being able to eat that food *ever again*. This is a fear of loss. This person might say, "I'm going to eat this piece of cake now because I'm going on a diet on Monday and won't be able to have cake again." The problem is, when Monday arrives, he or she never starts the diet.

My goal is to get you to adjust your mindset, to empower the part of you that wants you to be naturally thin and to be more in control; but also to honor the part of you that has these other needs. This is done by going to a *higher level*.

Einstein said that you can't solve a problem on the level it was created; you must go to a *higher level* where the solution exists. Then, with the solution in mind, you can return to the problem state with the answers you need. That's how CVR is going to help you bridge the gap.

Let's continue using the example of the woman who snacks. This individual said that her *positive intention* was to have more energy. She also acknowledged that eating healthier, more high-energy foods at mealtimes and exercising would give her more energy. In the past, she's taken the path of least resistance; she knows that the easiest way to spark energy is to eat between meals. Even though the latter has a negative outcome, it's the snacker's choice. Why? Because the other-than-conscious mind doesn't care about anything but the underlying *positive intention*. Therefore, it will take the path of least resistance and generate the behavior of eating between meals because it's a well-rehearsed habit.

The other-than-conscious mind will continue to create the desire for snacking until a new behavior that is equally as immediate and appropriate is used for a specific amount of time to replace the old behavior. This is where CVR comes in. When in a state of relaxation and using creative visualization to create a new pattern we are not subject to time—only sequence and experience. If the sequence and experience are convincing, the other-than-conscious mind will consider this new behavior the path of least resistance and will generate it effortlessly.

During the thought experiment, I will ask you to open your

hands in your lap. In one hand you will put the unwanted behavior. In the other hand you will put the new, more appropriate behavior. I will then ask you to recognize that at a deeper, more meaningful level the two different parts are really trying to accomplish the same thing.

Some of you will actually feel your hands being drawn together physically and others will do this mentally. Either way, it will condition your other-than-conscious mind to create a strategy of bringing these two together. In this way, just like the "Rolaids Effect," you will not be able to think or do the negative behavior without also knowing there is a more powerful, positive way to accomplish your goal or meet the positive intention.

## So How Do We Build the Bridge?

When our example client undergoes the CVR process, she will put her hands in her lap. She will be told to think of the one hand as representing "the you of the past"—or the part that enjoyed eating inappropriate foods and snacking. The other hand represents "the you of the future." This is the positive new behavior (the part that knows how to be naturally thin and agrees it would give her more energy). Then she will be guided through a relaxation process where these two parts are taught to communicate.

We are going to use a principal of physics that says *no two energies can occupy the same space in time.* The same principal is true of thoughts because thoughts are mental energy. When I say that thoughts are more than things because they create things, there is a scientific basis to this concept. Thoughts take up mental space and are composed of energy. They influence the firing of neurons in the brain and the release of neuro-peptides and other brain chemicals. Thoughts cause things to happen.

We're going to have these two different parts of you come together in a way that will bridge the gap between the sabotage thinking that says, "I can't believe I did that again!" and the part that says, "Hey, I have a new way over here!"

I believe that we all know what to do, we just don't always know how to make it fit into our lives. Because of stress, people don't always make the positive choice.

When we are in a mental state of stress, we usually don't have full access to all our skills. We tend to react instead of taking action. If, on the other hand, we are trained to bring a relaxed mind into stressful situations, we have access to all of our resources and can handle any situation appropriately. A relaxed mind can easily come up with creative positive solutions.

Your best thinking brought you to this moment, so it's obvious your best thinking in its current form can't help you. This is why the key to success is to get you thinking in a new way. For instance, when you think of eating a snack, you won't simply think of the immediate gratification. You'll think of the long-term effect of snacking and make a better choice.

Most people make immediately gratifying choices with no thought of the long-term results of those choices. For instance, they overeat (or eat the wrong types of food) and then they wonder why they're overweight. Through CVR, I'm going to introduce you to a new way of thinking that will allow you to be honest with yourself and think about the future repercussions of your actions. You're going to take the two feuding parts of your mind—with their *positive intentions*—and fuse them together. Then you're going to future-pace the result. That is to say, you'll take what you've learned about yourself and project it into the future. You're going to start thinking about future concepts, beliefs, and events as if they've already happened.

Once this has occurred, you'll be able to use this future as a memory. Don't worry, creating it as a memory happens naturally because your mind doesn't know the difference between real and imagined. You will recall this memory easily to make new eating decisions in the present.

**How to Get Comfortable Outside Your Comfort Zone**

You may have noticed that making any change, or even attempting to change, can make you uncomfortable. A perfect example of this is the person attempting to quit smoking cold turkey who gets so irritable that his family almost wishes he'd just smoke. This uneasiness all starts with the thought of change. Yes, a simple thought can make you feel increasingly uneasy. Studies of the brain have proven again and again that the subconscious can't tell the difference between real and imagined.

Whether you experience stress and tension in your mind or in physical reality, the internal effects are the same. If the change is too extreme, your physical and mental health can be affected. You can experience sleeplessness, indigestion, or fatigue. You may react with impatience, irritability, or anger. You will often feel as if you are on an emotional rollercoaster.

I know I've made this statement in an earlier chapter, but it bears repeating because it's so key to your success: *You Get What You Rehearse In Life; Not Necessarily What You Intend.*

If you want to achieve more and live the life of your dreams, you must increase your threshold for change—and you do this by rehearsing what you want. There is only one constant in the known universe and that is *change*. In order to succeed at any new endeavor, you must believe yourself capable of handling any situation. You do this by raising your aspirations, setting higher goals, and using CVR to make detailed plans to achieve them. CVR is where you rehearse what you intend for your life. You start by seeing yourself, and thinking of yourself, as a person who is highly flexible. You take charge of developing a new self-concept for change and look for ways to enjoy the journey.

## Risk Is The Key To Peak Performance In Life

Whenever you have a high self-concept, you perform well. If you enjoy your home life and it's working, don't make drastic changes. But if, for example, you're not enjoying your work life, step back and think about how you can improve it. Be willing to take the risk of helping on new projects or getting involved with your community. The secret is to start controlling your own change so you can meet life head on.

Whenever you feel tense or uneasy making a change, it means that you have a low self-concept in that area. If you don't feel comfortable when you are engaged in an activity, you probably avoid that activity as much as possible. This is a key factor in procrastination.

Use this chapter's thought experiment to practice this activity in your mind until you are comfortable with it. Imagine and visualize yourself as if you are already very good at what you wish to do. Create within yourself the feeling of success and accomplishment.

## Steve's Story

Steve Francisco is an entrepreneur at heart, but it wasn't always that way. He discovered the entrepreneurial spirit several years ago when he got involved with a start-up marketing and distribution company based in Dallas, Texas. During his involvement, the company opened 3,500 locations and earned $500 million in sales in its first four years. The company also opened up several countries and, according to Steve, "helped a lot of people around the world."

While Steve traveled for the company, however, he started to see a greater need. He regularly encountered business owners who didn't have the knowledge or financial resources to get involved with his business or to grow their own businesses, let alone make them thrive. These business owners needed help on an entrepreneurial level.

One night, while Steve was in Singapore, he woke up in the middle of the night with the urge to write down his dreams, goals, and objectives. A business idea started to gel in his mind, and he felt a surge in his heart.

Earlier that day, local business owners, who were intrigued by American business systems, had spent hours grilling him for information. They all had journals and were taking notes on everything he said. Steve was scheduled to fly out early the next day. He knew the group would keep him talking all night if they could, so at nine o'clock he finally told them he needed to go back to his room and get a good night's rest. Steve went to sleep that night thinking about these eager entrepreneurs and how he might help them. "I fell into a deep sleep and woke up about three o'clock in the morning with a vision for helping these entrepreneurs," Steve says. "I grabbed the pad of paper from my nightstand and, with total clarity, the ideas just rolling off the tip of the pen, I filled up eight or nine pages."

Steve's idea was to develop an integrated business platform for entrepreneurs to give them everything they need for success. He began to envision an entrepreneurial academy that included business education, coaching, visioning techniques, health and wellness, and financial wealth services. His goal was to set up a one-stop-shop for entrepreneurs where they could learn the skills necessary to realize their dreams.

From that night on, Steve put everything else on the back burner and started focusing on his dream. When Steve returned to the United States, he started to do some research into entrepreneurial success. He was shocked to discover that 90 percent of start-up businesses fail. Clearly, the existing model entrepreneurs were using was broken. New business owners didn't have the resources, knowledge, or money to see their dreams through to success.

Before Steve could succeed himself, though, he needed to use some of the skills for himself. In other words, it was Steve's turn to visualize his dream. He started to creatively visualize the kind of facility he would have, the type of people he wanted to bring together, and the kinds of programs he would offer. He envisioned people from all over the world joining his program and then going out and succeeding at business and in life.

When Steve started out, he had no idea how his dream would come to fruition; he just knew it would. In January of 2008, along with a small group of entrepreneurial experts, Steve launched Sognari International. "Sognari means 'to have a dream,'" Steve says. "I believe that people need to dream more today and stop lowering their goals to meet their circumstances."

In a few short months, hundreds of would-be entrepreneurs have joined the Sognari program—making it their entrepreneurial home; they are gaining knowledge, getting around the right experts, learning about state-of-the-art technology, learning how to dream, and how to creatively visualize what they want. Some are even going on to get their bachelors or masters degrees in business or entrepreneurship at an affiliated university.

Steve's dream was realized when he was able to recognize a dire need and then allow his creative mind to come up with a solution. "It all started that night in a Singapore hotel room with a pad of paper, a pen, and a dream," Steve says. "After that, I just kept visualizing my dream until it became reality."

**Thought Experiment: Finding Your Positive Intention Pattern**

Take your time in considering the following questions. Don't worry if you're not sure how to answer these questions at this point. The thought experiment will give you time to consider the answers. Take a few moments to relax, breathe deeply, and allow the information to come from that creative part within you. Imagine your mind has special internal messengers. When I use the term part, I am referring to the part of your personality that represents a tendency or habitual behavior. Your contemplation of these parts of you will help the thought experiment work as you bridge the gap from sabotage to empowerment.

**Step 1:**   What is your negative behavior or problem? _____

• When and where are you having the problem? _____

• What challenge has the unproductive behavior created?_____

• What evidence in the world proves to you that it is not useful for you to behave that way?_____

**Step 2:** What part is responsible? _____

Imagine the part that is responsible for generating the unproductive behavior. (Some people only need to think of times they displayed the unwanted behavior.) _____

_____

I am going to ask you to again pretend this is Drama 101 and you are playing a role. You are acting as the responsible part. Imagine it could tell you what it is trying to get for you.

What is the value or benefit from making you act and behave in this specific behavior? Ask the responsible part of you directly, "What did you wish to accomplish for me by displaying this behavior? In other words, what is the secondary gain you receive from this part creating that behavior within you?

_____

_____

Take as much time as you need to contemplate the part's responses.

**Step 3:** Is there any other way to meet the secondary gain with new behaviors?

• What if your positive intention or secondary gain could be met in another way? _____

• What would that be? _____

• When would it be most useful? _____

• How would you know it was a positive habit? _____

• When would you start using it? _____
• Is there any downside to the new behavior? _____

Keep asking the "what if" question until you get to the core belief or core value. When you get an answer, recycle it into another question, until you get to the core value. This core set of reasons drives the way you act in the first place. If your core values were being met they would not be problems. Behaviors only cycle into problems when they are out of alignment with your core values.

There are many examples of hidden *positive intentions*. The best examples are the ones you discover from your own inner investigation

## Thought Experiment: Bridging the Gap

For best results, record the following in your own voice. Speak slowly and allow yourself time to follow each instruction. Note that in today's creative visualization process, you're going to be asked to put your hands in your lap with the palms up.

*Go ahead and close your eyes… Take a few deep breaths, just letting go. Notice with each and every breath how easy it is for you to let go, and to go with the flow…*

(pause 10 seconds)

*Take a deep breath and as you exhale think about the part of you in the past that's been programmed to do things inappropriately… perhaps it's the part of you that enjoys snacking before bed… or can't resist the vending machine at the office … or the part that really needs to have dessert after you eat … or the part that procrastinates.*

*Take a moment and imagine energy filling one of your hands. Imagine this energy as a color. Allow the color to represent those past behaviors. Feel the energy flow from the core of your brain, unlocking these old behaviors, so a positive change can be made. Once you have a ball of mental energy take another deep breath in and then let it go.*

(pause 10 seconds)

*Now, its time to take the other hand. This hand is going to represent the part of you that has the answers, the part that knows how to solve your problems. The part that knows how to drink sufficient water ... how to eat sparingly ... how to avoid snacking ... how to exercise ... how to take action instead of procrastinating.*

*Take a moment and imagine energy filling the other hand. Imagine this energy as a color. Allow the color to represent the new positive behaviors. Feel the energy flow from the core of your brain, unlocking these resources so a dynamic change can be made. Once you have built that ball of mental energy take another deep breath and then let it go.*

(pause 10 seconds)

*Go ahead and scan your body. Let yourself go. Feel the power of your mind unlocking your creativity. Imagine as you focus on your hands, that the feeling, the color, and the sounds of these two very different parts of you are going to come together. Visualize the process of these parts communicating and allowing your hands to come together. You might do this mentally, In your mind's eye imagine these two different forces coming together.*

*This might start immediately and it might start some time in the future. Just know that no matter what happens, you're doing perfectly. Simply allow yourself to be guided through the process. The key is to believe that these two different parts of you have come together to bridge the gap between the saboteur and the successful person within you.*

*Take all the time you need to bring them together, working out a plan at the other-than-conscious level that will help you to succeed with resources you didn't know you had, triggered by experiences that you will have today and in the future.*

*Whether this happens physically... The hands come together. Or it happens mentally... the two colors mixing together in this visualization make a new powerful anchor. An anchor that will trigger this mental agreement to work together, solving the problems of the past with solutions found in the present and future.*

*Take all the time you need to imagine this powerful relationship getting better each and everyday... Better, bette, and better everyday in everyway.*

*When you are ready, imagine how they will work together in the next twenty-four hours... during the next week. When you have put this all together to the best of your ability, take a moment to visit your personal place of relaxation and then allow yourself to slowly return back into the room.*

*"Some say knowledge is valuable, but character is more valuable than knowledge. One may be a learned scholar, one may hold high positions of authority, one may be very wealthy or be an eminent scientist but if one has no character, all the other acquisitions are of no use at all. Sacrifice, love, compassion and forbearance are the sterling human qualities that should be fostered, shedding jealousy, hatred, ego and anger which are animal qualities."*

**- Sai Baba**

# CHAPTER
# ELEVEN

**Your Life – A Drama Worth Living**

## Your Life - A Drama Worth Living

Motivating you to take an active roll in the creation of success in your life is the primary goal of this book. Success is not a passive activity. You must plan and prepare for it; you must expect it. My friend and mentor, Jerry DeShazo, often starts his coaching sessions with the question, "If you could write the script for your life, what would be happening right now?"

With this question in mind, let's get down to the business of figuring out what your life would be like if you not only could write your own script but also have control over what gets cut and what is stored in your memory. Then we'll talk about how to make it happen.

The first step, as the beginning of this message states, is to plan. Dennis Waitley, motivational speaker and psychologist, says this about planning: "Expect the best, plan for the worst, and prepare to be surprised." What Dr. Waitley describes is the nature of the universe. We have very little control over what we see, hear, or experience in the outside world. This is why he admonishes us to prepare to be surprised.

Whether we like it or not, forces outside of our control always affect even the best-laid plans. How you deal with these challenges has a direct influence on your success or failure. You have an advantage, though, because you're reading this book. You're learning that, through CVR, you have limitless control over the three-pound universe that exists between your ears. In this inner space you are the king or queen of your domain—you even can be the court jester if you so choose. My job is to help you use the playground of your mind to plan success in the physical world.

Everything you see that was created by man was first a thought in the resourceful mind of an inventor. After the inventor had a vision, thought, or intuitive breakthrough, he or she had to devise a plan to bring it from the inner space of the mind to the physical space of our world. Success or failure for any inventor rests with the ability to translate thoughts into things. For the successful inventor, success is mandatory; frustration is optional.

Winning inventors, such as Edison and Einstein, used a subconscious trigger to help conquer the frustrations inherent in bringing an idea to fruition. Your plan might not be to explain the nature of physical space and time like Einstein did, or to invent the light bulb as Edison did, but your plan, whatever it is, follows the same invisible path from thought to thing. In order to succeed you, too, will need the assistance of your other-than-conscious mind to allay frustrations and maintain focus.

## The Cutting Room Floor

The true test of a movie is the final result. A film can have the best director, A-list actors, and a top-notch cinematographer, but what ends up on the cutting room floor and what ends up on the big screen is the difference between a Hollywood blockbuster and a filmmaker's nightmare. My hope is to train you in making the best decisions about which experiences or scenes to keep and which ones to leave on the cutting room floor. You will be the lead actor in the breakthroughs in your life as well as the editor of the final result.

## Creating Your Personal Promo Video

I recently had the honor of interviewing Bill Bartmann, who claims to be an expert in both success and failure. Bartmann went from living on the streets to being the twenty-fifth richest man in America. He says his mission is to share with the world how to overcome adversity—how to pick yourself up, dust yourself off, and move on.

One of the key methods he teaches involves putting together what he calls a success reel. He says that when you maintain an up-to-date success reel, focusing on the positive becomes easy. His message is a simple yet powerful one: Dwell on success and learn from your mistakes.

What Bill calls a success reel, I call your personal promo video. Your personal promo video is like a movie trailer in which all the best scenes are packed into one short clip, and it's what you use to sell yourself and others on the new behaviors you will display and the brand new life you will live. Using the thought experiments in this text will help you know what to keep in your promo video and what to cut. The truth is, you needed every experience you've had in your life to get to this moment, which means every life experience is valuable. But to get more out of your life, you must focus on what you want and let go of what you don't want. So now that you've decided on the story of your life, how do you tell it?

Even though movie trailers are only two or three minutes long, they always have a central theme. Start from the top and think of a single galvanizing idea that defines the life you've chosen to live. Think of this theme as the North Star that will help you navigate life's stressors so nothing can stop you from achieving your personal goal.

Next you will want to find the common thoughts, feelings, and actions that helped you succeed in the past. Armed with this information, you can move with a sense of purpose toward your future success. Every moment you live affords you the opportunity for adding to your promo video. Keep in mind that what you think about, you bring about.

Updating your promo video on a regular basis will lead you to live in a state of *positive expectancy*. In the same way a stressed out person anticipates stressful events, you will anticipate positive, life-enriching events. Moreover, with your other-than-conscious mind properly motivated, your dreams soon will turn into your reality.

## Nine Simple Steps for Programming Your Mind for Success

**Step 1:** Create an overall goal for creative-visualization. Be specific. Your mind loves attainable, measurable results. Your job is to picture the end result, step into it, and truly live the outcome.

Avoid being vague and saying I want to lose weight or I would like to stop smoking. Rather, your mind works best with an ultra-specific, tangible goal. Replace vague statements with specific ones such as: *I will return to my ideal weight of one-hundred-twenty-five pounds, or I will be tobacco-free by the first of January.*

**Step 2:** Make up your mind that achieving the goal is for *you*, and *you alone.* If this is something you're doing for a spouse, child, or boss, your old self-sabotage patterns could kick in. Once you determine that your goal is for you, unseen forces go to work to figure out how to get you that result.

**Step 3:** Make sure your plan works within the structure of *scenario planning*. In scenario planning, think of these five questions:

1. What will the accomplishment of this goal do for me?
2. Where will this success take me in the future?
3. When will I start developing this plan as action?
4. With whom will I share my success?
5. How often will I need to confirm my results to stay on track?

**Step 4:** Set realistic expectations. If your plan calls for you to win the lottery or borrow a large sum of money from a friend, it likely will never happen. Your goal is to bring your dreams into reality, not to live in a dream world.

**Step 5:** Know how accomplishing this goal will take effect in the world around you. We live in a world of mutual respect, which is linked to the Law of Cause and Effect. What you do or don't do has an effect on others. Humans have a strong need to be of service to others. If your plan meets this criteria, your other-than-conscious mind will support you.

**Step 6:** Be brutally honest about the upsides and downsides of this accomplishment. By stepping back to take a disassociated look at your plan, you will see flaws that you never knew existed. And you might find solutions to problems you never considered.

**Step 7:** If you took my earlier advice and found a mentor, ask him or her to review your plan. This adds another level of disassociation and puts the goal a step away from your emotions.

Your mentor, through the eyes of experience, can steer you clear of trouble spots. He or she can listen for limited beliefs in your conversation and add a comfort level that comes from bouncing an idea off an expert.

**Step 8:** Be willing to step outside your comfort zone. Leigh Curl, former two-time first-team academic all-American, 1984-85 Big East Scholar-Athlete of the Year, and team physician for the Baltimore Ravens had this to say: "The best mentors are the people in your life who push you just a little bit outside your 'comfort zone.'"

**Step 9:** Use the Law of Non-Attachment. Your job is to take the action steps that allow the unseen forces of the mind to figure out the best way to get you there.

**How Do You Program Success?**

What could you accomplish if you had a computer capable of taking in data and then, with uncanny accuracy, programming the most probable outcome for every decision you make? What if you could use these results to navigate through life? What if I told you that you have just such a computer and it is called the human brain? The human brain is a one hundred billion neuro-bit processor that either works for or against you at any given moment.

Wouldn't it be nice if we could just hire a software engineer, tell him the outcomes we want and then sit back and let it happen? A software engineer is someone with the knowledge and expertise to create a step-by-step list of instructions written for a particular computer architecture in a particular computer programming language. A layman's equivalent example might involve writing a specific, step-by-step list of instructions to teach humans who have never cooked before how to make a bacon, lettuce and tomato sandwich.

For example, the code needed for creating the software for building a BLT would be as follows:

**Bacon**
**Lettuce**
**Tomato**
**Bread (and of what type—white, wheat, rye?)**
**Access to a Toaster**
**Mayonnaise**
**A knife**

You also need to know the number of people who want a sandwich. Then your mind would require the step-by-step instructions on how to cook the bacon, cut the lettuce, slice the tomato, and toast the bread.

The software engineer would also need to know what type of knife, and the amount of pressure to apply to cut the lettuce and how to spread the mayonnaise, and so forth. And even taking all this into consideration some small detail might get left out. What about the plate? Or the temperature of the stove? What type of pan does one use?

At this point, I'm sure our food-preparing-challenged human would rather go down to the corner deli
and order a BLT on rye with a side of fries. After all, it's on the menu!

## Gail's Story

Gail Larson had a dream. She wanted to move to Los Angeles and build a career in television. She didn't believe it could happen, though, until a friend taught her to visualize her goals. "If you see it, and if you hold onto the vision, it will happen for you," the friend said.

Gail decided it couldn't hurt to give it a try. "Just a few minutes each day," her friend said, "and be sure to be specific."

The first time Gail tried it, she laughed. It felt silly.

"Don't laugh," her friend told her. "Your mind will take you seriously only if you behave as if your dream has already happened."

Every day Gail took a few minutes to visualize herself working at Paramount, appearing on Channel Four, and making $100,000 within the first year. And every time she visualized it, it became more real, more possible.

In June of 1986, she made the move to Los Angeles. The first two weeks were the most frightening of her life. "I'm going home," she said. "Nothing is happening for me."

Now it was her friend's turn to laugh. 'Two weeks, Gail?'" she asked. "You'd better get back to visualizing."

For the next two weeks Gail visualized the fulfillment of her dream several times each day. Then the phone call came and chills ran down her spine. She had a callback for an audition—and it is was at Paramount. Gail was twenty-six years old at the time, but she would be auditioning for the part of a sixteen-year-old on a show called the "Bronx Zoo." Every other part had been filled except that of an eccentric high school girl. Gail had never played a role like it, and she felt too old. She also had never performed in front of a camera. As she stood in the studio bathroom, she looked in the mirror and reminded herself that this was her dream. Even though she had never done film before, she knew she could do this; she had seen it in her mind's eye hundreds of times.

Gail turned out to be everything the director wanted for the role. He hired her on the spot. "There I was, in Paramount Studios, standing across from Ed Asner . . . Lou Grant . . . it was so surreal," Gail said.

After filming wrapped, Gail flew home to see her parents. No sooner did she get off the plane, though, and she had to fly back to Los Angeles. Paramount wanted her as a series regular on a show that would appear on Channel Four—a part for which they offered her $100,000 for the first season. Everything she had visualized was realized.

After that, Gail continued to use visualization to achieve her goals. She often refers to her visualization process as "holding my knowing." According to Gail, when you know you can do something, you're already halfway there.

When Gail decided she was ready for a serious relationship, she started visualizing herself already in it. She visualized the kind of man she wanted to meet. Within two weeks she met her husband; they've been happily married for twenty-one years.

Gail taught her daughters to visualize their goals as well. Her oldest daughter used creative-visualization to achieve her goal of getting into USC's broadcast journalism program.

Her younger daughter, Mattie, a gymnast, visualizes the successful completion of each of her meets. "From the time she was seven or eight years old, Mattie has played out the story in her head, the one where she walks into the gym, does her warm up, and then completes a perfect performance," Gail says.

Mattie arrives at her meets now confident in what she's doing because she's already seen it in her mind. Today Mattie uses CVR, along with the light and sound technology. Her goal? Nothing less than a gold medal at the Olympics. I fully expect to see her there, a medal around her neck and a beaming smile on her face.

Think of CVR as the time you spend creating your internal menus so that you can order what you want whenever you want it. Life, after all, is far more complex than the process of making a sandwich. Many times it seems as if we come with a certain operating system when we're born. If you're like most people, however, you could use an upgrade.

What do you need to upgrade your mental programming? How can you become a software engineer for your own mind? You need to think outside the box like Albert Einstein who said, "Anyone who has never made a mistake has never tried anything new."

Programming success involves evaluating and changing the response you get. As a software engineer for the human mind, you need to know your limitations—then push the limits to a point where you can learn and grow from them.

People often mistakenly confuse past successes or failures for knowledge and wisdom. In reality, though, nothing in the mind is real until the other-than-conscious mind has built a program around it. Some very successful people have written mental programs that have them *failing fast*. It may surprise you to know that failure of any kind can be a resource, but failing fast is probably one of the best you can have. Failing fast means you are quick to learn what doesn't work so you can find what does work without wasting time. I have known clients who started a diet each week for thirty out of fifty-two weeks a year for ten years. These folks could benefit from failing fast so they get to what works for them and stick with it.

People who think of entertainment as enlightenment also are making a mistake. By this I mean that some people live by the motto, "If it feels good, do it!" This is rarely an effective policy. The path of least resistance isn't always the best path.

Procrastinators often erroneously believe that analysis is learning. We all have strategies for success and failure. However, when you create an appropriate mental program—one that weighs the pros and cons of your decisions—you no longer stop the process of learning and growing. Keep in mind, too much analysis leads to paralysis.

Many adults also mistakenly believe that education happens only in the classroom. Nothing could be further from the truth. The most successful people I know consider *life* one big classroom.

By using the thought experiment in this section, you will

learn to magnetize to you everything you'll need to achieve your goals. This starts with a simple question. What will you need to do *today* to accomplish your daily goal?

Then you will need to follow up with an assessment of the facts. Will accomplishing this goal take outside help? If so, what will you need to do to start moving toward that goal?

## Four Steps to Become a Producer and Put More Learning into Your Life

1. Write down the five most important things you've learned in your life. How did you learn them?
2. Start a success journal and once a week write down a key learning experience. What was the most important thing you learned?
3. Become a mentor to someone else or involve yourself in community service. This is how you enroll in the classroom of life.
4. For one minute stare at yourself in the mirror. Ask: "How do I feel about my productivity today?"

## How Do You Play the Role of Producer?

Let's imagine you are a top Hollywood producer. Your first task is to review the project to determine if it's worth producing. The script you're looking over is the story of your life.

So, Mr. (or Ms.) Producer, is it a story worth telling? Would you buy it? If not, you can choose to rewrite it or throw it in the trash and start over. If you like the story, of course, you have the freedom to enhance it, expand upon it, and develop it into a full-blown success story. After all, you're the producer; you're the one making the investment.

Your next task is to enroll the cast. You might never have thought of your personal friends and coworkers as cast players, but they are. If you could step back from your life, you would see the drama between the characters. You have enrolled these characters in a very meaningful way. Is your current cast helping or hindering your success? If your characters aren't helping you live the life you want, you can recast them or find new characters.

As the producer, you also work with the writer. In fact, the great producers like to work with multiple writers on a project so they have more than one viewpoint. As this relates to your life, I want you to imagine you are given a blank script. How would you write your success?

If you don't have the answer, it's time for a little soul searching. You must know where you're going before you start any journey.

The most exciting thing you get to do as the producer is recruit and hire the talent who will work on the project with you. This is the most interesting part of our personal lives and it is an exciting part of the journey. Your friends, family, co-workers, and the thousands of other people you encounter throughout your life are there as supporting players in your drama of success. These cast members may sometimes appear as teachers or coaches and at other times they may appear as bill collectors, IRS auditors, or the policeman standing beside your car handing you a ticket. These are the people who make your world go round. Without them you would have few learning experiences and no growth or development.

The producer has the ultimate authority and say on the project. That's why you must know what you want so well that you are excited about stepping into this leadership role. Then, just like a leading Hollywood producer, you don't take on projects unless you have the final say. You can use this book as your coach until you can coach yourself.

The Hollywood producer also has the important job of keeping the studio's meddlesome suits out of the director's hair. Like any good producer, you might have to keep the saboteurs at bay. In your life, these could be certain foods, drinks, people, or activities.

You also control the budgeting process. You approve major

expenses and answer to the studio heads when problems arise. This means the buck stops with you. You have to develop a no-excuse policy. You have no one to blame but yourself because you chose the project, the cast, and the production company. Of course, you also get the credit for your success!

**How do you make sure your life becomes a drama worth living?**

With your knowledge of creative visualization, your role as producer continues through postproduction, into editing, scoring, marketing, and distribution. This is where you master the reframes of your life.

Early in my professional career I was told that there are two rules to the known universe.

1) Everything in the universe happens at the right time and in the right sequence for everyone concerned. And, if your life doesn't seem to be working that way, refer to Rule #2, which is . . .

2) Pretend that everything in the universe happens at the right time and in the right sequence for everyone concerned.

Even if you don't buy into this, it's a much better attitude than thinking that the world is out to get you!

This is your opportunity to take control and become the planner, programmer, and executive producer of the positive changes in your life!

**Thought Experiment : Making Your Life a Drama Worth Living**

For best results, record the following in your own voice. Speak slowly and allow yourself time to follow each instruction.

*Go ahead and close your eyes. Take a deep breath in and let it go with a sigh. As your body relaxes, create an overall goal for your visualization. Be specific here. Your mind loves attainable, measurable results.*
*Picture the end result, step into it and mentally see through your eyes, hear through your ears, and let your consciousness be there now. Allow your mind to be specific.*

*Make a mental list of all the reasons achieving the goal is for you, and you alone. Let go of the notion that you are doing this for a spouse, child, or boss. Allow the unseen forces to go to work figuring out how to get you the result you want. Notice the sense of peace in letting go and allowing the future to unfold with your success in mind.*

*In your mind's eye, see what accomplishing this goal is going to do for you personally. Allow your imagination to journey into the future. Become aware of where this success will take you in the future.*

*With this mental timeline in mind, notice what your first step will be in developing this plan of action. Allow your thoughts to expand and include the other people this change will affect. How will you share your success with the world?*

*From here, you are building into a dream sequence the ability to confirm that you are staying on track with your results. Each night, as you drift off to sleep, your other-than-conscious mind will review your day. With this review, you will measure your results toward attaining your goal; if a challenge should appear, you will dream of solutions—solutions that will allow you to attain this and other goals as easily as breathing and as naturally as your heart beats.*

*Notice the changes that need to be made so that you are willing to step outside your comfort zone. Allow the unseen forces of your mind to create the best outcome possible for you.*

*With this thought experiment in mind, it's time to take all of this information with you to your personal place of relaxation. In this place you can walk on a pristine beach. Make this as real as possible using your incredible imagination. Imagine the wind blowing through your hair. Even imagine the smell of salt as the golden light of the sun warms your body. Take all the time you need in your mental place—be in that space between the tick and the tock of the clock. Then, when you are ready, take three deep breaths and say to your self wide awake - wide awake, feeling fine and in perfect health. Then and only then return fully back into the room.*

*"Human beings, by changing the inner attitudes of their minds, can change the outer aspects of their lives."*

**- William James (1842 - 1910)**

# CHAPTER
# TWELVE

## Some Final Thoughts on How CVR
## Can Change the World

## Final Thoughts on How CVR Can Change the World

Within these pages, you have learned how to use creative visualization and relaxation, why it works, and how others have used it to change their lives and the world. If they can do it, so can you. It's your turn to step up, transform your life, and make a difference in the world—a world that is desperate for your help.

By using the thought experiments I've outlined, you have taken charge of the unconscious programming that used to control your life. By using these step-by-step processes, you have armed yourself with techniques that promote healthy thinking, constructive action, and freedom from the negative thoughts that may have limited you. You are on the fast track to personal satisfaction. You no longer follow the crowd because you are empowered with everything you need to alleviate stress, upgrade your thinking, and step up to the next level of personal evolution.

You should be warned, however, that once you apply the knowledge in this book, many of your previous beliefs, attitudes, and behaviors will be void. Once you are armed with these revolutionary concepts, there is no turning back. You have stepped up and taken personal responsibility. You won't have the luxury of blaming family, friends, or coworkers for your situation. You will know that your best thinking is what takes you to each moment, one moment at a time. The good news is that you are armed with information that sets you free to rewrite your future and live each day to the fullest.

Moreover, when you set a goal and then accomplish it, you will achieve a feeling of power. This incredible power will fuel you to even greater goals and to the acceptance of your real self-image. The truth is, ever since you first spit food back at a parent, you have been in control; you just didn't know it. Now that you have harnessed the power of your mind, anything is possible. And you can enjoy this incredible feeling of being in control of your personal destiny each and every day.

A mentor of mine, Dr. Gil Gilly, told me that you should never believe anything that you read or hear until you have tried out the ideas in your own life. With this thought in mind, I recommend that you go back to the first thought experiment in Chapter 3 and begin applying the principles—that is, if you haven't already done so. Each thought experiment builds on the one before, so that, step by step, you gain a greater understanding of yourself. I'm certain that you will come to the conclusion that you are only as limited as you decide to be. All you need to do is be honest with where you are now, be willing to outgrow old, limited beliefs, and be enthusiastic about embracing a great future for yourself, your loved ones, and the world.

Don't be fooled by the simplicity of the thought experiments. They are more than just daydreams; they are the threads that weave the right subconscious thoughts that bring your dreams into reality. When you read something at a conscious level, you may unconsciously resist taking action. This is because we are bombarded with so much information, it's hard to sort fact from fiction. Each thought experiment is designed to take you beyond the conscious mind to that inner place where you can contemplate your life, refine your dreams, and bring your solutions to reality. Be aware that this process is easier for some than for others. With practice, though, anyone can master the inner realms of their imagination and use thought experiments to create the life they want.

Understand that learning something consciously is one thing, but practicing it at the other-than-conscious level is something else altogether. When you combine subjective learning (book learning) with experiential learning (thought experiments), which makes use of your imagination and creativity, your mind sets up unconscious programs for using the new information in your daily routine.

Consider the advancement of knowledge in our lifetime; isn't it staggering? We can watch brain surgery on television, or we can numb our brains watching a sitcom. We can fire up our computers and solve complex equations, or we can waste hours surfing for trivia and gossip. Yes, technology has given us far more choices than ever before. Our responsibility is to step up and use that technology to improve our world. No doubt hardware and software will continue to advance. Gaming platforms will become more and more lifelike. I believe that one day, with a little help from a "mental coach," we will sit back, relax, and relive events in a kind of real-time holographic therapy. That day is closer than we think.

To become a better golfer, we would no longer need to imagine what Tiger Woods is thinking. With the right technology, we would simply go back and take a ride with him as he wins his twentieth Masters Tournament. Or we would be able to learn anything virtually, from playing the piano to flying an airplane to perfecting our tennis stroke. With this new technology, a twenty-minute dream may seem to last days or weeks.

Can you imagine having access to all the knowledge of the World Wide Web as easily as recalling what you had for dinner last night? Without the need for rote learning, schools could be modified with classes revolving around social skills and the betterment of the planet. Once the quantum computer is in production, problems such as scarcity of energy and other resources will disappear. Who knows, maybe one day soon we will actually see Star Trek-style "holo-decks," or holographic realities, that will be used in the classroom and the entertainment room.

Sounds like a pretty great future, doesn't it? And I've only touched on a few points of what's possible. But that future is possible only if we start today and make changes one day at a time, one choice at a time.

That's how a factory worker and hopeless alcoholic from Battle Creek, Michigan helped to change the world. *With one simple choice.* He decided to attend a class on relaxation and then apply what he learned. He not only overcame his alcoholism but also taught the techniques to his children. And several of his children have been teaching people this amazing mind technology ever since. That hopeless factory worker was my dad, and with one simple choice to help himself, he has influenced well over a million people who have been touched by this mind technology.

Each one of you has that same potential. As you learn to relax and use the power of your mind, you will influence your family and friends who will influence their family and friends, and so on.

I have found that the best way to change the lives of others is to change myself first. It is a natural progression for those you love to want what you have. When you first find peace within yourself, you will have what it takes to develop peace in the world. It's easy when you start small the way my dad did, then build your mental muscles by making gradual, steady changes in your life. Soon you will become a mentor to someone else. If you do your job with a true heart, that person will, in turn, mentor someone else. Think of it like the game, "Six Degrees of Kevin Bacon." In this trivia game, which is based on the idea that earth is a small world after all, players must link any actor through his or her film roles to actor Kevin Bacon. The assumption is that no actor is more than six degrees away from Kevin Bacon. Many believe this to be true for the world. In fact, the title for the game "Six Degrees of Kevin Bacon" is a play on words for "six degrees of separation," the term for this small-world theory.

So, let's take this concept a step further. What if you motivated every overloaded person you know (and that's probably almost everyone you know) to use the CVR techniques in this text? And what if those people shared it with their overloaded friends? And they shared it with their overloaded friends, and so on? In fewer than seven generations of networking, everyone in the country, and perhaps the world, not only would be thriving in overdrive, but also would be empowered to transform our precious planet into a world we can all love living on.

It has been said that spirit is simple, and man is complex. It is my hope that these simple yet complex ideas will transform the way you think about yourself and the future of the human race. My hope is that you, your family, and your friends will stand with me as a co-creator of health, wealth, and abundance. If knowledge is power, then may we share the wealth imbued upon us in this information age, and may we no longer be satisfied with being told what to think, but rather strive for new and better ways to think.

At night as you close your eyes and drift into sleep, keep in mind that the world's greatest computer—your human brain—is already working out the solutions to any problems you may be facing, helping you to awaken the dream that resides within you. And maybe, just maybe, it's the exact dream the world's been waiting for.

*"Keep away from people who try to belittle your ambitions. Small people always do that, but the really great make you feel that you, too, can become great."*

**- Mark Twain**

# CHAPTER
# THIRTEEN

## Additional Resources

# References

(1)     Isaacson, Walter, **Einstein, His Life and Universe** (Simon & Schuster, New York NY 2007) *(Page 17)*

(2)     Kessler RC, Chiu WT, Demler O, Walters EE. **Prevalence, severity, and comorbidity of twelve-month DSM-IV disorders in the National Comorbidity Survey Replication** (NCS-R). Archives of General Psychiatry, 2005 Jun;62(6):617-27. *(Page 21)*

(3)     Schoen, Marc, Ph.D. **When Relaxation is Hazardous to Your Health: Why We Get Sick After the STRESS is Over, and What You Can Do Now to Protect Your HEALTH**, (Mind Body Health Books, Calabasas, CA 2001)

(4)     Facts and Statistics. APA Help Center, www.apahelpcenter.org articles/topic.php.

(5)     Di Salvo, Carmelo Anthony, **Organizational Stress and What to Do About It,** Northstar Leadership Group, Leadership Renewal Seminar, (2007). *(Page 35)*

(6) Nadler, Beverly, **Vibrational Harmony, Why We Don't Get What We Want and How We Can** (Trafford Publishing 2001) *(Page 60)*

(7)     Oster, Gerald, **Auditory Beats in the Brain**, (Scientific American, 1973) *(Page 101)*

(8)     Cvetkovic, D and Cosic, I, **The Induced Rhythmic Oscillations of Neural Activity in the Human Brain**, (Proceeding (417 *(Page 101)*

(9)     Cady, Dr. Roger K. and Shealy, Dr. Norman, **Neurochemical Responses to Cranial Electrical Stimulation and Photo-Stimulation via Brain Wave Synchronization.** Study performed by the Shealy Institute of Comprehensive Health Care, Springfield, Missouri, 1990, 11 pp. *(Page 103)*

(10)     Blaylock, Russell, MD, **Excitotoxins: The Taste that Kills**, (Health Press, Santa Fe, NM 1997) *(Page 128)*

(11) Merzenich, Michael, Ph.D, **Video Games vs. the Aging Brain**, (Discover Magazine, May 21, 2007) *(Page 207)*

## Dr. Patrick Porter's
## Stress-Free Lifestyle Series

Stress is the most pervasive malady of our time. The effects on our health, productivity and quality of life are more devastating than most people care to admit. Luckily, you've just found the solution! CVR can help you see yourself as the healthy, happy, optimistic person you'd prefer to be. With this new image, your fears and frustrations fade away, your anxiety vanishes, and you no longer let small things stress you.

### Create Your Enchanted Forest for Stress Reduction
*Follow along as Dr. Patrick Porter guides you through your personal enchanted forest—a quiet, serene place where you have nothing to do but relax. Your other-than-conscious mind will massage away all tension, allowing you to release all negative thoughts and feelings. You'll return from your magical forest filled with positive feelings, able to enjoy and express your true inner peace.*

### Create Your Mountaintop Retreat for Stress Reduction
*Say goodbye to all stress and confusion as you take a trip to this breathtaking mountaintop retreat. When you listen to this restful process, using your mind to relax your body will become as comfortable and automatic as breathing. The stress, strain and confusion of everyday life will melt away as you awake refreshed, revitalized and renewed!*

A Complete List of
Stress-Free Titles
and full descriptions
can be found at
**www.PorterVision.com**

# Dr. Patrick Porter's
# Vibrant Health Series

Of all the cells in your body, more than 50,000 will die and be replaced with new cells, all in the time it took you to read this sentence! Your body is the vehicle you have been given for the journey of your life. How you treat your body determines how it will treat you. Taking good care of your body will go a long way in ensuring that your life is active, happy, and full of positive experiences. Dr. Patrick Porter will show you how, by using creative visualization and relaxation (CVR), you can recharge and energize your body, mind, and spirit. This series is for people who are looking for more than good health; it's for those who will settle for nothing less than vibrant health!

## Staying Focused in the Present

*Your emotions can either help your body stay healthy, or they can be the cause of disease. Negative feelings such as regret, worry, or anxiety about an upcoming event not only wastes your precious life, but also adds stress to the body, which makes you more susceptible to disease. In this CVR process, Dr. Porter will help you stay present and focused on the beauty of each moment and the gift each minute offers you.*

## Visualize a Heart-Healthy Lifestyle

*Heart disease is not a male issue alone; it is the top killer of American women. To protect your heart, you need a plan that includes movement, a healthy diet, and a positive mental attitude. You use an average of forty-three muscles to frown and only seventeen muscles to smile. You'll find smiling even easier now that you are taking an active roll in protecting the health of your heart. During this CVR session, Dr. Porter will show you how to celebrate the energy, passion, and power that are your birthright.*

Check Out The Complete
Vibrant Health Series
at **www.PorterVision.com**

# Dr. Patrick Porter's
# Life-Mastery Series

Throughout your life, from parents, teachers, and society, you were taught what to think. With the breakthrough processes of creative visualization and relaxation, you are going to discover how to think. With this knowledge you will literally become a software engineer for your own mind. On the Life-Mastery journey, you will explore the processes that best suit your needs for creating limitless personal improvement and success in your life.

## Ask, Believe & Receive
## Visualization

*The universe operates on specific laws. These invisible laws are always manifesting your physical reality. The universe never tries anything; it only does. This visualization calls upon the Law of Attraction, and helps you to become a conscious creator. You will discover how you designed, at the core of your being, to be an active participant in the enfoldment of your relationships, wealth and happiness.*

## The Secret Power of Self-talk

*On average, you give yourself over 5,000 messages a day. With this process you will discover how to weed your mental garden of negative thoughts and to sow new, more positive thoughts. You will use the same four-step process that has helped thousands of people neutralize fear, anxiety and worry. Using CVR, you discover the secret power of self-talk to easily create the habits, patterns, and beliefs that can put your success on autopilot.*

Check Out The Complete
Life-Mastery Series
at **www.PorterVision.com**

# Dr. Patrick Porter's
# Wealth Consciousness Series

## Inspired by the principles of Napoleon Hill's Think and Grow Rich

### Start Each Day with Purpose and Passion

*Napoleon Hill understood that people don't plan to fail; they fail to plan. Successful people know where they are going before they start and move forward on their own initiative. They have the power of intention, or what Napoleon Hill called "mind energy," on their side. Dr. Patrick Porter (PhD) will guide you in using this power of intention to focus your imagination on the success and prosperity you desire.*

### Commit to a Life Spent with Like-Minded People

*Together with Dr. Patrick Porter, you will use the power of intention to draw to yourself mastermind alliances that will support your dream. You will visualize setting up and using these mastermind alliances to help you attract goal-oriented people and create your success environment.*

### Trust the Power of Infinite Intelligence

*Do you sometimes feel as though negative thoughts and fear of poverty have control over you? During this CVR session, Dr. Porter will guide you through the principle of applied faith. All conditions are the offspring of thought, and you find it natural to visualize and realize the thoughts and actions that bring wealth and riches into your life.*

Check Out The Complete
Wealth Consciousness Series
at www.PorterVision.com

## Dr. Patrick Porter's
## Weight Control Series

Now you can design the body you want and the life you love. That's right, you can have the trim, healthy body you've always dreamed of by simply changing the way you see yourself and your life. Once you have a new image of yourself, everything else changes—junk

food and fast food lose their appeal, healthy foods become desirable, and you eat only when you're hungry. With Dr. Porter's System you will overcome common weight loss mistakes, learn to eat and think like a naturally thin person, conquer cravings, and increase your self-confidence. Each week you will take another step toward a lifetime of healthy living; losing weight is the natural byproduct of these changes. While the average diet lasts just 72 hours and focuses on depriving you of the foods you love, Dr. Patrick Porter supercharges your weight loss motivation with these powerful creative visualization and relaxation processes! You will eliminate the problem where it started—your own mind. There is simply no easier way to lose weight than CVR!

### Safely Speeding Up Weight Loss

*In this powerful process, you'll learn to safely speed up weight loss by thinking, acting and responding like a naturally thin person. Your sense of worth will improve when you discover and use inner resources you never even knew you had. Sit back, relax, and discover how easy it is to turn your body into a fat-burning machine—and keep the weight off forever!*

Check Out The Complete
Weight Control Series
at www.PorterVision.com

# Dr. Patrick Porter's
# Accelerated Learning Series

Whether you are an honor student or just having difficulty taking a test, this breakthrough learning system will help you overcome learning challenges and accelerate your current skill level. Imagine doubling your reading speed while improving your memory. Sit back, relax and allow your mind to organize your life, while you build your self-confidence and earn better grades with the our complete learning system.

## Setting Goals for Learning Success
*Dr. Porter's Pikeville College study proved that the more successful students are those who have an outcome or ultimate goal in mind. With this module you will learn the secrets of goal setting, experience a boost in motivation, and see your self-confidence in the classroom soar.*

## Being an Optimistic Thinker

*Henry Ford once said, "Whether you think you can, or you think you can't, you are right." It all starts with attitude. You will be guided into the creative state, where you'll discover ways of breaking through to your optimistic mind that will help you to think, act and respond with a positive nature even during your most difficult classes or around challenging people.*

## Six Steps to Using Your
## Perfect Memory
*Harness the natural byproduct of relaxing your mind by using the six steps that activate a perfect memory. You will discover creative ways to access and recall the information you need as you need it! Best of all, you will have this ability the rest of your life.*

Check Out The Complete
Accelerated Learning Series
at **www.PorterVision.com**

## Dr. Patrick Porter's
## Heart Healthy Lifestyle Series
*Inspired by the principles of*
*Dr. Michael Irving's*
*Twelve Wisdoms to a Healthy Heart*

Adversities and life challenges can be viewed as burdens or as gifts. A heart attack or diagnosis of heart disease is a dramatic wakeup call. Dr. Porter and Dr. Irving want you to see your diagnosis as the gift that it is—the opportunity to create a heart-healthy lifestyle and a brand new you!

*Download the Demo for Free!*
*Visit www.12WisdomsToAHealthyHeart.com*

### Gifts Found in Accepting the Challenges to Your Heart

*A heart crisis can be frightening, but it can also make you feel grateful to be alive and can increase your appreciation of life. These early changes will have you well on your way to living a vibrant life of energy and vitality.*

### Take Charge with a Strong Heart

*Taking charge is one of the most important components of heart health and recovery. Now you can take ownership of your own health and be the central director of your success, confident in your knowledge of heart health, and ready to make the decisions that fulfill your goals.*

Check Out The Complete
Heart Healthy Lifestyles Series
at **www.PorterVision.com**

# Dr. Patrick Porter's
# Freedom From Addiction Series

Addiction comes in many forms, but the underlying cause remains the same. For every addiction there is an underlying positive intention that the mind is trying to fulfill. Now you can use the power of your mind—through creative visualization and relaxation (CVR)—to find more appropriate ways to satisfy that positive intention without the destructive behaviors of the past. Dr. Patrick Porter's groundbreaking CVR program for overcoming addiction can work for just about any addiction including the following:

*Alcoholism*
*Anorexia & Bulimia*
*Codependency*
*Gambling*
*Marijuana*
*Narcotics*
*Prescription Drugs*
*Overeating*
*Overspending*
*Pornography*
*Self-Injury*
*Sexual Promiscuity*

## Personal Responsibility —Working With Your Other-Than-Conscious Mind to Manage Your Life

*Most people who struggle with addictions have, in reality, simply lost their power of choice. Dr. Patrick Porter (PhD) will help you discover why trying to force a change with willpower only perpetuates the problem and how visualization is what will lead you to realization and freedom. You will discover how, by tapping into the power of your mind, you can rebuild your confidence (even in uncertain times) and bring into your consciousness (with sufficient force) the appropriate memories and choices that will lead you to living an addiction-free life—which is your birthright.*

Check Out The Complete
Freedom From Addiction Series
at **www.PorterVision.com**

# Dr. Patrick Porter's
# Coping with Cancer Series

Being diagnosed with cancer is in itself a stressful event—so stressful it can suppress your immune system and worsen the side-effects of treatment. Fortunately, through guided relaxation, you can let go of your fear and anxiety, and take charge of your recovery. Creative visualization can help you regain an optimistic attitude, spark your immune system, and maximize your medical treatment. If you are ready to join the ranks of people who have discovered the mind/body connection and its healing potential, then the Coping with Cancer Series is definitely for you!

## Relaxation For Inner Healing

*For some people, relaxing while facing a serious illness may seem like an impossible task. In this first session, you will begin by simply clearing your mind of all negative or fear-based thoughts concerning your condition. At the same time, you will learn to allow the natural healing power of your body to take over. The benefits from relaxation are immeasurable when it comes to fighting cancer.*

## Rejuvenate Your Body Through Deep Delta Sleep

*During cancer recovery, many people have difficulty falling asleep or they may awaken in the middle of the night and struggle to get back to sleep. Your body naturally recharges and rejuvenates during sleep, which means a good night's rest is key to your recovery. This imagery will show you new ways to get maximum benefit from sleep.*

Check Out The Complete
Coping With Cancer Series
at **www.PorterVision.com**

## Dr. Patrick Porter's
## SportZone™ Series

Success in sports is about being the best you can be, and visualization plays a key role in getting there. Why is visualization so important? Because you get what you rehearse in life, but that's not always what you want or intend. This is especially true when you are facing the pressures of athletics. The SportZone program is designed to help you tap into the mind's potential and make your sport of choice fun and enjoyable while taking your game to the next level. Visualization for sports performance is nothing new to top competitors—athletes from Tiger Woods to diver Greg Louganis and a variety of Olympians have used visualization to bring about optimal performance, overcome self-doubt, and give themselves a seemingly unfair advantage over their competition. Now the SportZone series can work for any athlete, from junior competitors to weekend enthusiasts. Yes, you can get more out of your sport and, in the process, get more out of life.

### Using the "Zone" in Your Sport
*When competitive athletes slip into their "zone" everything seems to work just right. Dr. Patrick Porter will help you get to that place where everything comes together. With this process you'll learn to put yourself into a state of "flow," your own personal "zone," so you can stay on top of your game. The "zone" is as easy to access as a deep breath once you have mastered the mental keys.*

### Control Your Emotions
### and Master Your Sport
*It has been said that he or she who angers you conquers you; this is true even if the person who angers you is you! With this process you will learn a powerful self-visualization technique for keeping your emotions under control. With this easy technique you will no longer be giving away your power to others and will stop letting anger and frustration get the better of you.*

### Check Out The Complete
### SportZone Series
### at www.PorterVision.com

# Dr. Patrick Porter's
# Smoking Cessation Series

Kicking your smoking habit doesn't get any easier or more fun than this! When you use Dr. Patrick Porter's proven strategies, you'll find that making this life-saving change comes about simply and effortlessly. With the new science of creative visualization and relaxation (CVR), you will extinguish the stress and frustration associated with quitting smoking, and you'll conquer your cravings like the tens of thousands of others who have used Dr. Porter's processes.

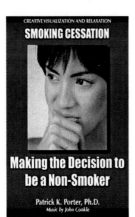

### Making the Decision To Be
### A Non-Smoker
*With this CVR session, you'll learn about the cleansing power of you own mind, and use it to take a "mental shower" that will wipe away all thoughts of tobacco. With this process, you'll gladly make the decision to be tobacco-free for life!*

### Making Peace With Your Mind
*In this powerful creative session, Dr. Patrick Porter will show you that, while you once had a positive intention for having tobacco in your life, you no longer need it to live the life you desire. The smoker of the past will make peace with the clean air breather of the future in order to create a new, vibrant you!*

### Plan Your Life As A Non-Smoker
*Every goal needs a plan, and in this process, Dr. Patrick Porter will guide you in visualizing and working a plan for your tobacco-free life. This motivational session will allow you to remember to forget cigarettes forever. You'll awake convinced being a nonsmoker is as easy as taking a breath of fresh air!*

### Check Out The Complete
### Smoking Cessation Series
### at www.PorterVision.com

## Dr. Patrick Porter's
## Mental Coaching for Golf Series

Efficient golfers know how to relax and let their minds take over. Now, thanks to these creative visualization and relaxation (CVR) processes, you'll learn to see yourself as a calm, confident golfer. You deserve to take pleasure in your time on the course. Thanks to CVR, you'll finally be able to let go of frustration and focus on every stroke—meaning you'll not only play better, but you'll also enjoy the game more than ever!

### Optimize the Risk Zone for Golf

*You've never experienced a practice session like this one! Follow along with Dr. Patrick Porter as he guides you onto the driving range in your mind. Once there, you'll practice each swing, letting go of negative thoughts and allowing the clubs to do what they were designed to do—send the ball straight to the target.*

### Develop the Attitude of a Champion

*Champions understand that good outcomes come from good shots. With this dynamic process, you'll find it easy to think positive thoughts and accept each shot as it comes. You'll no longer spend time feeling distracted, over-analyzing your game, blaming the conditions of the course, or getting angry over a bad lie.*

### Concentration: Your Key To Consistency

*Most golf professionals consider concentration to be the key to playing golf...but almost no one teaches it. In this energizing process by Dr. Patrick Porter, he'll teach you to achieve the concentration you need simply by sitting back, relaxing, and letting go of all stress and confusion.*

Check Out The Complete
Mental Coaching for Golf Series
at **www.PorterVision.com**

## Dr. Patrick Porter's
## Enlightened Children's Series

Seven-year-old Marina Mulac and five-year-old Morgan Mulac, who have come to be known as the world's youngest marketers, were the inspiration behind this Enlightened Children's Series. When they met Dr. Patrick Porter, they had one question for him: Why had he created so many great visualizations for grown ups and nothing for kids?

Dr. Porter told the two little entrepreneurs that if they put on their thinking caps and helped him design a program for kids, together they could help children from around the globe to use their imaginative minds to become better people and help improve the world. Together, Marina, Morgan, and Dr. Patrick Porter put together this series that uses guided imagery, storytelling, and positive affirmations to help children see the world as a peaceful and harmonious place where everyone can win. If your goal is to develop a happy, healthy child of influence in our rapidly changing world, this series is a must-have for your child.

### Building Optimism in Your Children

*Every day your child is forming his or her view of the world based on life experiences. Now is the time to help your child build a positive outlook that will serve him or her for a lifetime. Optimists believe that people and events are inherently good and that most situations work out for the best. Dr. Porter will show your child how to see the good in every situation and how to be open to experiencing new things.*

Check Out The Complete
Enlightened Children's Series
at **www.PorterVision.com**

# Dr. Patrick Porter's
# Medical Series

## De-Stress and Lower Blood Pressure

*The physiological benefits of deep relaxation and visualization are well documented. During this creative visualization process you will learn to achieve the relaxation response—a state known to unlock your brain's potential for de-stressing your body and returning your blood pressure to a healthy level. Known benefits of the relaxation response also include a lower respiratory rate, a slower pulse, relaxed muscles, and an increase in alpha brain wave activity—everything that makes for a healthier you!*

## Pre-Surgery Calm for Better Healing

*For years physicians and therapist have used guided relaxation, intense concentration, and focused attention to achieve deep relaxation and heightened states of awareness prior to surgery. Now, through the science of creative visualization and relaxation (CVR), you can easily benefit from these powerful processes. Patients using these techniques are known to have less pain, require less pain medication, and enjoy a more rapid recovery.*

## Post-Surgery Stress Relief for a
## Healthy Mind and Body

*CVR is a relaxation technique that uses concentration and deep breathing to calm the mind and put your body in the best possible state for repair and healing. What could be easier than to sit back, relax, and let the stress of surgery and recovery melt away?*

### Check Out The Complete
### Medical Series
### at www.PorterVision.com

## Dr. Patrick Porter's
## Professional Airlines Blue Sky Series

The airline industry has long been considered a "glamour" industry, but those working in the business know that, once it becomes your job, you are in a constant battle to maintain the health of your body and mind. An airline professional's stress can come in many forms — from dealing with exhausting schedules and unruly passengers to the underlying fears related to travel during uncertain times. For this reason, Dr. Patrick Porter, has created the Blue Sky Series, which is designed to help airline professionals regain balance in their lives through deep relaxation and creative visualization techniques.

### Sleep on Any Schedule
*In the airline industry, flying across time zones, arriving late at night, and being expected to awaken early the next morning are all part of the job. While the occasional traveler is able to get over jet lag with relative ease, in the airline business, jet lag is part and parcel to a day's work. Unfortunately, this regular disruption of the sleep cycle can result in chronic fatigue, headaches, body aches, and a lowered immune system.*

### Clear Out Flight Noise and Return to Health
*With this visualization, you will be guided through some mental balancing processes to help you deal with the impact of that constant barrage of jet engine noise. During the process you will clear your mind, reset your attention, and focus on health. You will learn to de-stress, relax, and have fun after a flight.*

Check Out The Complete
Blue Sky Series
at **www.PorterVision.com**

# Dr. Patrick Porter's
# Pain-Free Lifestyle Series

Persistent pain can have a costly impact on your life. It can lead to depression, loss of appetite, irritability, anger, loss of sleep, withdrawal from social interaction, and an inability to cope. Fortunately, with creative visualization and relaxation (CVR), pain can almost always be controlled. CVR helps you eliminate pain while you relax, revitalize, and rejuvenate. You deserve to be free of your pain—and now you can be, thanks to CVR!

### Tapping into a Pain-Free Lifestyle
*Dr. Patrick Porter will guide you through a simple exercise to transform pain into relaxation. You'll tap into your body's innate ability to heal itself, allowing the healing process to happen while you take a relaxing mental vacation. Pain will lose all power over you as you learn to relax away your pain and enjoy your life free from discomfort.*

### Activate Your Mental Pharmacy
*In this dynamic process, you'll unlock your body's natural pharmacy, flushing pain from your body and neutralizing all discomfort. You will so galvanize your mind's healing capacity, all you'll have to do is say the word to release pain, fear and anxiety. Most importantly, you'll have this healing power at your fingertips—when and where you need it most.*

### Starting the Day Pain-Free
*In this motivational session, Dr. Patrick Porter will show you that living pain-free is as simple as saying, "So-Hum." Which means, transporting yourself to a pain-free state can be as easy as breathing! You'll be able to bury your pain in the past and awaken each morning pain-free.*

Check Out The Complete
Pain-Free Lifestyle Series
at **www.PorterVision.com**

## Dr. Patrick Porter's
## Stress-Free Childbirth Series

Bringing a child into the world should be an amazing life experience. Sadly, for many women, the joy of the event is lost due to fear, stress and pain. Also, research has shown that a fetus can actually feel the stress, worry, and negative emotions of the mother during pregnancy. Fortunately, with the discovery of the mind/body connection, women have an alternative—creative visualization and relaxation (CVR). This breakthrough series is designed to help the mother-to-be to relax, let go of stress, and enjoy the entire process of pregnancy, delivery and motherhood. In addition, the listener is taught to use the power of thought to create an anaesthetized feeling that can transform pain into pressure throughout labor and delivery—making the entire process stress-free for the entire family.

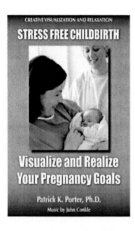

### Visualize and Realize Your Pregnancy Goals
*Take this journey of the imagination where you'll train your brain to stay focused and on task. With this process, you'll start experiencing the relaxation response, set healthy priorities, and prepare your body for the many changes it will go through for the next nine months and beyond. This is the foundation session for the complete Stress-Free Childbirth program.*

### Mental Skills for Pregnancy and Delivery
*With this session negative thinking melts away and a calm state of emotional readiness replaces fear. The power of positive expectancy will lead you to positive results. Once you experience this mental training, and gain the relaxed mindset and inner confidence you need for motherhood, others may actually look to you for support!*

Check Out The Complete
Stress-Free Childbirth Series
at **www.PorterVision.com**

# Dr. Patrick Porter's
# Mind-Over-Menopause Series

For many women mid-life can be a time of uncertainty and loss. For some the loss of fertility and the perceived loss of youth can cause depression and anxiety. At the same time, the body's response to the decrease in hormones can create any number of symptoms—hot flashes, night sweats, weight gain, itchy skin, mood swings, lost libido, headaches, and irregular cycles are just of few of the menopausal challenges women face. In the midst of all these changes, relationships can suffer as loved ones start to ask, "What happened to the caring, loving woman we once knew?" Now you can reclaim that woman, along with all the strength, confidence, and wisdom you gained in the first half of your life. This series takes you way beyond mind over matter—it's mind over menopause!

## Balance Your Mood,
## Balance Your Life
*With this session you will use creative visualization and relaxation to help balance your mood, harness positive mental energy, and use your innate creative power to produce much-needed balance in your life during this time of change and uncertainty. You will stop focusing on what you've lost, and discover all that you've gained!*

## Creating Harmony
## With the Cycles of Life
*Using your mind you will activate the powerful calming effects produced by your own brain chemistry.*

## Mental Skills to Help You Master Menopause
*With this creative visualization and relaxation process, you will be given time to plan your life from a new perspective. You will learn to view menopause as a rite of passage—one that gives you confidence and inner worth. With new ways to handle situations at work, and with family and friends, you'll discover that mid-life can bring forth a whole new you that's been there all along just waiting to blossom!*

Check Out The Complete
Mind-Over-Menopause Series
at **www.PorterVision.com**

# Dr. Patrick Porter's
# Sales Mastery Series

Discover the powerful selling methods of sales masters! When you use this amazing series, you'll build your self-confidence, master your time, and learn to overcome all objections. Visualize and realize your brighter sales future today.

## Sales Confidence through Self-Confidence

*To have confidence in your sales skills, you need confidence in yourself. In this dynamic session, Dr. Patrick Porter will show you how to generate resources you never knew you had. Take control of your own self-confidence in order to organize your thoughts, put priorities in place and take control of your sales... and your life!*

## Supercharge Your Sales Skills

*You already have all the abilities you need to become a sales superstar. This exciting process will help you organize those resources to eliminate cold-call reluctance and discover the secrets known by true sales pros. Sit back, relax, and find out how to supercharge your sales skills!*

## Enjoying the Prospecting Game

*All sales masters know networking is the key to finding a need and helping prospects fill it. This refreshing process by Dr. Patrick Porter teaches you to develop your infinite referral system and make all the money you desire. When you approach sales with the mindset of a child, prospecting is not only easy...it's fun!*

Check Out The Complete
Sales Mastery Series
at **www.PorterVision.com**

## Entrepreneurs Wanted

*Are You Ready For The Most Innovative & Successful Entrepreneurial Support System EVER Created?*

If you own a business or have always dreamed of owning a business but have yet to achieve the success you want, I know how you're feeling, and it's NOT your fault, because until now you've never had a mental motivation system available to you - but that's all changed!

I am going to connect you directly with my Internet marketing coaches Stephanie and Greg Mulac. What they will show you will cut years off your learning curve. I have teamed up with them to create a CVR support system that will put cutting edge mind tools to work for you to support you every step of the way.

For years they have watched some of the best and brightest online marketers fail - not because they lacked a great product, not because they couldn't create killer sites and NOT because they failed to drive traffic to those sites and make sales...

The #1 reason these talented people went bust is because:

*They lacked a support system!*

For the past several years Stephanie and Greg have produced over 26 products and online events, traveled the country speaking at seminars, held workshops and mentored hundreds of private clients to do the same...

And for most of 2008 they have been on the road in a motorhome traversing 26 states across the U.S.

If you want to set your own hours, take vacations (at will) to some of the most desirable places on earth, like Stephanie and Greg, you will want to go online and check out all the details at:

**www.90percentattitude.com**

## Add Powerful CVR Programs to Your Existing Business Introducing the PorterVision Business Expansion Package!

Imagine adding the powerful tools of CVR with light & sound technology to your existing spa, medical practice or wellness center. The package includes unlimited usage of Dr. Porter's breakthrough CVR programs for in-office use. This is not a franchise or a joint venture; its your business and we coach you to success every step of the way.

### YOU ALREADY HAVE MOST OF WHAT'S NEEDED TO ADD$1,000.00 A WEEK OR MORE TO YOUR BOTTOMLINE

With PorterVision's CVR System, you can offer high-demand support services that will greatly benefit your clients and contribute to your bottomline!

With our Deluxe Package you will work directly with world-renowned and award-wining author, Dr. Patrick Porter. Your first step starts with a 3-day intensive where he will share with you his experience in building the world's largest network of lifestyle improvement centers.

You will get conference calls and regional training and learn how to grow your business with the latest breakthroughs in mind technology. The programs you will be offering include weight loss, stop smoking, stress reduction, pain management, mental coaching for golf, Sportszone series and more. For a full list visit www.PorterVision.com.
You already have the basics:

- *An existing business*
- *Competent office help*
- *A list of current and past clients*
- *Space for clients to relax and enjoy the processes*

Benefits of using the PorterVision System:

- *Special pricing on PorterVision products*
- *Discounts on seminars and training*
- *Access to online training and support*
- *Inclusion in Dr. Porter's referral network*
- *Revenue sharing on all your client's downloads*

**Check out the latest details at www.PorterVision.com**

## Attend Dr. Porter's VisionQuest Weekend

Who should attend? Anyone who wants to experience a life-transforming weekend that's fun and inspiring. *No advanced training is required.*

Are you ready to unlock your mind's potential? Dr. Porter has combined the best of his research in Neuro-Linguistic Programming, hypnosis, and visualization into one of the most powerful weekends you've ever experienced.

### *12 Reasons to Attend VisionQuest Weekend*

1. You will learn how to uncover your life's purpose and how to fuel your creative mind.
2. You will learn the four questions to which you must know the answers to super-charge any suggestion. Warning--you can use this powerful information to motivate others as well as yourself.
3. You will learn how to affect change using the other-than-conscious mind, a power that can either enslave you or set you free. After VisionQuest Weekend, it'll be entirely up to you!
4. You will learn the easiest way to harness positive thoughts and how to eliminate the negative.
5. You will learn the advancements in mind science that will have you manifesting anything and everything your heart desires.
6. You will discover the freedom in letting go of judgment.
7. You will leave with a working knowledge of the most powerful communication tools on earth.
8. You can either cry your way or laugh your way to enlightenment. After the weekend, it'll be your choice. Discovering the key to happiness allows you to live life to its full potential.
9. You will discover why happiness is your birthright and how to master it.
10. You will learn to stop unwanted behaviors. Because of the nature of the seminar, you can focus on improving any part of your life.
11. You will learn Tai Chi for the mind and achieve emotional freedom. Imagine learning how to choose your emotional states and stop being a victim of how you feel.
12. You will master the techniques in this text and learn to thrive in overdrive.

**Check for dates for the next training
at www.PorterVision.com**

## PorterVision **Master Distributor** Program
### *Territories Available for a Limited Time . . .*

**Will You Act Now . . .**
**Before the Lucrative Territory You Want is**
**Snatched Up by Another Savvy Entrepreneur?**

The personal health & wellness industry is on target to reach **$1 TRILLION** by 2010. Are you ready to claim your share?

Forget about the recession. Become the creator of your own reality by joining one of the undisputed leaders in the personal improvement field!

**No other company offers this many self-improvement services!**

Consider your current circle of acquaintances. How many of them smoke or are overweight? How many suffer from chronic stress or anxiety? How many are golfers or some other kind of sports enthusiast? How many have careers in sales? How many fear the dentist? Here's a biggie for you: How many suffer from insomnia? PorterVision offers genuine solutions for all of these and more, including:

- o   Controlling Chronic Pain
- o   Vibrant Health
- o   Wealth Consciousness
- o   Life Mastery
- o   Freedom from Alcohol & Addiction
- o   Stress-free Childbirth
- o   Mind-Over-Menopause
- o   And Dozens More!

Even children can benefit with Dr. Porter's amazing Enlightened Children's and Accelerated Learning programs. Which means a case could be made that PorterVision products and services can benefit nearly every human being. And that translates to a veritable gold rush for your Master Distributor business.

# PorterVision Master Distributors
# earn income in FOUR unique ways!

1.　*Receive a one percent override on all PorterVision sales in your territory.* Which means you get paid a commission on hundreds if not thousands of sales to customers you've never even met.

2.　*Sell PorterVision products retail to 40+ business models for untold profits.* Since you never pay more than the wholesale rate, your profit potential is infinite. How much you earn is totally up to you.

3.　*Earn generous commissions through retail, professional license, and affiliate enrollments.* If you're good at motivating people, you can make a fortune through the efforts of others.

4.　*Use PorterVision as your entrée for conducting training sessions, demos, seminars, shows, and home parties.* Everything you earn is yours to keep.

Why waste years trying to climb the ladder of success? With the Master Distributor Program, you start out at the top. Will this be the year you make it big?

Is the territory you want still available? Do you qualify for the Master Distributor program? You can find out in one simple step. Go to **www.pvmasterdistributor.com** provide your name and email and we'll get back with you in less than 24 hours.

*p.s. When you become a Master Distributor, we'll include 400 of Dr. Porter's CVR programs absolutely free.*

*p.s.s. PorterVision is a people-helping organization. What's more rewarding than helping people achieve their dreams?*

*p.s.s.s. We have aggressively priced our territories to sell quickly. Territories won't last long. Act now!*

# Welcome to The Gift of Love Project

**The Gift of Love** is a poetic writing that has its own beauty ... and upon further examination, it may lead one to a contemplative process, creating balance and harmony in one's everyday life. Over time, this process can also create subtle positive change in the recipient of **The Gift**.

My guidance leads me to distribute this writing to one billion people within the next two years. Hopefully, many people will be led to practice the contemplative process. If **The Gift of Love** resonates with you, please share it with others. As we gather and hold the **power of love** in our consciousness, we will dramatically reduce the level of anger, fear, and hatred on our planet today. -- Jerry DeShazo

### The Gift of Love

*I Agree Today*
*To Be The Gift of Love.*

*I Agree to Feel Deeply*
*Love for Others*
*Independent of Anything*
*They Are Expressing,*
*Saying, Doing, or Being.*

*I Agree to Allow Love*
*As I Know It*
*To Embrace My Whole Body*
*And Then to Just Send It*
*To Them Silently and Secretly.*

*I Agree to Feel it, Accept it, Breathe It*
*Into Every Cell of My Body on Each In-Breath*
*And On Each Out-Breath*
*Exhale Any Feeling Unlike Love.*

*I Will Repeat This Breathing Process Multiple Times*
*Until I Feel it Fully and Completely*
*Then Consciously Amplify In Me*
*The Feeling of Love and Project It to Others*
*As The Gift of Love.*

*This is My Secret Agreement –*
*No One Else Is To Know it.*

For more about The Gift of Love Project and to view the videos, please visit www.TheGiftofLove.com. You will also be given access to a special 9-minute Creative Visualization that will align you with the **Power of Love** and supercharge your day. Together we will change the world one person at a time.

CPSIA information can be obtained at www.ICGtesting.com
Printed in the USA
BVOW041440100313

315081BV00003B/11/P